# INDUSTRIAL DEVELOPMENT
# THROUGH URBANIZATION

University of New Orleans Press
Manufactured in the United States of America
All rights reserved
ISBN: 978-1-60801-162-9


Translated by Inge Fink


This publication was printed with financial support by Center Austria at the University of New Orleans, the Vice Rectorat for Research and the International Relations Office at the University of Innsbruck.

The original version of the book was published in German in 2015 and translated by Inge Fink, Director of the Writing Center in the Department of English at the University of New Orleans.

**UNIVERSITY OF NEW ORLEANS PRESS**

unopress.org

# INDUSTRIAL DEVELOPMENT THROUGH URBANIZATION

## A NEW THEORY ON POVERTY AND PROSPERITY

FRANZ MATHIS

UNIVERSITY OF NEW ORLEANS PRESS

# CONTENTS

# INTRODUCTION

Poor countries – rich countries, First World – Third World, exploitation, rural flight, slums. We read about these things every time we deal with global economic development. The average per-capita income in the US is still 8 times that of India; the Swiss income is almost 30 times that of Mali.[1] We are still told that the prosperity of the First World depends on the exploitation of the Third. Every day, thousands of poor people leave their rural environment, hoping to find employment and income in the growing mega-cities. Most of them, initially, find themselves in the ghettos or slums as middle and upper class residential areas continue to spread at the same time.

Researchers have been trying for years to explain these and other *related phenomena of economic development*. Legions of scholars in different disciplines have tried to explain these issues; even a mere summary of their findings would fill a book.[2] The dynamics of economic development have not only been the subject of countless academic studies but they have become a part of common knowledge as well. As a result, I will not need to present them in great detail here nor do I need to analyze their origins. And yet, I will briefly introduce and discuss the most important findings later in this chapter. However, I would like to point out that *previous attempts to explain* these phenomena do not hold up to scrutiny because the examples supporting their arguments are refuted by too much evidence to the contrary. The claim that the prosperity of the First World depends on the poverty of the Third and vice

---

1   According to estimates of the International Monetary Fund and the World Bank for 2016. List of countries (GDP).

2   David S. Landes in Landes (1969) was one of the first to tackle this question, and he presented his findings again 30 years later in Landes (1998). In addition to those mentioned below, the following represent more recent analyses: Bradberry/O'Rourke (2010), Cameron/Neal (2003), Clark (2007), Diamond (1998), Maddison (2001), Maddison (2007), Berend (2006).

versa is one of them. Similarly, the argument that industrialization depends on a country's access to raw materials does not hold up if we look closer; neither do claims that certain religions or mentalities produce more entrepreneurs than others or that climatic and other conditions in Europe favored its economic development. I will analyze the real reasons for the advantageous and much broader economic development and try to show why this has been denied to all but a few countries. My investigation focuses on globalization, industrialization, and urbanization, concepts that need to be explained in some detail before I move on to show the connections between them.

## GLOBALIZATION

Much has been written on the subject of *globalization* in recent years. The question of whether this is a fairly new phenomenon – as is generally assumed – or something that has existed for centuries depends on the depth and variety of global relationships that are essential for globalization. Nobody doubts that regions, countries, and continents are much more closely connected today than they were at time of Christopher Columbus around 1500. Yet, it makes sense to look for the origins of globalization in the explorations at the end of the 15th century, which expanded European horizons beyond Europe, North Africa, and Asia and, in turn, made people in America and large parts of Africa and Oceania aware of a much larger world than the one they had hitherto known. These explorations extended European trade relationships beyond Asia and the Mediterranean even though they did not exceed domestic trade for a long time. However, they also laid the groundwork for the conquest of many non-European countries and their domination, both politically and economically, by European colonial powers.

Five hundred years of globalization pose a variety of questions: How important were the commodities derived from their colonies abroad for the economic development of European nations? In what way did non-European countries serve as a market for European goods? To what degree did the imported precious metals and the profits gained in the trade with non-European countries expand the capital invested in the European economy? How much did European exports handicap successful industrialization elsewhere? Did Europe deprive these countries of goods they needed for their own economic development? How much did the capital outflow to Europe prevent investments in the domestic economy? How is it possible that some former colonies – such as the US, Canada, or Australia – developed high-level economies but most of the others did not? How come two independent (i.e. never colonized) countries like China and Japan experienced such different economic development? On the other hand, why did the first colonial powers, Spain and Portugal, develop much less than the more recent colonial powers, England, France, and the Netherlands? Questions upon questions arise in the wake of globalization, and we will have to investigate them.

# INDUSTRIALIZATION

The common denominator of these questions is that they all point to *industrialization* as the key to our current prosperity.[3] Granted, high incomes have become common in other fields as well, such as agriculture, banking, insurance, transportation, tourism, and especially public service. However, these achievements would not have been possible without successful industrialization. The Industrial Revolution initiated the transition from manual to machine-based production, which – supported by the use of new forms of energy – increased human production both quantitatively and qualitatively. Thanks to more efficient production methods, we manufacture ever more and better goods than we did in the past. Increased productivity has multiplied the supply of goods, which has decreased their prices

---

3    Jeffrey D. Sachs, the well-known economist and former special advisor to UNO Secretary-General Kofi Annan, has recently pointed out the tremendous significance of industrialization for economic and social modernization and for the increase of the annual national product. Two hundred years ago, the differences in per-capita production between individual countries and regions were not nearly as large as they are today. It was not until industrialization, which happened at different times in different countries, and which promoted economic growth in some countries more than in others, that the gap widened as much as it did. Sachs (2005), based on Angus Maddison's calculations (Per Capita GDP). Kenneth Pomeranz (2000), among others, argues that Europe and China, which recently has come into sharper focus, did not develop in different directions until the 19th century.

and boosted the profits of those who produce them. Wherever industrialization happened, people had more, cheaper, and mostly better products at their disposal, and they could afford them thanks to their higher incomes. Admittedly, they first had to struggle for a more even distribution of income between employers and employees, but their higher incomes ultimately depended on increased productivity.

Due to mechanization and automatization, *increased productivity* made itself felt in other parts of the economy, too. Railroads, automobiles, and steam boats replaced horse-drawn carts and sailboats, which, thanks to larger quantities of goods being transported, decreased transportation prices and thus increased the profits of the shipping industry. The same is true in agriculture, where various machines and tractors increased productivity. As a result of increased productivity and income in these and other areas, tourism, banking, and the insurance business profited from the people's increased purchasing power. In addition, taxes and social security contributions benefitted education, health care, and public service. In addition, thanks to increased productivity, all of this could be accomplished in less time, which led to shorter work days, weeks, and years. Industrialization was not only the beginning of modern economic development but its cause; it brought about the widespread and – compared to pre-industrial centuries – much higher prosperity that First-World countries have enjoyed for several decades and of which Third-World countries have only seen the rudimentary beginnings.

However, upon closer inspection, statistics of per-capita incomes in countries reflect a distorted view of reality. If we look more closely, we discover that industrialization is not a national development involving entire countries but more of a *regional phenomenon*.[4] For example, per-capita incomes differ significantly between northern and southern Italy, between Catalonia and Andalusia, between Mecklenburg-West Pomerania and Bavaria, or between coastal China and its hinterland, which makes it impossible to talk about Italian, Spanish, German, or Chinese industrialization in generic terms. National statistics reflect the sum of various regional developments, which, in turn, depend on similar and/

---

4    Pollard (1981) points out the importance of regions in the industrialization process. See also Mathis (2012).

or different structures. Some countries have agricultural and little-industrialized regions as well as highly-developed or tourism-based areas. Their development often depends on neighboring regions in other countries rather than on the national economy. The availability of raw material, as well as the touristic attractiveness of mountainous and coastal terrains, is as much a regional phenomenon as the accumulation of cities and factories in certain places. And if urban centers are imperative for successful industrialization, as I will show below, they often sprang up in countries whose borders have shifted considerably throughout the course of history. All of these observations, along with the fact that there are still significant economic differences between certain areas despite their governments' efforts to eliminate them, relativize the influence of national economic politics on a country's economic development.[5] Consequently, we have to investigate the regional, natural, and historically-developed socio-economic structures if we want to explain different economic developments. This is particularly true when we speak of a region's degree of urbanization.

## URBANIZATION

As the term is used here, *urbanization* indicates the origin, expansion, and growth of towns and cities, all of which are connected to an absolute and relative increase of urban versus rural populations. However, urbanization did not take place everywhere in the world at the same time. On the contrary, there are clear differences between individual regions with regard as to when they began to urbanize and how quickly they did it. Population density is an important (but not the only) factor in the development of these differences. The more people lived in a certain region, the more one could expect the development of urban settlements. Push and pull factors caused people to leave rural areas and move into towns, where they hoped to improve their economic situation.

An important *push factor* is the relative *overpopulation* in rural areas, which arose from the imbalance between an ever-increasing population on the one hand, and limited resources

---

5    For a recent discussion of the role of economic politics, which has often underestimated if not altogether ignored the manifold relations between supply and demand at the basis of the economy, see Weigl (2011).

and sources of income on the other. Still, this alone would not have provided sufficient motivation for rural flight. The push factor of overpopulation needed to combine with a pull factor, namely the hope that employment in non-agrarian industries would provide people with a better income. Economic success away from the farm required a sufficiently large number of *potential consumers* for the goods these migrants produced or the services they offered, which were more readily available in more densely populated regions.

Communities with denser populations saw more trade and traffic and, increasingly, necessitated administration and jurisdiction, both of which were concentrated in conveniently located towns that attracted permanent and temporary migrants. As *trade and administrative centers grew*, they became even more powerful pull factors for potential migrants because a rising number of inhabitants constituted a larger market and thus a better chance for improved income. Just to name a few, Hamburg, New York, Osaka, or Bombay serve as examples of trade centers; Madrid, Berlin, or Tokyo represent administrative centers, and Vienna, London, or Buenos Aires exemplify both.

The role these two factors – the push factor of relative overpopulation in the country or the pull factor of potential customers in town – played in the emergence of non-rural settlements and later towns differed from case to case. Geographically and historically, however, the emergence of almost all urban settlements depends on at least one of them. Even towns that were founded deliberately were successful only if they could attract migrants from rural areas and if their location made them suitable for a commercial and/or administrative center. Because people's desire to flee the country and move to the town differed from region to region, urban settlements varied in size. I will show when, where, and to what extent urban settlements emerged and expanded in different parts of the world and how urbanization connects with industrialization and globalization.

## NO INDUSTRIALIZATION WITHOUT URBANIZATION

Successful industrialization depends on the infrastructure provided by *urban settlements*, which, where and whenever they emerged, became centers of trade and manufacture, as opposed to rural areas, where homesteading and subsistence farming dominated despite occasional non-agricultural activities. Profiting from the division of labor that marked their occupations, *urban artisans* developed the specialized technical skills necessary for their trade as they supplied goods to the surrounding and occasionally trans-regional areas. Their technical knowledge would later facilitate the development, construction, and operation of machines. Insufficiently urbanized areas that lacked the specialized skills of artisans found it much more difficult to industrialize.

In addition to skilled workers, industrial production depended on the presence of *entrepreneurs* willing to invest in its development. Besides their willingness to take risks, the founders of factories had an above-average desire to attain independence, financial gain, and prestige—they had the entrepreneurial spirit. During the pre-industrial era, the social group in possession of these qualities included mostly town-based merchants who specialized in foreign rather than local trade. Investing in foreign trade meant taking greater risk, but it brought social prestige and increased profits due to the lack of competition. In addition, because these merchants bought and sold their goods in foreign markets, they knew these much better than those who traded only locally.

No other group in pre-industrialized societies resembled later entrepreneurs as much as did these *merchants*. While aristocrats owned the capital necessary for industrial investment, they were more inclined to spend it on goods and services befitting their social status rather than on trade or, later on, factories. A few exceptions notwithstanding, peasants did not participate in trans-regional trade and industrial investment for two reasons: On the one hand, they were mostly occupied with subsistence farming and not much interested in trade, let alone foreign trade; on the other, agrarian methods of production are radically different from commercial practices. Artisans, on the other hand, whose professions were more closely related to industrial production, depended on local markets and did not readily develop the entrepreneurial spirit we find in merchants trading internationally; still, they readily cooperated with merchants in the establishment of factories.

Urban settlements were the backbone of regional and trans-regional trade,[6] which depended on an adequate *transportation infrastructure*. In this way, urbanization created a network of traffic routes on land, rivers, and oceans, which facilitated later industrialization that depended on trans-regional markets to buy raw materials and sell mass-produced

---

6    See also Lopez (1971), 60.

commodities. Modern means of transportation, like railroads, steam boats, and automobiles, which did not become commonly available until decades after industrialization had already begun, contributed significantly to its expansion. Finally, the transition from a barter to a monetary economy – another indispensable condition for industrialization – did not occur in the framework of subsistence agriculture but in the market economy of the city.

All of these factors – market orientation based on the division of labor, technical know-how, the merchants' pursuit of commercial profit and entrepreneurial spirit, a network of traffic routes, and the transition from barter to a monetary economy – were important *conditions for industrialization*, but they were not sufficient by themselves. Towns existed in antiquity and in medieval times, outside of Europe and in all parts of the world, but they never industrialized. A second phase of urbanization was necessary, one that transcended the mere emergence and expansion of towns. In some parts of Europe, it started as early as the second half of the 18th century, in North America and Japan in the 19th century, and on other continents often as late as the second half of the 20th century.

The second phase of urbanization depended on the expansion of existing towns into *big cities*, whose population grew from a few thousand inhabitants to several hundred thousand and more. Cities like London, then Paris, Berlin, or Vienna in Europe, New York, Boston, Philadelphia, or Chicago in America, Tokyo and Osaka in Japan, and most recently the young Third World metropolises provided an additional, and in this case decisive, condition for successful industrialization. Only large cities such as these offered sufficiently large and expandable *markets* that made the mass production of commodities both reasonable and profitable. Industrial mass production required a mass market, which existed in modern big cities whose populations increased as a result of rural flight[7] and which promised large

---

7  Professional sources mention the role demand plays in the industrialization process only in passing and alongside other, more highly valued factors. This is true for older studies like Gilboy (1932), quoted in Rule (1992), 252, or Everley (1967), but it also applies to more recent analyses such as Pollard (1981), Matis (1988), Wallerstein (1989), 6 and 11, Menzel (1993), Buchheim (1994), 61 f, Evans (1996), 115, Pierenkemper (1996), 15 ff, Jones (2002) or Bayly (2006), 217. Demand is rarely mentioned in connection with towns, and just about never with the concentrated purchasing power of big cities. Bayly (2006), 228-245, for example, devotes a large chapter to the cities of the world, but without as much

profits to entice potential entrepreneurs to invest in factories and expensive machinery. As the urban settlements grew larger and larger, more and more investors decided to establish factories in places that provided not only a market but also the necessary technical skills and knowledge.

If the market of one big city attracted industrial investment, a cluster of *several big cities* that were fairly close to one another – which reduced transportation costs – drew even more potential entrepreneurs. This, in turn, created industrial landscapes rather than merely isolated industries in largely rural area, which stimulated industrialization on a much larger scale. Take, for example, southern and northern Italy: On the one hand, industrialization

---

as a hint about their significance for the process of industrialization. Similarly, Eigner (2011) omits the role of big cities in his recent collection about the development of the European economy over the last 1000 years, a work intended for students, teachers, and the interested public. Ehmer (2011), 140 f and others mention the most important big cities and their population numbers but they do not connect them with industrialization. According to Bairoch (1991), 250, some researchers view urbanization as a contributing – albeit not a "particularly significant" – factor for the industrial revolution, and Bairoch (1991), 257 himself thinks it "rather improbable that cities would be useful in explaining industrialization in England" even though he emphasizes that "cities provide markets for industrial commodities." Bairoch (1991), 257. Pollard (1981), 211 f even goes a step further and claims that big cities, especially on the fringes of Europe, influenced industrialization negatively. In his long article on urbanization in the Cambridge Economic History of Modern Europe, Malanima (2010) ignores big cities of more than 100,000 inhabitants and their potential influence on industrialization. Instead, he focuses on developing and comparing inner-European urbanization rates, based on cities with more than 10,000 or 5,000 inhabitants. Vries (1984) did more or less the same earlier. Unlike Bairoch (1991), 252 and Sachs (2005), 36, Phyllis Deane sees urbanization not only as a result but as a possible cause of industrialization. In Deane (1998), 49 she opines that "the demand of city dwellers for food, fuel, and basic commodities … stimulated the development of trade and industry." Yet, she does not mention the special role of big cities either. North (1961), 166-170 discusses the growth of urban centers as a favorable condition for the industrialization of the American Northeast, but he is looking at the time before 1815, when American cities (like those in many other parts of the world) were still too small to stimulate industrial mass production.

occurred around the city of Naples but did not spread further; on the other, industrialization in big cities like Milan, Turin, and Genoa, along with other medium-sized cities, involved much more people than we would find in the more agricultural south. Similarly, in western and central Europe, as well as the Northeast in the US, industrialization occurred as a result of the big cities mentioned above, and it intensified and expanded thanks to a network of additional mid-sized cities.

In addition, *consumer demand* in big cities and their neighboring industries stimulated industrialization in other – sometimes even remote – regions, especially those that had the necessary raw materials such as coal or iron ore, which, for centuries, had not been mined at all or only on a relatively small scale. It was not until modern industries demanded massive quantities of these resources that industrial regions like the Ruhr area in Germany could develop; in turn, these newly developed regions spawned yet more cities, which stimulated industrialization even more.

Both diachronic and synchronic analyses show that the *mining of raw materials* depends on the demand generated by the big cities. Despite the emerging European and North American industries, which could have served as models for other parts of the world, other countries did not mine their natural – often much larger – resources for a long time. This did not change until modern vehicles brought down the cost of long-distant transport and until cities developed in these areas whose demand stimulated industrialization.

While some areas boasted natural resources, others could supply relatively *cheap labor*. The same principle applies to both: Cheap labor attracted investors only if there was a market for the goods they produced, such as the consumer demand generated by a big city. Like other regions, industrialization in parts of Switzerland or the neighboring Vorarlberg depended, to a large degree, on the availability of cheap labor, which resulted from overpopulation in these areas. Because they could not make a living from farming, the people took factory jobs that were not very appealing because of low wages and bad working conditions.

My *global approach* in this book will show that the causes of and conditions for successful industrialization were more or less the same in western and central Europe as in other parts of the world later on. I intend to show that global models of industrialization existed in the past and still exist today. These models will permit the formulation of a *theory of economic development* that explains industrialization whenever it happened in the past and will shed some light on the future as well. Such a theory perceives globalization not as a collective development in which individual regions are connected by a global system of dependency, and in which some areas develop at the expense of others.[8] Instead, I intend to look at specific regional conditions when trying to explain the causes, development, and results of economic development in general—and industrialization in particular. These developments are global in the sense that they follow the same or similar patterns everywhere in the world.

## GLOBAL INTERRELATIONS

Still, it cannot be denied that, in addition to local conditions, multi-faceted *economic relationships* exist between different regions, today more than ever. However, in order to prevent hasty generalizations, we need to weigh them with regard to time and place. This is especially true for the popular opinion that the so-called First World developed at the expense of the Third World and, through exploitation, retarded its development. However, the arguments in support of this theory do not hold up under close scrutiny.

---

8    Among others: Frank (1978), Frank (1978a), Wallerstein (1989), Senghaas (1981), Menzel/Seng-haas (1986), Amin (1997a). Menzel (1993) offers a comprehensive bibliography of over 3,000 titles of scholars who share their theory of economic development. This theory is based on the belief that countries and large regions connect with each other in a global system and that they depend on each other to varying degrees (dependence theory). Due to a global division of labor, they differ from each other in that some have become highly-developed metropolises while others on the (semi-)periphery have developed less. According to the proponents of this theory, foreign trade has had a much greater influence on the economic development of a country or region than its domestic trade even though exports, especially in larger countries, account for only a small percentage of the gross natural product. O'Brien (1982), 4 points out that exports in European countries around the end of the 18th century accounted for only 4 percent of the gross national product. In addition, those who subscribe to this theory tend to see economic development as a consequence of economic policies or sweeping social decisions and less as the result of thousands of individual decisions on the part of economic subjects, who are much more influenced by the chances, challenges, and limits of the market than by the economic policies of governments.

For one, according to this theory, the European colonies served as *purveyors of cheap raw materials* for the industrialization in Europe.[9] This is wrong on several counts. Starting in the 16th century, the goods that were imported from America included food and luxury items like sugar, coffee, tobacco, and cacao on the one hand, and wood and furs on the other. Neither was necessary for industrialization; they supported the lifestyles of a small elite or were used to build ships. Granted, items such as corn and potatoes, which were much more important in feeding the European population, originally came from America, but they were soon grown in Europe and were not part of the international trade.

The only raw material worth mentioning with regard to early industrialization is raw cotton. For a long time, the Levant supplied whatever limited demand existed in the pre-industrial era, but by the end of the 18th century, the newly invented looms created an increased demand for raw cotton, which was imported from the American South. Even though Great Britain had its own cotton-producing colonies in India, British and European importers decided in favor of the cheaper American cotton. Granted, the exploitation of African Slaves at the hands of the American plantation owners contributed to the lower price, but the British colonialists exploited Indian tea plantations in a similar way. In the end, we assume that it was cheaper to ship cotton from the US, an independent nation since 1776/83 than from India, the British colony.

As was the case with *crude oil* a hundred years later, the example of raw cotton shows that colonies were not a necessary source of raw materials. Before World War I, the countries of the Middle East, one of the most important purveyor of crude oil to date, was largely part of the Ottoman Empire until they gained their independence soon after. The same is true for other oil-exporting countries such as historically independent Persia or Mexico and Venezuela, independent since the beginning of the 19the century, and Nigeria and Indonesia, independent since the second half of the 20th century. Global trade does not depend on colonies. Economic interests and expected gains sufficed to create business relationships between potential suppliers and their clients. Other important raw materials like iron ore and coal, indispensable for the second phase of the industrialization process that

---

9    Among others, see Frank (2005), 58, or Senghaas (1982). Elsenhans (1982) provides a critical perspective.

began around the middle of the 19ᵗʰ century, were supplied by European sources until far into the 20ᵗʰ century.

In addition, contrary to popular opinion, the European colonies overseas did not provide an important – let alone indispensable – *market* for the emerging industries. Admittedly, it has been sufficiently demonstrated that the mass production of the fledgling European industries needed some mass demand, which, however, did not really exist overseas. According to the Irish economic historian Patrick O'Brien, only a quarter of the European foreign trade included other continents at the end of the 18ᵗʰ century: Asia represented 5% of the trade, North America 10%, South America 8%, and Africa 1%. The rest of the trade involved European countries, and this changed very little in the course of the 19ᵗʰ century.[10]

With the exception of Asia, non-European countries did not have the necessary *population rates*, which explains O'Brien's findings. Around 1800, America, Africa, and Oceania had a combined population of about 128 million, compared to 188 million in Europe.[11] In addition, the people living outside of Europe – many of them still hunters and gatherers or self-supporting peasants – did not have enough purchasing power to buy the European goods, which were made even more expensive through high transportation costs. This is also true for most Asians, even though a part of their 638 million population lived in urban settlements like Europeans.[12] For a long time, they were able to meet their demand for

---

10    O'Brien (1982), 4, and Fischer (1985), 170. Early on, Everley (1967) and later Evans (1996), 113 relativized the importance of foreign markets. According to Evans, British foreign trade even declined by 6% between 1775 and 1784. Landes (1973), 64 records a decline in British exports in the third quarter of the 18th century, but he still attributed a good deal of importance to foreign trade. The same is true for Vries (2011), 430-434, who deals with this question in great depth and detail. Lipsey (1972) found that around 1869, the exports from the US accounted for only 6% of the gross national product and that imports made up only 11% of all the goods bought in the US. Much of the overrated importance of foreign trade for the beginnings of industrialization probably results from the later increased growth rates for exports , which, however, do not say anything about the much-larger volume of the domestic trade.  See Frank (1978), 74-77.

11    Mathieu (2011), 87.

12    Mathieu (2011), 87.

industrial goods on their own. Even when, in the course of the 19th century, cheaper, indus-trially-produced foreign goods crowded out their own, exports to Asia accounted for only about 10% of all European exports.[13]

In this way – at least in total and independently of the high profits of individual mer-chants and businesses – the *profits* mentioned above derived less from trade outside of Europe than from the larger exchange between European countries. When these profits were used as capital for industrial investments – which was not always the case, however – they did not depend on foreign trade or markets outside of Europe.

The same, eventually, holds true for *silver*, which was often used as currency. It had come to Europe in large quantities from Potosi (today a part of Bolivia) since the mid-16th century, but it was mostly used for decorative items and as currency for spices and luxury goods from Asia. The money necessary for industrial investments had existed in Europe herself for centuries, especially since small, fledgling factories did not need a lot of capital initially.[14]

If European industrialization depended on existing conditions in Europe, the same is ultimately true for the delay of *industrialization in Third World countries*. Their trade with Europe, which was partially forced on them and was partially supported by their social elites for their own benefit, would have left them in possession of enough raw material to build their own industries. Despite the fact that some of their workers were exploited by native and foreign entrepreneurs, the revenues from exports in food and crude oil would have supplied enough capital for industrial investment, at least in some of these countries. Admittedly, the competition of foreign goods hampers the development of a domestic in-dustry.[15] However, countries like Canada, the US, Australia, or Japan demonstrate that it was possible to industrialize against these odds. The absence of industrial investment is not necessarily a result of a shortage in raw materials and/or capital, nor of overwhelming foreign competition. As I will show in detail, the real reason is that, for a long time, there

---

13    Fischer (1985), 170.

14    See Evans (1996), 110.

15    See Frank (1978), 92-139, Frank (2005), 65, or Bayly (2006), 226 on the restriction of the domestic market as a result of the over-emphasis on foreign trade.

was no sufficient mass demand in large urban settlements. The lack of incentives to invest in manufacturing industries led to continued investment in agrarian production and mineral raw materials for the export trade, as well as to an outward flow of capital to foreign countries that offered expanding markets and opportunities for profitable investment. It was not until recently that large and mega-cities emerged in Third World countries; they provided incentives for industrial production and thus stimulated industrialization. As late as 1940, all of the five mega-cities with more than five million inhabitants were located in the First World; 60 years later, at the turn of the 21st century, 34 of 45 such cities were part of the Third World.[16]

## TRADITIONAL EXPLANATIONS

I intend to analyze the degree of industrialization in different countries on a *global scale*, which will not only reveal similar causes for their industrialization, but it will also enable me to question the explanations that have traditionally been given for the differences between them.

The fact that industrialization began in Europe around the end of the 18th century led many historians and economists to look for *specifically European* or Occidental reasons for the process.[17] Even a cursory glance at the countries that underwent industrialization reveals that the question as such is the wrong one to ask. For one, there is – and always has been – a big difference between heavily and less industrialized nations in Europe. If anything, we would have to ask if there were specific western, central, and northern European factors that promoted wholesale industrialization in these areas and not in the still less developed regions of southern and eastern Europe. On the other hand, examples like the US, Canada, Australia, or Japan, as well as the younger industrial nations of South Korea, Taiwan, or Singapore, illustrate that industrialization is not restricted to Europe and thus a

---

16    Bronger (2004), 20.

17    See Landes (1973), 26-46 and, more recently and representative for many others, Jones (1981), Jones (2002) or Mitterauer (2003).

particularly European phenomenon. The argument that the population in the US, Canada, or Australia is of largely European stock is not convincing either because the same is true for the less industrialized nations of Latin America.

The same can be said about the popular opinion that certain *religious orientations* supported industrialization more than others. Following Max Weber, scholars attribute the "spirit of capitalism" in Great Britain and the US to a specific brand of Protestant ethics,[18] which, in a nutshell, maintains that economic success and wealth in this world is a sign of being among the elect and thus encourages entrepreneurial endeavors. This theory has been used to explain the difference in development between the predominantly Protestant US and the Catholic countries of Latin America,[19] but it ignores non-Protestant industrial countries and the fact that international merchants thought in decidedly capitalist ways long before the Reformation. The former category includes France, Belgium, Northern Italy, Austria, the Catholic regions of Germany and Switzerland, and even Shinto-Buddhist Japan. The latter category includes the medieval European merchants and bankers, such as the Fugger, the Medici, and many others, who demonstrate that a profit-oriented attitude and entrepreneurship existed long before the start of the Industrial Revolution at the end of the 18th century. We need to ask why, for centuries, merchants in and outside of Europe focused their energies on trade – a few exceptions notwithstanding.[20] However, their religion and culture do not explain why they preferred international trade to similarly profitable industrial mass production.[21]

The much-cited theory that *climatic conditions* influenced industrialization does not fare any better.[22] It has often been used to explain the allegedly different work ethic in tropical as compared to more temperate climates. Admittedly, besides Singapore and Taiwan, there are

---

18    A reissue of Weber (2006). See also early Landes (1973), 35 f.

19    For a critical analysis see Frank (1978), 25-33.

20    See Pollard (1981), 63-78 and, more recently, Cerman (2011) on the subject of proto-industrial production, involving a small group of merchants that hired a relatively large number of artisans to produce various textiles for them to sell.

21    Grondana (2002) takes a very different view.

22    See Sachs (2002), 60-62.

very few industrial nations (albeit not regions) in the tropics; however, Japan, South Korea, and Australia are important examples of successful industrial nations in the sub-tropics. In turn, there are quite a few less industrialized countries in more moderate climates to their north and south. More importantly, it is difficult to prove the causal connection between climate and industrial production. If such a connection exists at all, one would expect to find it in agricultural work, which largely takes place outside, and not in indoor factory production.

We can make a similar case for the *institutional framework* conditions of economic production.[23] Even though a degree of legal certainty is indispensable for industry investments, this is true for all economic activity. Without doubt, legal conditions play a big role in economic development that can be hampered by war or political unrest. Yet, like religion, culture, or climate, these factors do not explain the uneven global distribution of industrialization.

*Raw materials* play a more important role in industrialization. It goes without saying that they are a necessary condition for the manufacture of any goods. However, experience shows that they do not have to be part of the natural resources of the country in which they are processed. Take cotton, for example: One of the oldest raw materials, it was supplied by the Levant, India, and, since the end of the 18th century, by the American South. Obviously, the cotton mills in the industrial countries were able to procure the necessary raw materials abroad. The same is true for iron ore and coal, the most important raw materials and sources of energy in the iron and steel industries. Some later industrial nations had plenty of these resources, but countries like Japan, South Korea, Taiwan, Italy, and Switzerland did not. Likewise, crude oil, which came to replace coal as a main source of energy, was more often imported than produced in industrial nations. Obviously, wherever there was a demand for raw materials, there were enough suppliers to provide it, worldwide if necessary, and despite the occasional inconvenience of blocked trade routes in times of war. Existing natural resources could stimulate industrialization, but they were not a necessary condition, and many countries that owned a lot of raw materials failed to industrialize.

---

23    Standing in for others: North (1988), North (2005), Acemoglu/Robinson (2014); for an overview, see Resch (2011).

Just like raw materials could be supplied worldwide, the distribution of *technological innovations* knew no borders, neither at the end of the 18th century nor today. If entrepreneurs lacked the technical know-how for industrial projects, they found it somewhere abroad. There is no doubt that technological inventions were as necessary a condition for industrial production as raw materials, but they were not sufficient by themselves to trigger large-scale industrialization.[24]

*Capital* constitutes another necessary (albeit not sufficient) condition for widespread industrialization. Generally, only the rich had it, and they used it in different ways. The landed gentry and the upper classes spent their money on their lavish lifestyles while merchants re-invested it in their businesses. We must therefore ask what conditions and impulses inspired them to invest their income in industrial enterprises instead. Obviously, the affluent groups in many countries that profitably exported food and/or raw materials lacked the incentive to invest much of their profits in their native industries. Besides, fledgling industrial enterprises did not initially need a lot of starting capital, and what they needed was relatively easy to get; it was not until later that reinvested and additional capital from outside turned them into big businesses.[25]

Besides sufficient starting capital, successful industrialization required a large *workforce*. Despite opinions to the contrary,[26] an adequate number of workers would have been available before the accelerated population growth that started around 1750. The large numbers of people working in the decentralized putting-out system before the Industrial Revolution support this theory; they might as well have been employed in factories. However, if the locally available labor force proved insufficient for the growing production, employers could easily obtain workers elsewhere. There are plenty of examples to support this: The workers who came from the east of the former German Empire and settled in the Ruhr area; the workers in the Vorarlberg textile industry who came from the formerly Austrian province

---

24    On the role of technology see Landes (1973) and Pollard (1981), 143-148, and, more recently among others Sachs (2005), 31 f. and Weitensfelder (2011), who goes into great detail. For an analysis of how technology furthered the Industrial Revolution in England, see Allen (2009).

25    On the subject of relatively low initial capital requirements see Evans (1996), 110.

26    See Wallerstein (1989), 6.

of Trentino; and, most recently, the legions of guest workers from Southern Europe who were recruited after World War II into German, Austrian, and Swiss businesses. On the other hand, available cheap labor could induce potential entrepreneurs to build or expand factories in some regions, but only if there was a market for their products. The millions of people who leave their rural homes in search of work in big cities illustrate that the presence of a local work force does not by itself inspire entrepreneurs to build factories that would employ these people.

In conclusion, one can say that the traditional explanations for the genesis of industrialization include important and at times indispensable requirements for industrial production, but they were not sufficient – by themselves or in combination – to trigger it. As will be shown in this analysis for the first time on a global scale, successful industrialization requires a sufficiently *large market* and a demand for mass-produced goods that will guarantee profits. When scholarly sources discuss the importance of markets at all, they either talk about colonial markets outside of Europe or refer to the rapid population growth in Europe since the 18th century. I have already shown that the colonial market was not large enough to absorb the great quantities of mass-produced goods and thus stimulate the production of more. The European market, however, could not develop as long as population growth occurred in areas that lacked large urban centers. The transportation costs created by the distance between the supplier and the consumer undercut potential profits. It was not until the 18th and 19th century that large cities – first in Europe and North America and then in other parts of the world – provided the concentration of potential consumers in a relatively small area, in other words, the mass market necessary to bring about and sustain industrial production. In the following chapters, which are organized by continents, I will support this new theory that big cities play a central and causal role in the industrialization process.[27]

---

27   This will also close the gap indicated by Jürgen Osterhammel in Osterhammel (2010), 913, who claims that "in the last three decades, nothing essentially new has been added to the older or 'classic' theories of industrialization."

# EUROPE

## URBANIZATION IN ANTIQUITY

It is impossible to estimate the *total population numbers* in pre-Christian Europe with anything approaching accuracy.[28] Yet, scholars have been trying time and again. Most recently, the British economic historian Angus Maddison[29] estimated the population of Europe around the time of Christ's birth at a scant 30 million (his estimate excludes the territory of the former Soviet Union). This would have been one-seventeenth of today's population. By Maddison's calculation, most of the people – about two thirds – would have lived in present-day Italy, Spain, France, and Germany. Even if the numbers are not entirely reliable, we can safely assume that population density in western and southern Europe was higher than anywhere else, which coincides with the fact that there were also more towns in these parts.

Obviously, the population density in the Mediterranean was high enough for *quasi-urban settlements* to develop as early as the first millennium BCE. The most documented of these were located in ancient Greece and the subsequent Roman Empire, where towns sprang up in present-day Italy, on the Iberian Peninsula, and as far as the British Isles in the west. We tend to find fewer ancient towns outside of the Roman Empire, i.e. in eastern and northern Europe. If industrialization had been possible at this time, one would have expected it to occur in the western and southern parts of Europe rather than the mostly agrarian or pre-agrarian areas outside of the Mediterranean.

Indeed, most of the *conditions necessary for industrialization* already existed during the Greek and Roman periods.[30] Craftsmen, artisans, and merchants lived in these ancient

---

28    Houtte (1980), 14-16.

29    Maddison (Population).

30    See Mathis (2011), 100-108.

towns and would for centuries afterwards. They had technical know-how and the entrepreneurial spirit to invest in commercial enterprises, as is illustrated by their architectural accomplishments and the fact that they traded far beyond the borders of their home countries. They had natural resources such as metals and textiles, as well as capital ready for investments. They had plenty of people looking for work and an efficient traffic infrastructure on land and sea. They were able to produce or import sufficient food supplies for their urban communities, and they probably would have been able to feed additional non-agrarian population groups without any problems.

The only thing that prevented the emergence of *industrial mass production* was the demand created by large urban mass markets, which could have inspired risky and expensive investments for the sake of profit. However, the population numbers of these ancient cities were not large enough to create such a mass demand. An overwhelming number of Roman cities – if we include their surrounding communities – had between 2,000 and 10,000 inhabitants, which means that the number of those who lived within the city walls was significantly smaller.[31] Only a few urban settlements – such as the fore-runners of present-day Milan, Aquileia, Padua, Lyon, Trier, or Cádiz – had over 50,000 inhabitants and were thus larger cities in our sense of the term.[32] More than 100,000 citizens lived in the European part of the Roman Empire only in Rome, whose population is estimated to have been between 250,000 and more than a million. Similarly, Constantinople, after it became the capital of the Empire, is assumed to have had between 300,000 and a million inhabitants in the 6th century CE. In the light of the fact that 3rd-century Rome occupied an area of 13-14 square kilometers (5-5.5 square miles) and Constantinople hardly more than 10 square kilometers (3.8 square miles), which is considerably smaller than a city the size of present-day Innsbruck, the low population estimates appear much more realistic.[33]

Thus, in ancient Europe, two factors hampered the development of the kind of *mass market* necessary for industrialization: for one, Rome and Constantinople, the two cities

---

31    Vittinghoff (1990), 197.

32    Vittinghoff (1990), 198.

33    Kolb (1984), 191 and Kolb (2006), 93.

that would have been the likeliest candidates, were too small (compared to the big cities in Europe and the US in the 19[34] century); in addition, they were located too far apart to stimulate profitable mass production.[34]

## URBANIZATION IN THE MIDDLE AGES AND THE EARLY MODERN ERA

The size and number of ancient cities did not change after the fall of the Western Roman Empire in 476 CE. On the contrary, instead of growing in numbers, the European population shrank as a result of the increased warfare that accompanied the Migration Period and the frequent plagues of the 6th and 7th centuries.[35] Not least because of frequent plundering, the number of towns decreased along with their populations and the urban lifestyle in general, which amounted to an economic and social *counter-urbanization*. Although the process was more strongly felt in the more remote regions than in the Mediterranean, the former center of the Roman Empire, it drove the degree of urbanization well below previous standards. Rome shrank to some 10,000 inhabitants; Constantinople eventually suffered the same fate by the end of the Middle Ages.[36]

The trend probably reversed in the 8th or, at the very latest, in the 9th century. The *population of Europe* increased in all its larger regions, but it took until the end of the first millennium to supersede the numbers at its beginning.[37] The steady growth suffered a setback around 1347/50, when the Bubonic plague, which had hitherto appeared only sporadically, reduced the population by a third of its former size.

Up to this point, the increase in population coincided with the cultivation of additional land on the one hand, and the revival of old *urban settlements* and the construction of new ones on the other.[38] The growing population and the reappearance of clerical and secular

---

34    Mathis (2011), 111.

35    See Houtte (1980), 16 and 119 f; Cameron/Neal (2003), 59.

36    Bairoch/Batou/Chèvre (1988), 47. On the controversy regarding Constantinople's number of inhabitants, see Wikipedia (Constantinople).

37    Maddison (Population).

38    See Houtte (1980), 121-124.

elites increased trade and spawned a number of commercial and administrative centers that grew steadily as they attracted more and more people. However, as they did in ancient times, these centers remained relatively small by today's standards. Disregarding much higher and unrealistic estimates, it is to be assumed that the largest of them probably had no more than 100,000 inhabitants. According to the lists compiled by Paul Bairoch, Jean Batou, and Pierre Chèvre, Europe had eleven cities of more than 50,000 inhabitants around 1300.[39] Only two of these – Paris and Cologne – were located north of the Alps; the others were in Italy – Milan, Genoa, Venice, Florence, Naples, Palermo – and in Spain – Córdoba, Granada, and Seville; The latter profited from their centuries-old proximity to Islamic urban traditions. As a matter of course, the number of cities with population rates between 20,000 and 50,000 inhabitants was markedly larger (see Table 1).

Even though the population numbers for some of these urban settlements are based on estimates rather than exact calculations – and might thus be a little too high – we can see a clear trend with regard to the *geographic distribution* of the 92 cities under discussion (see Map 1). Almost half of them are located in two rather small areas north and south of the Alps: London, Paris, Speyer, and Cologne define the first of these in the north-west of Europe, and Genoa, Milan, Venice, and Rome make up the north-Italian cityscape. Around 1300, each of these areas boasted about the same number of cities with more than 20,000 inhabitants as could be found in eastern and southern Europe outside of Spain, and almost twice as many as in the larger Iberian Peninsula.

---

39    Bairoch/Batou/Chèvre (1988).

Map 1: Cities with Over 20,000 Inhabitants in Europe Around 1300

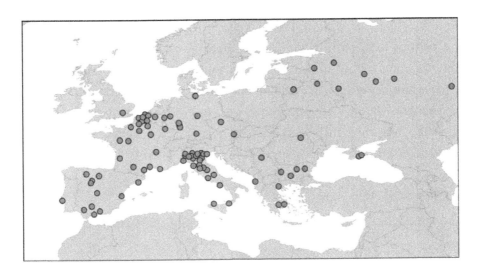

Tirol Atlas – Designed by Klaus Förster based on Table 1.
Map background: World Borders Dataset - http://thematicmapping.org/downloads/world_borders.php

The *center of urbanized Europe* had gradually shifted from the Mediterranean toward central and northern Europe. If urbanization had been an important prerequisite for subsequent industrialization, northern Italy and north-west Europe would have been in a better position than the rest of the continent, where urban settlements were spread over a much larger area and where, consequently, the degree of urbanization was lower. However, even in the more economically advanced regions, the cities were still too small to abandon traditional artisanal methods of production that supplied the local demand and produced some goods for the foreign trade.

Pre-industrial *artisanal manufacture* continued over the next four to five centuries. After the decline of population size around the middle of the 14th century, the numbers rose again and, according to Maddison and others, reached 80 million by 1500, which was slightly higher than before the Bubonic Plague epidemic.[40] From then on, the population grew rather slowly until it stalled at 120 to 140 million people by 1750, the eve of the Industrial Revolution. The degree of urbanization increased in proportion with population density. By 1750, according to Bairoch/Batou/Chèvre, there were 154 cities with more than 20,000 inhabitants (as compared to 92 in 1300), and some of them were growing rapidly (see Table 2).[41] This number included 15 capitals and important commercial cities that exceeded 100,000 inhabitants. Besides London and Paris, both of which had grown beyond a half million people, these cities included (in order of their size) Naples, Amsterdam, Lisbon, Vienna, Madrid, Rome, Venice, Moscow, Dublin, Milan, Palermo, Lyon, and Berlin.

Map 2: Cities with Over 20,000 Inhabitants in Europe Around 1750

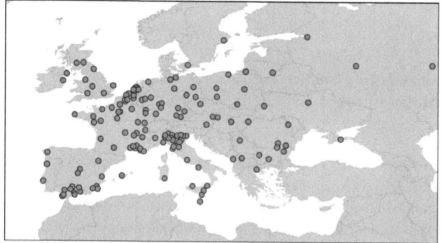

Tirol Atlas – Designed by Klaus Förster based on Table 2.
Map background: World Borders Dataset - http://thematicmapping.org/downloads/world_borders.php

---

40    Maddison (Population); Mathieu (2011), 87.

41    Bairoch/Batou/Chèvre (1988).

As was the case around 1300, the *density of urban settlements* was above average in some European regions (see Map 2). The formerly rather small urban landscapes in northern Italy and north-west Europe had not only grown denser, but they had also expanded to include surrounding areas in France, Belgium, the Netherlands, and Germany. As a result, a kind of urban belt stretched from the Netherlands to northern Italy. Urban density tended to decline with a region's distance from this belt, albeit not everywhere to the same degree.[42]

## URBANIZATION AND INDUSTRIALIZATION IN THE LATE 18TH AND THE LONG 19TH CENTURY

The increasing density of the urban landscape – a few large cities notwithstanding – was still not enough to provide the *mass market* necessary for – or at least conducive to – industrial mass production, which happened only as a result of the massive changes of the next few decades. In just hundred years, between 1750 and 1850, the number of cities with more than 20,000 inhabitants doubled to 417 (333 if we do not count Great Britain); this number had only grown by 70% throughout the previous 450 years.[43] Accelerated population growth intensified urbanization. Thanks to declining mortality rates, the European population doubled to a scant 270 million during this time period.[44]

*Great Britain*, where cities with over 20,000 inhabitants multiplied tenfold, has to be treated as a special case. Britain's remarkable urban expansion was no longer a mere prerequisite for but already a result of industrialization, which started there in the 1770s. However, the number of British cities of 20,000-plus inhabitants had already tripled between 1750 and 1800.[45] And still, the exponential growth of the British capital was probably a more important factor than the expansion of mid-size and larger towns. While it still lagged behind Paris in 1600, *London*, with 575,000 inhabitants, had surpassed the French metropolis

---

42    See also the map in Bairoch/Batou/Chèvre (1988), 239.

43    Bairoch/Batou/Chèvre (1988).

44    Fischer (1985), 12.

45    Bairoch/Batou/Chèvre (1988).

as Europe's biggest city by 1700. A hundred years later, the population of London had grown to one million while Paris held steady at approximately 550,000 inhabitants.[46] No other European city at this time could compete with London, and they all lagged behind Paris as well. We can make a strong case that a city the size of London created the kind of mass demand needed to spark industrialization sooner than it happened on the Continent. Between 1772 and 1815, the number of warehouses – an indicator of a rapidly growing market – increased six-fold from 120 to 729.[47]

Because industrialization in Great Britain – as it did later in many other countries – started with the mechanization of the *cotton industry*; the well-documented method of processing raw cotton serves as a reliable indicator of its development. Between the mid-18th century, when cotton was processed by hand, and the end of the century, when the new mechanized spinning frames were already in use, the volume of cotton processing increased almost twenty-fold in the United Kingdom alone.[48] Between 1770 and 1815, the production of cotton goods increased more than twenty-fold thanks to the new spinning frames and, not much later, mechanized looms.[49] During the first decade of the 19th century, Great Britain produced about four times more cotton than the more populous France, and, in the late 1830s, almost 20 times more than the lands of the later German Empire.[50]

Industrialization soon spread to other trades. Thanks to the steam engine and railroads, which were operating since the 20s and 30s, machine production developed hand in hand with *the iron and steel industries*. In 1840, about half of the European railroad network was concentrated in Great Britain and Ireland.[51] The production of pig iron tripled in Great Britain in the mere 30 years between the 1780s and the first decade of the 19th century.[52]

---

46   Bairoch/Batou/Chèvre (1988).

47   See Mathis (2006), 227 f. and Chapman (1990), 31 f..

48   Mitchell (1975), 427 f.

49   Rule (1992), 35.

50   Mitchell (1975), 428. See Table 3 for the population numbers for individual countries.

51   Fischer (1985), 157 and Mitchell (1977), 514.

52   Mitchell (1975), 391.

Before, it had lagged behind the French production. In the 1820s, Britain produced three times the amount of pig iron as France and seven times as much as Germany.[53]

The iron, steel, and machine-building industries and railroad construction boosted the *coal mining industry*. Because of the increased use of steam engines, coal took the place of charcoal, water, and animal power as the main source of energy. Great Britain had an even greater head start in coal mining than in the production of pig iron. By 1815, Britain produced 18 times as much coal as France, and about 13 times as much as Germany.[54]

The rapid progress of industrialization in Great Britain, as illustrated by these few examples, reduced the number of people working in agriculture and forestry, which shrank to a scant 25% by the middle of 19th century.[55] By contrast, half of the *workforce* was employed in manufacturing industries. In other European countries, agriculture still represented a much larger percentage of the economy: about 50% in western and central Europe and more than 60% or even 70% everywhere else.[56]

It thus comes as no surprise that the *per-capita economic production* between 1700 and 1820 grew nowhere as fast as in the United Kingdom. Maddison estimates the growth to be about 36%, compared to 25% or less in France, Germany, and other countries. The difference would have even been greater if the time period under discussion did not include several pre-industrial decades with comparatively slow economic growth.[57]

Throughout the 19th century, none of the large cities on the *European continent* could compare to London. Paris, the second-largest city in Europe, was not even half as big as the growing British metropolis. Still, they all expanded much faster than they did before. Around 1800, there were only 18 cities with more than 100,000 inhabitants; by 1850, their number had grown to 32 (see Table 4). The inhabitants of these cities rose from 3.6 to 7.3

53    Mitchell (1975), 391 f.

54    Mitchell (1975), 360 f.

55    Fischer (1985), 126.

56    Fischer (1985), 126; Kahan (1985), 520; Berend/Ránki (1985), 615; Delivanis/Sundhausen (1985), 655; Bernecker/Segura (1985), 670; Serrao/Thomas (1985), 694.

57    My calculations are based on Maddison (Per Capita GDP).

million. One million of these lived in Paris alone while the others – except St. Petersburg – had fewer than half a million people in 1850.[58]

Map 3: Cities with Over 100,000 Inhabitants in Europe Around 1850

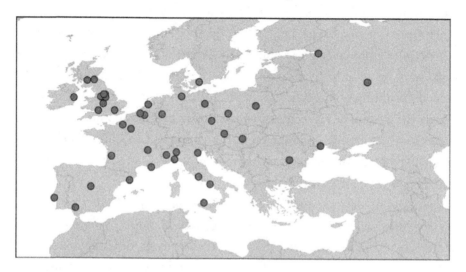

Tirol Atlas –Designed by Klaus Förster based on Table 4.
Map background: World Borders Dataset - http://thematicmapping.org/downloads/world_borders.php

Around the middle of the 19th century, these cities were concentrated in continental western and central Europe, occupying an area that extended from Copenhagen in the north, to Amsterdam and Rouen in the west, to Marseille and Genoa in the south, and Venice, Budapest, and Breslau in the east (see Map 3). This area included most of the cities with over 100,000 inhabitants, with the rest of them distributed over much larger areas in northern, eastern, and southern Europe.

As a result, one could expect the *mass demand* for industrial goods to develop in western and central Europe much more than in the rest of the Continent – even more

---

58    Bairoch/Batou/Chèvre (1988).

so since the distribution of medium-sized cities of 20,000 to 100,000 inhabitants shows a similar pattern, with a much larger supply of potential entrepreneurs and skilled workers in western and central Europe. While not all regions in this part of Europe experienced the same degree of urbanization at the same time, they profited more from it than northern, eastern, and southern Europe, where industrialization was limited to the metropolitan areas of a few far-flung cities. Depending on the number and size of areas that experienced industrialization, the overall industrial production differed from country to country.

Like Great Britain before them, different regions on the Continent began *mechanizing* their *manufacturing production*. And like Great Britain, the mass demand of urban populations stimulated economic activity not only in the cities and their immediate surroundings, but also in neighbouring regions which offered two-fold advantages to potential entrepreneurs: existing raw materials and a large supply of skilled and unskilled workers. Smaller and mid-sized cities provided most of the skilled workers while overpopulated regions supplied most of the unskilled (and cheap) labor force. However, in order to make a profit for entrepreneurs, factories should still not be too far away from the large cities, which provided the market for the goods they produced.

As was the case in England, the development of the textile industry – as well as coal mining and the steel and iron industries – illustrates the beginnings of industrialization on the Continent. Thanks to an increase of mechanized spinning frames between the beginning and the middle of the 19th century, France increased its annual rate of *processed raw cotton* from 8,000 to 65,000 tons, Germany from about 9,000 tons in the late 1830s to almost 70,000 tons by 1860, and the Habsburg monarchy from about 12,000 tons to over 40,000 in the same time span.[59] Despite their distance from the center of European industrial production, the Russian cities of Moscow and St. Petersburg stimulated industrialization in Russia, where annual cotton production rose from less than 1,000 tons at the beginning to over 21,000 tons around the middle of the century.[60] Considering that the British cotton industry already had these kinds of production numbers at the turn of the century – and

59   Mitchell (1975), 428 f.
60   Mitchell (1975), 428 f.

would push them to almost 300,000 tons by mid-century – we can see that these other countries were still only at the beginning of the industrialization process.[61]

The production numbers for *coal and lignite*, which around 1800 barely amounted to a million tons in countries outside of Great Britain, show similar increases: By the mid-19th century, Germany produced 6.9 million tons, France 4.4 million, and Belgium 5.8 million, but all of them lagged behind Great Britain, which mined 50 million tons of coal annually.[62] The production of *pig iron* on the Continent increased steadily after the turn of the century, but with less than half a million tons even in the larger countries by 1850, it lagged far behind Britain's 2.3 million.[63]  Lastly, *railroad construction*, both an indicator and motor of industrialization, increased on the Continent, but it could not compete with Britain: With roughly 10,000 kilometers of railroad lines, Great Britain still owned almost half of the European railroad system, followed by Germany with about 6,000, France with around 3,000 and Austria-Hungary with approximately 1,400 kilometers.[64]

*Railroads* also indicated a country's degree of industrialization. Around 1860, when almost all European countries had started building them, the countries with the highest per-capita railroad density – Great Britain, Germany, Belgium, France, and Switzerland – were located in urbanized western and central Europe (see Figure 1).

---

61    Mitchell (1975), 428 f.

62    Mitchell (1975), 360 f.

63    Mitchell (1975), 391 f.

64    Mitchell (1975), 581 f.

Figure 1: Railroads in Europe Around 1860 (Km per 1 Million Inhabitants)

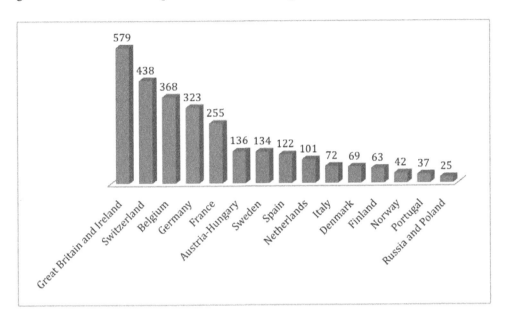

Calculations based on Fischer (1985), 14 and 157.

The difference in development between western and central Europe and the rest of the Continent persisted throughout the second half of the 19th century, up until the eve of World War I. However, the relationship between *urbanization and industrialization* was about to change. In the past, industrialization was triggered by a higher degree of urbanization and the formation of large cities, but now industrialization stimulated further urbanization in turn. Factories were concentrated in urban areas and enticed people to leave their rural homes and move to town. The pull factors of hoped-for jobs in the city, along with the push factor of a rapidly growing population, resulted in rural flight. In the 60 years between 1850 and 1910, the population of Europe increased by two thirds to roughly 450 million people.[65] Due to push and pull factors, cities grew even more quickly, which increased the demand for industrially produced goods. Urbanization, mass demand, and industrialization no longer appeared in

---

65　Fischer (1985), 12.

succession but stimulated each other simultaneously, a phenomenon that emerged in Great Britain as early as the first half of the 19th century and on the Continent during the second half.

In addition to an increase in the number of *big cities* with over 100,000 inhabitants, Berlin, Vienna, St. Petersburg, Moscow, and Glasgow became cities with over a million inhabitants, next to London, which had grown to more than seven million, and Paris, with almost three million inhabitants.[66] As was the case in England, the Continent now also saw the rapid growth of cities in the wake of industrialization, such as Dortmund, Duisburg, Düsseldorf or Essen in the Ruhr Valley, all of which profited from the increased demand for coal, which was mined there, and the iron and steel industries that followed. Taken together, European big cities had over 45 million inhabitants right before World War I, or almost four times as many as they did in 1850. This means that the number of people living in big cities grew four times as much as the total population.[67] Such a strong increase of potential consumers (especially if we add the inhabitants of smaller and medium-sized cities) could not fail to bring about further industrialization.

It comes as no surprise that this process happened primarily in *western and central Europe*, where about two thirds of all European cities over 100,000 inhabitants were located at the turn of the 20th century.[68] Industrialization in these regions happened more quickly and more extensively than it did elsewhere in Europe, where the process was limited to individual cities and their immediate surroundings. England in the first half of the 19th century and northern Italy in the second serve as examples for widespread, Russia and southern Italy for limited industrialization. While a densely urbanized industrial landscape developed between London and Manchester – and later between Milan, Genoa, and Turin – an agricultural economy dominated the region between Moscow and St. Petersburg as well as southern Italy outside of Naples and Palermo.[69]

---

66    Mitchell (1975), 76-79. According to Bairoch/Batou/Chèvre (1988), 283 the list of urban agglomerations with more than a million inhabitants included Birmingham and Manchester around the turn of the century.

67    My calculations are based on Fischer (1985), 12, Mitchell (1975), 76-79 and Bairoch/Batou/Chèvre (1988), 283.

68    Mitchell (1975), 76-79 and Bairoch/Batou/Chèvre (1988), 283.

69    See Mathis (2006), 229 and Mathis (2007).

Figure 2: Processing of Raw Cotton in Europe, 1909/13 (Kg per Capita, Annual Averages)

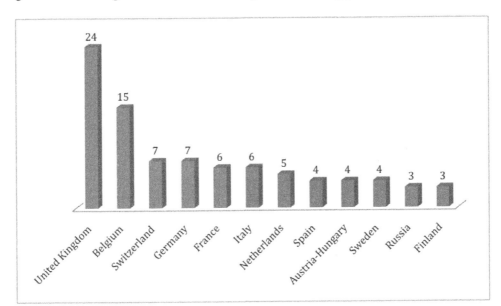

Calculations based on Fischer (1985), 14 and 151.

The production numbers of individual countries reflect the regional differences in urban density and industrialization, which still depended heavily on the *expansion of the cotton industry*. We can see this most clearly in the processing of raw cotton, which continued to increase in the second half of the 19th century, albeit not everywhere at the same pace. Figure 2 shows that the cotton industry in western and central Europe had made the most progress. This is even more evident if we consider that over 90% of Italian cotton spindles were located in Piedmont, Liguria, and Lombardy, that most of Spain's cotton goods were manufactured in Catalonia, and that the Austrian-Hungarian cotton industry was concentrated in the western part of the empire, especially in the Sudetenland, Vorarlberg, and the Vienna area – all of them regions bordering on the core zone of western and central Europe.[70]

---

70　Mathis (2007), 338; Nadal (1977), 395; Matis/Bachinger (1973), 203.

Figure 3: Production of Pig Iron in Europe, 1910/13 (Kg per Capita, Annual Averages)

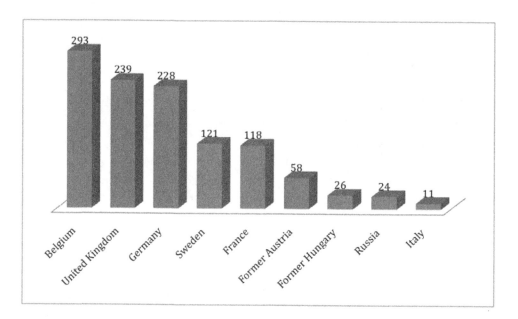

Calculations based on Mitchell (1975), 19-24 and 393 f.

The second phase of industrialization, the modernization of the *iron and steel industries* and their related trades, presents a similar picture (see Figure 3). Although the pig iron industry depends, to a degree, on the presence of iron-ore deposits, the per-capita production in Russia and Austria-Hungary – both of which had large quantities of iron ore – shows that the development of extensive iron and steel industries depends less on natural resources than on a demand for iron and steel. These industries grew with the increasing use of machines and the expansion of the rail network, which explains why they developed more robustly in western and central Europe than elsewhere on the Continent.

The size of a *railroad network* depends on the demand for more efficient transportation. Industrialized and urbanized regions produce more goods and thus stimulate trading, which, in turn, increases the demand for transportation. This explains why half of European railroads were built in western and central Europe, where by 1913 per-capita pig-iron production was much higher than in the larger rest of Europe.[71]

The same is true for overall *per-capita industrial production.* It ranged between 76% and 51% of the British numbers in Belgium, Germany, Switzerland, and France; in all other countries between 9% and 29%.[72] And since industrialization increased *per-capita incomes,* it is no surprise that on the eve of World War I the wealthiest countries were also located in western and central Europe: Great Britain, Switzerland, Belgium, the Netherlands, Denmark, France, Germany, and present-day Austria. The per-capita gross domestic product was slightly lower in Norway, Sweden, and Italy, but significantly lower in the other countries, especially those in eastern and southern Europe.[73]

# INDUSTRIALIZATION IN THE 20TH CENTURY

Throughout the late 18th and especially the 19th century, the *industrialization process,* which did not happen the same way everywhere, had intensified the existing differences between western and central Europe and the rest of the Continent. This did not change drastically throughout the first half of the 20th century, with the exception of the Soviet Union and Scandinavia. In fact, the gap between them widened even more until the middle of the century.[74]

For one, Europe continued to *urbanize* due to ongoing rural flight and despite slower population growth.[75] The number of cities with more than a million inhabitants rose from seven to 17 in the years between 1910 and 1950; the number of people living in them doubled from a scant 19 to over 40 million.[76] Ten of these cities were located in

---

71  Fischer (1985), 14 and 157.

72  Fischer (1985), 149.

73  Maddison (Per Capita GDP).

74  See Maddison (Per Capita GDP).

75  The population of Europe, which had more than doubled in the course of the 19th cenury, grew by a scant 80% to 728 millions in the 20th. Mathieu (2011), 87.

76  My calculations are based on Mitchell (1975), 76-79.

western and central Europe, between Glasgow, Milan, Budapest, and Copenhagen; the other seven were distributed over the much larger area of eastern and southern Europe between Leningrad, Moscow, Athens, and Madrid (see Map 4 and Table 5). In addition, the general degree of urbanization, measured by the number of people living in cities with more than 20,000 inhabitants, was also definitely higher in western and central Europe than elsewhere.[77]

As was the case in the past, western and central Europe had a much higher demand for *industrially-produced* bulk commodities. In addition, railroads lowered transportation costs and enabled established businesses or industrial regions to ship goods to more remote markets, which made it difficult for new suppliers to get a foothold in the business. In this fashion, enterprises in western and central Europe profited from their head-start while the less-industrialized countries in eastern and southern Europe fell further behind.

The *Soviet Union* took a different route. After the Bolshevik Revolution and the introduction of a planned economy, the industry was detached from domestic or international market forces and developed unhampered by competition from abroad. According to calculations done by Paul Bairoch and Angus Maddison, nowhere in eastern and southern Europe did per-capita income rise as much as in the Soviet Union, where manufacturing increased eight-fold between 1913 and World War II.[78] Before 1928, per-capita industrial production amounted to about one-sixth to that of Great Britain; by 1953, it had risen to one third. While still ranked behind Hungary and Czechoslovakia, the Soviet Union was ahead of Poland, Rumania, Bulgaria, and Yugoslavia, as well as Italy, Greece, Spain, and Portugal.[79] Increased industrialization influenced the average per-capita income of the Soviet population, which lived mostly in Europe. From 1913 to 1950, the per-capita gross domestic product almost doubled in the Soviet Union while it increased by only 25% in other eastern European countries and by even less in southern Europe.[80]

---

77   Fischer (1987), 54.

78   Bairoch (1982), 302 and 331; Maddison (Per Capita GDP); Lal (1988), 201.

79   Fischer (1987), 137, after Bairoch (1982), 302 und 331.

80   Maddison (Per Capita GDP).

Map 4: Cities with Over a Million Inhabitants in Europe Around 1950

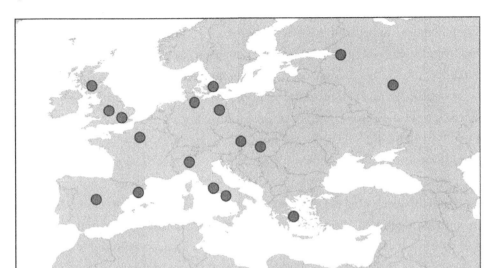

Tirol Atlas – Designed by Klaus Förster based on Table 5

Map background: World Borders Dataset - http://thematicmapping.org/downloads/world_borders.php

Thanks to the unprecedented increase of both the *steel and cotton industries*, the Soviet Union, at the beginning of the 1950s, approached the British, German, and French standards and ranked fourth behind Belgium, Great Britain, and Switzerland in cotton processing.[81] The numbers for the *electricity* industry are similarly impressive: The per-capita production of electrical energy in the 1950s far outstripped the production of the 1920s and thus the remaining countries in eastern and southern Europe – but it still did not come up to western and central European standards.[82]

*Western and central Europe* continued to industrialize successfully throughout the 20th century despite two World Wars and the Great Depression. Still, the wars did not influence the economies of the different countries in exactly the same way. Countries like Germany and Austria, whose

---

81    My calculations are based on Mitchell (1975), 19-27, 402 and 432.

82    My calculations are based on Fischer (1987), 12 f. and 120.

per-capita economic output was no higher in 1950 than it was in 1913, contrasted with countries like Switzerland, Sweden, Norway, Denmark, and Finland, which more than doubled their pre-war production numbers. In between these two extremes, we find France, Belgium, the Netherlands, Italy, and Great Britain, whose per-capita gross national product grew between 30% and 50%.[83]

Apparently, from the 19th century on, the *Scandinavian countries* managed to profit from the increasing demand coming from central Europe. As early as 1913, Sweden's, Norway's, and Denmark's share in the European export trade was four to six times higher than Spain's and six to twenty times higher than the shares of Romania, Bulgaria, Portugal, and Greece.[84] This gap continued to widen until right before World War II; even Czechoslovakia and Hungary, despite their proximity to central Europe, lagged behind the Scandinavian countries. The export trade not only complemented the dominant domestic trade but also increased the profits and thus the purchasing power of export enterprises and their employees, which stimulated the domestic demand even more. Apparently, the domestic market and the additional purchasing power generated by the export trade contributed to the industrialization of the Scandinavian countries as they had done before in the Benelux countries and Switzerland, which are of comparable size. In 1953, Sweden's per-capita industrial production – though still far behind Great Britain – came close to Switzerland and ranked third among the European industrial countries, with Denmark in fourth, Germany in fifth, and Norway in sixth place.[85]

The beginnings of industrialization in *eastern and southern Europe* were much more modest until the mid-20th century. Right before the beginning of World War II, the per-capita industrial production in these countries amounted to less than 15% of the British production. Only Hungary and the Soviet Union had slightly and Czechoslovakia significantly higher numbers.[86] It was not until after the war that eastern European countries started to catch up, partly as a result of their command economy. In 1973, per-capita industrial production in southern and eastern European countries amounted to 30% to 50% of the British standard, which had by now doubled; the Soviet Union came up to even

---

83   Maddison (Per Capita GDP)

84   My calculations are based on Fischer (1987), 12 f. and 157.

85   Fischer (1987), 138.

86   Fischer (1987), 137.

65%.[87] The east-central European countries Hungary, Czechoslovakia, and the German Democratic Republic had, by now, closed the gap with central Europe. Along with industrialization, urbanization increased markedly as the two influenced each other. In 1980, the metropolitan areas of 35 European cities had more than a million inhabitants; a good third of them were located in the command economies of eastern Europe.[88]

Naturally, the process of catching up influenced the average net product of eastern and southern European countries. If their *per-capita gross domestic product* in 1950 amounted to the standard western and central European countries had already achieved by 1870, it took only twenty years to raise it to – or above – the 1950 mark of their more-developed neighbors.[89] Their swift and comprehensive industrialization process turned eastern and southern European nations into industrial countries, whose per-capita gross domestic product had increased more than seven-fold since the early 19th century.[90] Still, they were never quite able to catch up to the western, central, and northern European countries, which also continued to grow rapidly after the war.

The continuing backlog is apparent in the different development of *older and newer branches of industry*. The cotton and crude-steel industries serve as an example of the former; the electric appliance and automobile industries illustrate the latter. The *traditional cotton industry*, measured by the per-capita processing of raw cotton, had reached its zenith in both England and Belgium by the 1930s, and in most of the other countries in western, central, and northern Europe soon after World War II, and was consecutively replaced by the production of more profitably consumer goods. In eastern and southern Europe, however, it continued to increase almost invariably through the 1970s and 1980s (see Figure 4). Still, with the exception of the Soviet Union and southern Europe, the current production average of individual regions still lay below the peak performance of western and central European countries. Because of their more industrialized western and northern regions, the German Democratic Republic, Italy, and Czechoslovakia are treated as a part of central Europe in Figure 4 and in the following comparisons.

---

87   Fischer (1987), 137.

88   Fischer (1987), 52 and List of cities (individual countries).

89   Maddison (Per Capita GDP).

90   Maddison (Per Capita GDP).

Figure 4: Processing of Raw Cotton in Europe, 1930-1983 (Kg per Capita, Annual Averages)

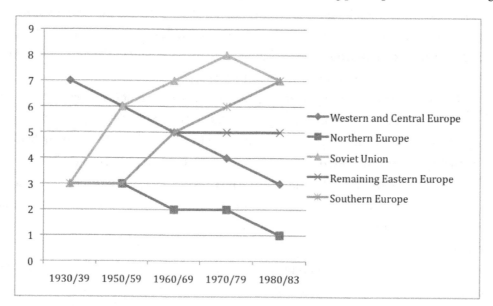

Western and Central Europe: Austria, Belgium, Czechoslovakia, Germany, France, Ireland, Italy, Luxemburg, Netherlands, Switzerland, United Kingdom. Northern Europe: Denmark, Finland, Norway, Sweden. Remaining Eastern Europe: Bulgaria, Hungary, Poland, Romania, Yugoslavia. Southern Europe: Greece, Portugal, Spain. Calculations based on Fischer (1987), 12 f. and 135.

The *production of crude steel* experienced a much more significant growth spurt. On the one hand, industrialization in the 20th century was increasingly dominated by capital-goods industries as more and more machines replaced human labor. On the other hand, the command economy of the Soviet Union, which spread to other eastern European countries after World War II, insisted on the increased production of primary commodities as the foundation for a national consumer-goods and armament industry. Unlike the cotton industry, which had been stagnating in western and central Europe since the 1920s and had, until the 1980s, merely tripled in the rest of Europe, the steel industry grew much more significantly in all countries (see Figure 5).

Figure 5: Production of Crude Steel in Europe, 1920-1998 (Kg per Capita, Annual Averages)

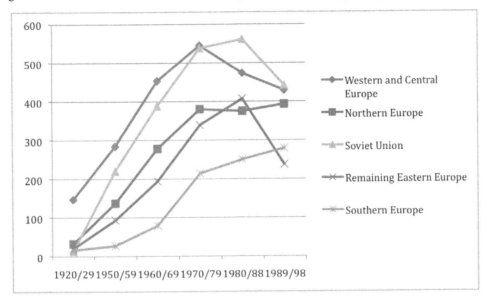

Regions as in Figure 4. See Table 6.

The already large per-capita production of crude steel in western and central Europe doubled between the 1920s and 1950s and then again by the mid-1970s. It grew even more significantly in less industrialized regions, where steel production in the 1920s amounted to only a small fraction of that in western and central Europe. About 60 years later, the Soviet Union surpassed western and central Europe, and the rest of eastern Europe outstripped Scandinavia, which had been growing steadily as well. Only the three southern European countries – their strong postwar growth notwithstanding – lagged behind the rest of Europe. As a result, the production of crude steel reached its apex in the 70s and 80s and, like the cotton industry before it, partly decreased in the following years. The decline was particularly marked in eastern European countries, due to the transition from a command to a market economy. In the new century, the steel industry continued to grow only in a few countries, especially the Netherlands, Austria, Spain, Finland, Belarus, and the Russian Federation.[91]

---

91    List of countries (Steel).

While eastern and southern Europe caught up with its neighbors in the production of goods typical for early industrialization, it continued to lag behind with regard to more recent consumer goods, such as electric appliances and automobiles. Even though the *electronics industry* developed at different rates in different countries, eastern and southern Europe produced much fewer television sets, refrigerators, and washing machines than western and central Europe – only about half as many per capita during the 1970s and early 1980s.[92]

The *automobile industry* is an even better indicator of advanced industrialization, albeit mostly in larger countries because smaller nations could not compete due to their limited domestic markets (see Figure 6). During the 1950s, Germany, France, and Great Britain produced by far the most cars per capita. Even though other countries managed to catch up later, between 1980 and 2000, Germany and France still topped the list of auto-producing countries by a wide margin. Only Sweden and Spain came close to German and French levels, while the automobile production in eastern European countries (including the Soviet Union) lagged far behind and only managed to grow recently when production was outsourced to countries like Slovakia (see Table 7).

Figure 6: Production of Automobiles (Passenger Cars and Trucks) in Europe, 1950-2009 (Annual Averages per 1,000 Inhabitants)

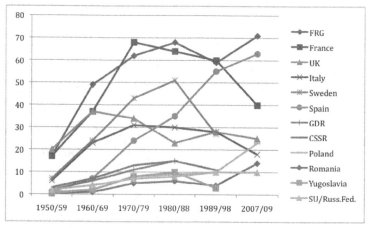

See Table 7.

---

92    My calculations are based on Fischer (1987), 130 f.

Besides a country's automotive industry, its *density of passenger cars* (both domestic and imported) is also connected to its degree of industrialization and its per-capita income. Cars are the most expensive items the general public can afford to buy, which makes them an excellent indicator of a country's prosperity (see Figure 7). In 1949, only a few years after the end of World War II, Great Britain and France, respectively, had 42 and 37 cars per 1,000 inhabitants, followed by Sweden, Switzerland, Belgium, Denmark, and Ireland, which had between 26 and 28 (see Table 8). The distribution of automobiles followed the path of industrialization in western and central Europe, with the exception of Germany and Austria, which back then had only six to seven cars per 1,000 inhabitants as a result of the economic setbacks caused by the war. The numbers were even lower in eastern and southern Europe. After the war, automobile density rose rapidly everywhere and, by 1988, had reached more than 400 cars per 1,000 inhabitants in Italy, Germany, Switzerland, and Sweden, and more than 300 in the rest of western, central, and northern Europe (excepting Ireland). Still, the numbers were significantly lower in southern and eastern Europe and lowest in the Soviet Union, which had fewer than 100 cars per 1,000 inhabitants, quite certainly the result of a command economy that neglected consumer goods. Later on, the southern European countries managed to catch up with western and central Europe, but the eastern European nations, including the former Soviet Union, still lagged behind at the beginning of the 21st century (see Table 8).

Besides automobile density, the prosperity gap between western, central, and northern Europe on one side and eastern Europe on the other is further reflected in the per-capita *gross domestic product* at its root.[93] In this regard, Greece, Portugal, and above all Spain came out ahead of eastern Europe, when, by 2008, they had attained – and partially exceeded – the western, central, and northern European standard of 1990. The development in eastern European countries took a very different course: Their economic growth slowed down during the final years of their command economies and was temporarily interrupted due to their transition to a market economy at the beginning of the 1990s. Even though they saw renewed growth before the turn of the millennium, by 2008, their per-capita gross domestic product had just about reached the standard that the more industrialized

---

93    Maddison (Per Capita GDP).

European nations had attained by the 1960s and 1970s – a few exceptions like Slovenia and Estonia, and some significant regional differences, notwithstanding.

Figure 7: Passenger Cars per 1,000 Inhabitants in Europe, 1949-2006 (Larger Countries)

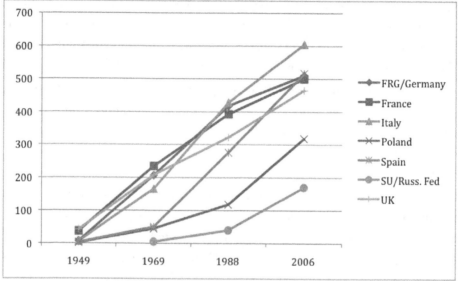

See, also for smaller countries, Table 8.

Figure 8: Computers per 1,000 Inhabitants in Europe, 2006 (Larger Countries)

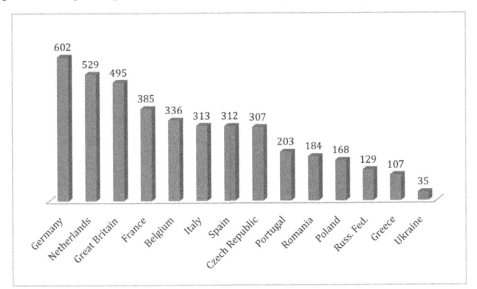

Welt in Zahlen (Computer). For smaller countries see Table 9.

Finally, the differences between the industrial frontrunners and the other European countries can be seen in the density of *computers*, which is a powerful indicator of the more recent economic development. In 1995, on average, one in four western Europeans owned a computer; in the Mediterranean countries, the number was one in ten, but the Czech Republic, Hungary, the Russian Federation, and Rumania, respectively, had only 53, 39, 18, and 5 computers per 1,000 inhabitants.[94] While some of these countries caught up to the West in subsequent years, the gap in computer density was still larger than the gap in automobile density during the first decade of the 21st century (see Figure 8 and Table 9). Next to the frontrunners Switzerland, Luxemburg, and Sweden, which boasted more than 700 computers per 1,000 inhabitants, there existed a middle group with numbers between 300 and 600+, which, among others, included some of the eastern and southern European countries. In most of these, however, only about one fifth (or less) of the population owned

94    Berend (2006), 210.

a computer; in the southern parts of the former Yugoslavia, and also in Albania, Moldavia, and the Ukraine, the number comes to fewer than 10%.

However, there were marked *regional differences* within the individual countries, which yet again underscore the prevailing income gap inside of Europe.[95] In 2015, in a comparison of the per-capita gross domestic product of 276 regions, 46 exceeded the European average by 25% or more, and 86 regions came in at least 25% below. The former group were all located in western, central, and northern Europe including the Bolzano region in northern Italy, as well as the metropolitan areas of Prague, Bratislava, and Bucharest. The less affluent regions, with the exception of southern Yorkshire, west Wales, and the Tees Valley and Durham, were all located in eastern and southern Europe, including the seven southern Italian regions of Molise, Campania, Apulia, Calabria, Basilicata, Sicily, and Sardinia.

## FROM AN INDUSTRIAL TO AN URBAN SERVICE SOCIETY

The fact that Italy, despite its relatively large number of less affluent regions, had the largest per-capita number of automobiles[96] indicates that continuing economic development could no longer predominantly be measured by a population's material possessions alone. After a certain point in the 1960s and 1970s, people in the more industrialized areas of Europe began to spend less of their ever-increasing disposable income on additional consumer goods. The market was partially saturated and the demand for consumer goods grew more slowly than before. At the same time, thanks to technical innovations, productivity increased both quantitatively and qualitatively. As a result, fewer people were needed to meet the slow-growing demand for industrial goods, but incomes continued to rise. Many – albeit not all – workers who lost their industrial jobs found employment in the *service industry*, which enjoyed a growing demand as incomes and taxes – in both the private and public sector – continued to rise.[97] The distribution of wage earners in the three main economic sectors reflects this development most clearly.

---

95    BIP pro Kopf 2015.

96    See Table 8.

97    On the subject of massively increased public expenses see Berend (2006), Table 5.1.

The number of people earning a living in *agriculture*, the primary economic sector, decreased consistently in the wake of industrialization. On the one hand, technical innovations had decreased the demand for agricultural workers; on the other, the demand for industrial goods at the time was so high that manufacturing, the secondary economic sector, could accommodate increasing numbers of workers. It was not until the demand for industrial goods decreased and an ever-growing amount of income was spent on services that the tertiary economic sector, the service industry, grew at the expense of the secondary. Naturally, this phenomenon occurred earlier in countries that had industrialized sooner. In addition, the service industry attracted workers from the primary sector as well, which prompted a further decrease of the agricultural work force, which shrank to less than 10% just about everywhere in Europe. Rumania, Macedonia, Croatia, Greece, and Poland were the only countries where, in 2013, more than 10% of wage earners still worked in agriculture.[98]

Maximum *employment in the secondary sector* was reached between 40% and 50% of all wage earners, most of whom worked in manufacturing. Most of the countries in western, central, and northern Europe reached this status in the 1960s; those in eastern and southern Europe in the 1970s and 1980s.[99] Even though the demand for industrial goods still exists, especially in less developed countries, the number of employees in the secondary sector has fallen just about everywhere thanks to increased productivity and international trade relations. It meanwhile fluctuates between 20% and 30%; the numbers are slightly higher in some eastern European countries.[100]

Everywhere, however, fewer people than before work in manufacturing,[101] which means that the *industrialization process* has been completed just about everywhere in Europe, at least with regard to the number of wage earners. By the end of the 20th century, most of Europe had successfully industrialized and attained a standard of living that far exceeded

---

98    Beschäftigungsstruktur 2013.

99    My calculations are based on Fischer (1987), 93, Mitchell (1975), 153-165, Mitchell (1992), 141-156 and Mitchell (2003), 145-162.

100    Statistisches Jahrbuch (2013), 576.

101    Mitchell (2003), 145-162.

that of the pre-industrial era.[102] Yet, as I have shown, not all Europeans profited equally from the growing prosperity. In addition to the inequality between individual regions, there were significant differences between individual countries. In 2008, the per-capita gross domestic product – and thus the average income – in countries like Rumania, Serbia, Albania, Macedonia, Moldavia, and the Ukraine was only between one fifth and one quarter that of the other eastern European countries, whose numbers – a few exceptions notwithstanding – were, at most, only half of what they were in western, central, and northern Europe.[103]

Both industrialization and a higher standard of living coincided with accelerated *urbanization*, which was both a reason for and a result of industrial development.[104] Around 2010, about 40% of people in Europe – including the Russian Federation – lived in cities with more than 100,000 inhabitants.[105] Despite significant differences between the degrees of urbanization in individual countries, the large European regions had become very much alike. As a result, we can no longer explain the continuing gap in prosperity by referring to the different numbers of the big cities, as we were able to do at the beginning of the industrialization process. The quickly growing demand for industrial goods resulting from the emergence of large cities no longer increases employment in the industrial sector. On the contrary, thanks to increased mechanization and computerization, the number of wage earners in manufacturing has decreased despite growing demand, both relatively and absolutely, in favor of the service industry.

In the course of continued competition, not all industrial enterprises managed to increase their *productivity* at the same rate. Those in early-industrialized regions were more successful than those in less developed areas. If we calculate the per-capita production of wage earners in the secondary sector, based on the 2006 non-agricultural production of goods and the number of wage earners, European countries fall into four groups based on their degree of "industrial" production.[106] Next to the special case of Norway, which

---

102   Maddison (Per Capita GDP).

103   Maddison (Per Capita GDP).

104   See Fischer (1987), 54.

105   My calculations are based on List of cities (European Countries)

106   These estimates are based on my own calculations, which are based on Welt in Zahlen (Industrieproduktion), Beschäftigungsstruktur 2013, WKO Länderprofile and Maddison (Population).

topped the list with $235,000 thanks to its oil and gas production, the other Scandinavian countries were the most productive, with an industrial production between $100,000 and $120,000 per wage earner. The western and central European countries follow at $80,000 to $100,000; Spain and Italy had at this point caught up to them, but not Portugal or the Czech Republic, which—like other eastern European countries including the Baltic States—had a production of only $20,000 to $40,000 per wage earner. Only Slovenia and Greece came in markedly higher, ranging from a scant $50,000 to more than $60,000. Slovakia, and especially Bulgaria, Romania, Macedonia, and Albania, as well as Russia, Belarus, the Ukraine and Moldavia, lagged behind at $10,000 or less.

Thanks to the longer *tradition* and their accumulated *industrial knowledge*, the front runners in western, central, and northern Europe managed to develop and increase their productivity in a way that allowed them – not least due to new products – to maintain their status as most productive industrial regions. The other regions were able to catch up part of the difference, but only a precious few made it all the way. Higher production resulted in higher income, which could be spent on higher-quality services. In this way, the increase in productivity was not limited to the manufacturing industry but spread to the tertiary – and now largest – economic sector. Despite the decreasing importance of industrial production for the national product, the entire economy of a country profited from the increase in industrial productivity, which, in turn, increased the productivity of the service industry and resulted in higher income averages in the more productive countries.

AMERICA

Like Europe, the two American continents were only sparsely populated for thousands of years. The indigenous people first hunted and gathered and, as the *population density* increased, they settled into an agrarian way of life, growing crops and breeding cattle.[107] Here and there – especially in today's Peru and Mexico and in areas south of these – urban settlements developed in the centuries before and after the birth of Christ in the early Aztec, Inca, and Mayan civilizations, which resembled the early cultures of the ancient Middle East. These urban settlements expanded agricultural production by adding trade and artisanal manufacture, but they were too small to constitute a mass market for industrial products.

This situation did not change much after European seafarers and conquistadors discovered both Americas around 1500. Though exact *population numbers* or broad estimates are even more difficult to calculate than they are for ancient Europe – Maddison estimates about ten million for North and South America each; Mathieu estimates 42 million for both[108] – we can assume that the greater part of the Americas was populated by relatively few hunters and gatherers. And even in the economically more developed areas of the ancient civilizations, low population numbers made industrialization as unlikely as it was in the ancient Mediterranean or in medieval Europe.

In addition, the already *low population density* in the Americas was further decimated by military conflicts with the conquistadors and the diseases they brought with them. In the long run, the indigenous population of South America, despite their losses, was able to

---

107    Salisbury (1996), 1-10.

108    Maddison (Population); Mathieu (2011), 87. According to Newson (2006), 143, a total of 50 to 60 million people lived in the Americas. Couturier (1994), 5, estimates up to 18 million inhabitants in North America north of the Rio Grande. According to Newson (2006), 144, the total estimates range between 8 and 112 million.

defend itself better than the natives of North America, where, by 1865, the number of Native Americans had shrunken to 350,000 in the areas that today are the US and Canada.[109] Still, in the course of the 18th century, population numbers – aided by European immigration and the African slave trade – went back to where they were in 1500, except in Mexico and Peru.[110]

As they developed further, the two Americas went *separate ways*. Between 1700 and 1820, the population in South America including Mexico – known today as Latin America – increased from about ten to twelve million to over 20 million. On the other hand, in the area of today's USA and Canada, population numbers increased more than five-fold, from about two million to approximately 11 million in the same time frame.[111] Throughout the 19th century, the two populations continued to grow at different speeds, largely because North America attracted a much larger number of European immigrants. By 1913, the population of the USA and Canada increased almost ten-fold to 100 million[112] while the Latin American population (distributed over a larger area) increased only four-fold to about 80 million.[113] If increased population density can spark urbanization and the emergence of a mass market, this was more likely to happen in North than in South America.

Besides, the fast-growing population in North America was concentrated in a relatively small area, which promoted *population density* and *urbanization* even further. Most of the European immigrants landed in the Northeast – in port cities like Montreal, Boston, New York, Philadelphia and Baltimore – most likely because they were closer, which reduced transportation costs. Despite their initial plans to become independent farmers, not all of the immigrants moved inland. Many preferred to stay in the port cities, which offered opportunities to find and make a living. But even those that planned to move inland initially settled near the coast. Toward the end of the 18th century, almost all of the US population lived on the Atlantic coast, as did most Canadians.[114]

---

109    Salisbury (1996), 11.

110    Maddison (Population).

111    Maddison (Population) and Mathieu (2011), 87.

112    According to Maddison  (Population) 97,6 million in the USA and 7,85 million in Canada.

113    According to Maddison (Population), 80, 8 million.

114    Haines (2000), 189 and Cardin/Couture (1997), 41.

# USA

Thanks to the robust influx of immigrants and the relatively high population growth it brought about, the *population density* on the East Coast caused villages to grow into larger and smaller town even outside of the port cities. These growing urban centers, in turn, attracted increasing numbers of migrants. Even though many of them eventually migrated west, almost three quarters of the total population of the US and about 90% of the country's urban population lived in the states along the East Coast around 1830.[115]

During the following decades, the population density – especially in the expanded Northeast – continued to increase while the South remained behind. While, in 1790, the US population was fairly evenly distributed between the Northeast and the South, 100 years later almost two thirds of the population lived in the Midwest and the "old" Northeast between North Dakota, Kansas, New Jersey, and Maine; less than a third, however, lived in the "old" and "new" South between Delaware, Florida, and Texas.[116] The differences in population density brought about differences in the *degree of urbanization* in the North and South – about 60% in New England and the Mid-Atlantic States New York, Pennsylvania, and New Jersey and about 33% in the Midwest; in the Southeast and Southwest, the rate amounted to less than 20%.[117]

The higher degree of urbanization in the Northeast promoted a relatively early and stronger *market integration* among its population, despite the fact that subsistence farming dominated the economy for a long time. In the South, by contrast, most of the above-average profits of the export-oriented plantation economy went to a relatively small number of land owners while slaves and subsistence farmers earned very little or no money. As a result, around 1840 – and thus before the start of large-scale industrialization – per-capita incomes in the South ranked 25% below the national average; those in New England and the Mid-Atlantic states exceeded the national average by over 30%.[118]

---

115  Haines (2000), 189.

116  Haines (2000), 189 and Heim (2000), 94.

117  My calculations are based on Haines (2000), 189.

118  Gallman (2000), 53.

Map 5: Cities with Over 100,000 Inhabitants in the USA and Canada Around 1900.

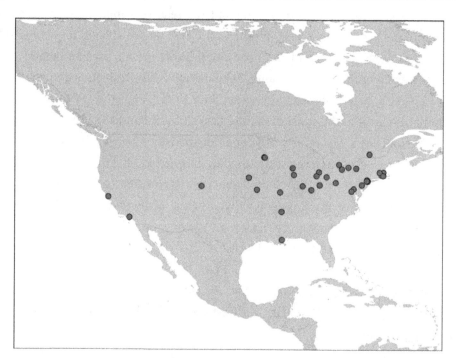

Tirol Atlas – Designed by Klaus Förster based on Table 9.

Map background: World Borders Dataset - http://thematicmapping.org/downloads/world_borders.php

Increased urbanization in the Northeast created favorable conditions for industrialization, triggered by the emergence of *big cities* as had been the case in western and central Europe. In 1850, the US had six cities with more than 100,000 inhabitants; by 1900, there were 34 of them.[119] By the turn of the century, New York City, Chicago, and Philadelphia counted more than a million inhabitants, followed by St. Louis, Boston, Baltimore, and Pittsburgh with about half a million each.[120] Like all the other big cit-

---

119    Mitchell (1998), 46-53.

120    Mitchell (1998), 46-53.

ies, they clustered in a relatively small area between Boston, Chicago, St. Louis, and Washington, D.C. (see Map 5 and Table 10).[121]

*Industrialization* occurred sooner and on a larger scale in the urbanized Northeast than it did in the South. It started – as it did in early 19th century Europe – with the cotton industry. Even though Southern plantation owners grew raw cotton and had enough ready capital to become potential entrepreneurs, the first cotton mills sprang up in New England, where rapidly growing markets rendered investments profitable. Industrialization spread from New England to the Mid-Atlantic states and then to Ohio, Michigan, Indiana, Illinois, and Wisconsin, all of which were densely populated. Industrial mass production soon included other industrial branches besides the cotton industry.[122]

Only a small portion of the US industrial production took place in the *South*, both before and after the Civil War. As late as 1909, about three quarters of industrial production came from New England and the above-mentioned states in the Northeast and Midwest, even though less than half of the total population lived in these areas.[123] At the same time, the percentage of people employed in agriculture decreased to 12%-13% in New England and the Mid-Atlantic states while it remained at about 60% in the South.[124] The difference in average per-capita income reached an all-time high at the turn of the century, when it was almost three times higher in the Northeast – and twice as high in the Midwest – than it was in the South.[125]

The transportation industry, indispensable for the expanding trade, reflects how much the *Northeast* had grown into the commercial center of the USA. The amount of freight shipped on the Erie Canal between Albany and Buffalo, which connected the East Coast to the Great Lakes, increased almost six-fold between the early 1840s and 1880, amounted to almost

---

121    Of the 16 cities with more than a quarter of a million inhabitants, besides Baltimore and Washington, which bordered on the Northeast, only one of them was in the South: The well-situated port city of New Orleans.

122    Engerman/Sokoloff (2000), 373 f. and 383.

123    Heim (2000), 117.

124    Margo (2000), 213.

125    Gallmann (2000), 53.

half of all cargo transported on the country's canals.[126] Railroads saw a similar upturn in business and soon replaced canal and river navigation as the prime method of commercial transportation. When, in the 1840s, railroad construction began on a larger scale, 60% of railroad lines were in New England and New York, from where they soon spread to other northeastern states.[127] Around the middle of the century, New York, Pennsylvania, Ohio, Illinois, and Indiana were among the leading states in railroad construction,[128] but even later, between two and three times as many railroad lines were built in the Northeast and Midwest than in the Old South.[129] As a result, with 4,200 kilometers of railroad lines per one million inhabitants right before World War I, the US had a much denser rail network than any European country including Great Britain.[130] The Northeast and Midwest were also largely responsible for the country's rapidly growing per-capita industrial production and high per-capita income. The gross national product more than quadrupled after 1820 and has invariably exceeded that of every European nation since 1905.[131]

However, in the course of the *20th century*, the gap between the more and less developed regions in the USA changed. First, the total population numbers continued to increase, and did so markedly faster than in Europe. They rose from a scant 100 million to almost 300 million people between 1913 and 2003, thanks to continued immigration from all parts of the world and to much lower rates of casualties in the two World Wars.[132] The population increased predominantly in the Old South and on the West Coast, which had been attracting an enormous number of migrants since the trans-continental railroad lines were completed in the second half of the 19th century (see Table 11). While the population in the Northeast and Midwest more than doubled between 1900 and 1990, it increased 3.5-fold in the Old South and even fifteen-fold on the West Coast.

---

126    Fishlow (2000), 562.

127    Fishlow (2000), 584.

128    Niemi (1997), 74.

129    Niemi (1997), 74.

130    My calculations are based on Maddison (Population), Mitchell (1977), 514 and Cameron/Neal (2003), 201.

131    Maddison (Per Capita GDP).

132    Maddison (Population).

In a parallel development, urbanization in the South and West increased more than in the Northeast, from 18% to 69% in the South and from 45% to 89% on the West Coast, which allowed these regions to catch up with – or exceed – the Northeast and Midwest (See Figure 9 and Table 11).

In the wake of urbanization, the number of *big cities* increased, which stimulated industrialization in the South and West like it had done before in the northern and eastern regions. In 1950, almost all of the 14 cities with over a million inhabitants were located in the Northeast and Midwest, but Baltimore, Washington, Los Angeles, and San Francisco had at this point passed the one-million mark as well (See Map 6 and Table 12).

Figure 9: Urban Population in the USA, 1900-1990 (Percent of Population)
Heim (2000), 141.

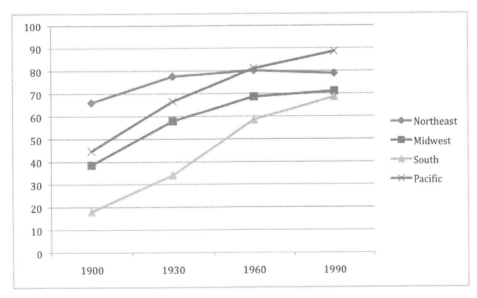

Among the 14 big cities with over half a million inhabitants, five were already located in the South and four in the West (see Table 12). In the wake of urbanization, industrial production and the amount of people working in the industry increased in the South and West, which especially in California created similar economic structures as it did in the eastern part of the country.[133]

Map 6: Cities with Over a Million Inhabitants in the USA and Canada Around 1950

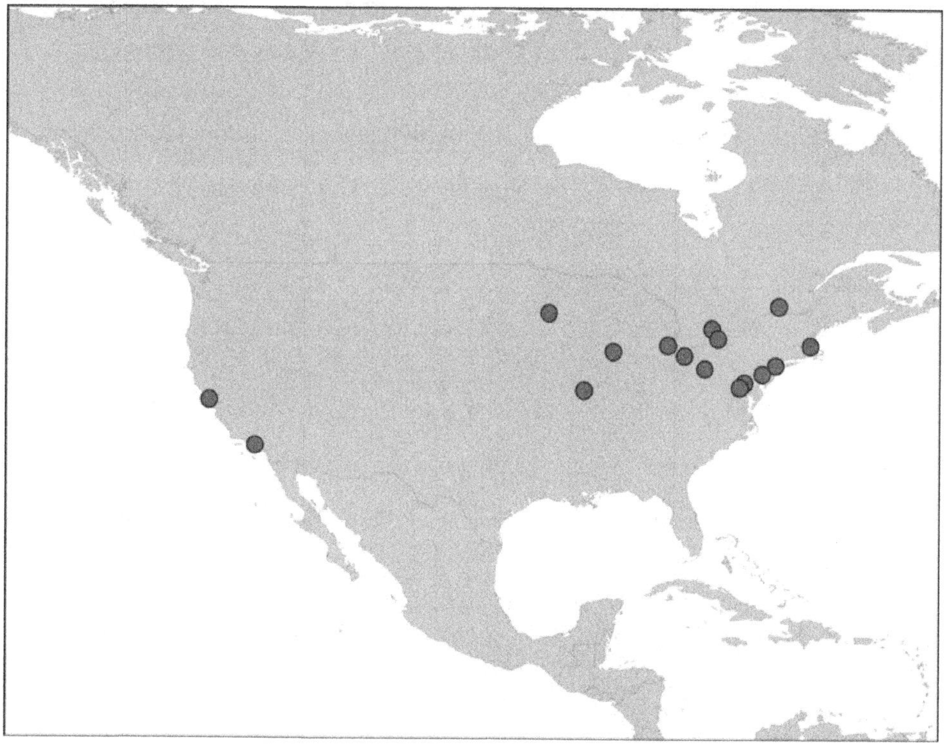

Tirol Atlas – Designed by Klaus Förster nach Tabelle 12.

Map background: World Borders Dataset - http://thematicmapping.org/downloads/world_borders.php

---

133    Heim (2000), 116 f.

The share of *manufacturing* in the overall employment of workers did not attain the peak rates of the Northeast, but with 23% on the West Coast and 24% in the Southeast, it came much closer than before (see Figure 10). After 1950, the percentage of people employed in manufacturing decreased in all the large regions in the US, as it did in Europe, as a result of increased automatization and the gradual transition to a service economy.

Figure 10: Employment in Manufacturing in the United States, 1900-1990 (Percent of Economically Active Population)

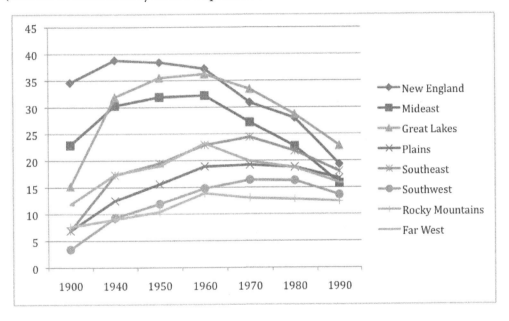

See Table 13.

*Productivity* in the South and West caught up with the industrial frontrunners and managed to increase the per-capita income in these regions. In the South, this process started gradually, but, after World War II, it closed the gap almost entirely.[134] The rates for the West Coast, which urbanized sooner and on a larger scale, already slightly

---

134    My calculations are based on Heim (2000), 101 and 117 f.

exceeded those of the Northeast at the beginning of the century. The process of catching-up influenced the average per-capita income in all of the large regions as well. In 1900, per-capita income in New England and the Mid-Atlantic states was almost three times as high as it was in the southeast of the US; in 1970 and 1990, it was only one third higher.[135] Industrialization in the US had reached almost all areas of the country and had brought about a regionally balanced and highly developed service economy that resembled that of western, central, and northern Europe on the other side of the Atlantic.[136]

## CANADA

Canada's development resembles that of the USA, with only one difference: Due to its geography, the country did not have a southern region that lagged behind the rest of the country. It was *settled* by European immigrants, who first settled in the east and gradually spread west, albeit more slowly and on a smaller scale than in the USA. At the beginning of the 19th century, fewer than 400,000 people lived in the former British colonies that would become Canada. Fifty years later, there were 2.4 million,[137] with only a few thousand descendants of the indigenous population among them. At first, immigrants settled on a small strip of land on both sides of the St. Lawrence River, which served as a central gateway.[138] A significantly smaller number of people settled in the maritime provinces of Nova Scotia, New Brunswick, and on Prince Edward Island in the far east. Québec and, *Montreal* were the first larger urban settlements to develop on the St. Lawrence River. Montreal, which had about 22,000 inhabitants in 1801, developed into the region's commercial center.[139]

---

135    Heim (2000), 102.

136    See Maddison (Per Capita GDP) for the slightly smaller differences between the countries of western, central, and northern Europe.

137    Köllman (1965), 44 and Couturier (1994), 1, 5 and 114.

138    McInnis/Horn (1982), 303.

139    McInnis/Horn (1982), 205.

People then settled further southeast, populating the initially narrow regions north of Lake Ontario and Lake Erie.[140] In this area, *Toronto* became the commercial and administrative center. With a population of fewer than 1,000 people in 1812, Toronto grew to 96,000 inhabitants by 1880; Montreal, in the meantime, had grown to 155,000 inhabitants.[141] While this was still a relatively small number, there were enough people for factories to spring up, first in the Montreal metropolitan area and later in Toronto.

Like in Europe and the USA, the *textile industry* came first, soon to be followed by others, especially the manufacture of agricultural tools and machines.[142] While the growing cities stimulated the textile industry, the large number of farmers, who grew food for themselves, the people in the cities, and the export trade, supported the production of tools and machines. After the first cotton factory was established in Sherbrooke east of Montreal in 1844, their number grew to 2,000 by 1881 and to around 4,000 ten years later, by which time the total population had reached 4.8 million.[143]

Even though Montreal retained its status as the country's biggest city, the *focus of development* soon shifted to the Great Lakes in the Province of Ontario, which, in 1851, had more people than the Province of Québec.[144] Urbanization advanced more quickly in Ontario as well. The number of cities with more than 2,500 inhabitants grew to more than 31 between 1851 and 1871; in Québec, it grew to only eight.[145] Montreal and Toronto grew at about the same rate. Both of them had more than 200,000 inhabitants by the turn of the century.[146]

The rapidly advancing urbanization coincided with an equally rapid *industrialization*. In 1912, the number of cotton spindles had grown to 800,000, a seven-fold increase in

---

140    McInnis/Horn (1982), 303.

141    Köllmann (1965), 124 and McInnis/Horn (1982), 205.

142    McInnis (2000), 86.

143    Couturier (1996), 89.

144    McInnis/Horn (1982), 301. 50 years later, around 40% of the Canadian population lived in Ontario and about 30% in Québec. Köllmann (1965), 122.

145    McInnis (2000), 89.

146    Köllmann (1965), 124 and Mitchell (1998), 51 and 53.

30 years.[147] In Toronto, the number of industrial enterprises grew from 561 to over 2,000 between 1871 and 1891; the number of workers employed by them increased from 9,400 to almost 25,000, and the annual production from a scant $14 million to $42.5 million.[148] Besides Montreal and Toronto, which accounted for more than half of Canada's industrial production, many other cities established production facilities in different industries.[149] The number of industrial workers increased by 80%, at twice the rate of the general population in the same time period; their production increased by 138%.[150] As in Europe and the USA, the railroad infrastructure had quickly expanded since 1850, parallel with the increase in industrialization: In 1865, Canada had 3,600 km of railroad lines; twenty years later, it had grown to 16,500.[151] Driven by the urban demand in the east, industrialization progressed rapidly: By the end of the century, the Canadian per-capita industrial production exceeded that of Germany and France; only Great Britain, Belgium, and the USA were still ahead.[152]

Along with the continued growth of the total population, *urbanization* and *industrialization* continued unabated. By 1920, Montreal and Toronto had surpassed the half-million-inhabitants mark, and four other cities, at more than 100,000 inhabitants, qualified for big-city status.[153] Overall, more than half of the Canadian population of over 7 million people lived in cities at the time.[154] The industrial gross national product increased almost four-fold in 25 years.[155] As is typical in economies with widespread and advanced industrialization, the iron, steel, and metal working industries grew vigorously alongside the

---

147    Kerr (1990), Plate 7.

148    Couturier (1994), 213 and Couturier (1996), 89.

149    Kerr (1990), Plate 1.

150    Couturier (1996), 89 and McInnis/Horn (1982), 405.

151    Couturier (1996), 85 und McInnis (2000), 83.

152    McInnis (2000), 58.

153    Köllmann (1965), 268.

154    Canada Year Book (1997), 31.

155    McInnis/Horn (1982), 437.

traditional textile industry.[156] Right before World War I, Canada's per-capita gross national product ranked fifth behind the USA, Australia, New Zealand, and Great Britain.[157]

A kind of domestic division of labor had developed *within Canada*. The southern parts of the population-dense and highly industrialized provinces of Ontario and Québec complemented the western provinces, which supplied mineral raw materials and products from agriculture and forestry, most of which were exported, which increased the purchasing power of the western population. In 1929, the average per-capita income in Manitoba, Saskatchewan, Alberta, and British Columbia were at or slightly below the national average. However, there was little additional demand for industrial goods because of the low population density; for the longest time, not even a tenth of the Canadian population (and still less than a third by 1931[158]) lived in the vast area of the western provinces. Most of the demand was generated by the urban populations in the eastern provinces: Around the turn of the century, almost the same number of people lived in Montreal and Toronto as did in all of the western provinces taken together; 30 years later, the population in these cities was twice the size of that in the provinces.[159] By the beginning of the 20th century, no less than 80% of all industrial workers were employed in Ontario and Québec.[160]

*Industrialization* in the west did not increase until the following decades; in these areas, population rates continued to grow exponentially, especially after the opening of the first trans-continental railroad in 1886.[161] Populations grew more quickly in the cities than they did in the country, especially in Vancouver, the major trans-shipment center on the West

---

156   Couturier (1994), 240.

157   Maddison (Per Capita GDP).

158   Köllmann (1965), 122 und 265.

159   0.5 and 0.6 and 1.45 and 3 million respectively. Köllmann (1965), 122, 124, 265 und 268.

160   Kerr (1990), Plate 13.

161   McInnis (2000), 97 und Kerr (1990), 31. In 1891, only 7% of the Canadian population lived west of Ontario; by 1911, the number had grown to 24%. By 1961, 26% of the total population, which had grown to 18.2 million, lived in the western provinces. Couturier (1994), 271, Kerr (1990), Plate 4 and Köllmann (1965), 122 und 265.

Coast.[162] In 1961, like Québec and Ontario, British Columbia and Manitoba produced more industrial goods than other kind.[163] Twenty years later, Canada produced eight times more industrial goods than agricultural products.[164] Unlike Ontario and Québec, where a number of industrial towns – Hamilton, Kitchener, Windsor, London, or Oshawa – had sprung up in addition to the metropolitan areas of Montreal and Toronto, the western industry clustered around a few far-flung big cities.[165] In 1957, nearly half of the local industrial employees worked in Vancouver and Winnipeg; an additional 14% in Edmonton and Calgary.[166] However, only relatively few people lived outside of the big cities, unlike in eastern and southern Europe and in many other parts of the world, as will be shown below. As a result, industrialization in Canada, which was triggered by big cities and created jobs and income, prevented a larger developmental gap between east and west. On the contrary, average per-capita incomes in British Columbia and Alberta were slightly higher than that in Ontario and a scant 18% higher than those in Québec, Saskatchewan, and Manitoba by the end of the 1970s. The numbers were substantially lower in the less industrialized Atlantic provinces.[167]

Overall, because of their smaller populations, the western provinces lagged behind the *old industrial centers* with regard to industrial production and the number of industry workers. Even though most of the raw materials were produced in the west, the processing industries clustered around the population-dense urban markets in the east. By the mid-1990s, Ontario and Québec, where 60% of the total population lived, provided more than 75% of Canada's industrial production and employed 75% of industrial workers.[168] An additional 10% worked in British Columbia, and 10% in Alberta, Saskatchewan, and Manitoba taken together.　Because of the two population-dense and highly developed provinces in the east,

---

162　Köllmann (1965), 124 and 268; Couturier (1994), 241; Kerr (1990), Plate 4.

163　Kerr (1990), Plate 3.

164　Green (2000), 237.

165　Kerr (1990), Plate 51.

166　Kerr (1990), Plate 51.

167　McInnis/Horn (1982), 682.

168　My calculations are based on Canada Year Book (1997), 210 and 366 f.

Canada has been able to maintain its status as one of the world's most highly-industrialized nations, with a per capita gross domestic product which ranked fourth (with Australia) behind the USA, Norway, and Ireland in 2008.[169]

Like other industrialized countries, Canada had by now made the transition from an industrial to an *urbanized service industry*. In 2011, when the total population had risen to 33.5 million, Toronto and Montreal – not counting their surrounding areas – had more than 5 and 3.4 million inhabitants, respectively. Vancouver had over 2 million and Calgary and Edmonton around a million each.[170] These cities had obviously grown much faster than the total population of the provinces that surrounded them. Until recently, almost half of the Canadian population lived in the six metropolitan areas with over a million inhabitants.[171] Three quarters of all workers were by now employed in the service industry, with only small differences between east and west.[172] The individual provinces' average per-capita production ranged between 31,000 CAD in Alberta and a scant 24,000 CAD in Québec and Saskatchewan, which indicates a balanced economy that compares to that of the USA.[173] Only the Atlantic provinces in the far east, which comprise only 8% of the population, lagged behind in their economic development with an average per-capita production of 20,000 CAD. If we measure economic prosperity by the number of passenger cars, the west and far east, with 712 and 628 cars per 1,000 inhabitants, surpass the central areas of Ontario and Québec with 545 cars; the national average is 601 cars per 1,000 inhabitants.[174] This further shows how much the individual parts of Canada have adjusted to the high national average.

---

169    Maddison (Per Capita GDP).

170    Wikipedia (Canada).

171    Next to the big cities listed here, the Ottawa-Gatineau metropolitan area. List of Cities (Canada).

172    Canada Year Book (1997), 210.

173    My calculations are based on Canada Year Book (1997), 77 und 282.

174    My calculations are based on Canada Year Book (1997), 77 und 401.

# LATIN AMERICA

If Canada's more recent economic development resembles that of the American Northeast, the development in *Latin America* resembles that of the American South. Both remained sparsely populated for a long time. Until the 20th century, the cities grew more slowly and were located at greater distances from each other than was the case in the American Northeast and eastern Canada. As a result, Latin America depended on a subsistence economy and did not produce much of a surplus for urban markets. As was the case in the American South, the rural population had very little buying power, consisting as it did of small farmers and slaves, who had been brought over from Africa. The profits of a small number of export-oriented plantation owners, who grew sugar, coffee, tobacco, and cocoa, were reinvested in the agricultural industry or used to purchase industrial goods that were imported from Europe and, later, from the US. The few big cities did not offer enough incentives for more than sporadic industrial investments.

For a long time, the two *Americas* were no different from each other in this regard. Around 1800, Latin America was very thinly populated: An estimated 5 million inhabitants lived north and a scant 20 million south of the Rio Grande.[175] Urban settlements developed very slowly after the destruction of the ancient civilizations. During the early decades of the 19th century, the population in the north grew more rapidly thanks to increased immigration from Europe. Around 1900, over 80 million people lived in the US and Canada; in Latin America, there were only 65 million (see Table 14).[176] In addition, the population in North America was concentrated on a much smaller area than in Latin America – and herein lies the important difference. In contrast to the American Northeast and Canada, no single region developed in the south that drew most of the immigrants; instead, migrants settled in various regions between the Rio Grande and the southern tip of the continent, which meant that nowhere in Latin America a single region achieved the population density seen between Montreal, Chicago, St. Louis, and Washington.

The lack of population density hampered the development of *larger cities*, which here, too emerged as centers of export trade and the capitals of the new Latin American countries.

---

175    Mathieu (2011), 87.

176    Maddison (Population).

Even though these cities grew quickly during the second half of the 19th century, they trailed behind the large cities in North America in both size and number (see Tables 10 and 15). While the American Northeast and the Midwest counted 27 cities with over 100,000 inhabitants by 1900, the much larger region between Mexico City and Buenos Aires had only 13 (see Maps 5 and 7). Not only were these cities spread much further apart, but only a scant 6% of the total Latin American population lived there; in the American Northeast and the Midwest, over 25% of the population lived in these big cities.[177] In addition, until railroads were built in Latin America in the second half of the 19th century, they were not efficiently connected with each other.

---

177    My calculations are based on Mitchell (1998), 50-57, Maddison (Population) and Heim (2000), 101.

Map 7: Cities with Over 100,000 Inhabitants in Latin America Around 1900
Tirol Atlas – Designed by Klaus Förster based on Table 9.

Map background: World Borders Dataset - http://thematicmapping.org/downloads/world_borders.php

Because most of the population was not very urbanized and thus lacked strong market integration, modern *industrial production* developed only slowly and sporadically. The lack of urbanization limited the number of affluent consumers, whose demand for industrial products was met by imports from Europe and the US and by rural and urban artisans.[178] Although since the 18th century, the production of cotton goods (organized by large suppliers,

---

178    Bulmer-Thomas (1994), 130.

as was the case in Europe) developed alongside the traditional wool industry in the "obrajes de paño"[179], cotton spinning mills were not mechanized until the 1830s, and, in the case of the cotton weaving mills, not until the 1890s. Mexico led the way in this regard; it had a significant wool-processing industry in Puebla before 1800 and, by 1843, 59 mechanized cotton processing mills with a combined total of over 100,000 spindles.[180] Around the same time, the first cotton factory started production in Bahia in Brazil, but even ten years later, the country had only eight cotton spinning mills with a combined total of 4,500 spindles. During the following decades, these industries moved production from the cotton-growing areas in the north to the rapidly-growing urban centers like Rio de Janeiro and São Paolo in the south of the country.[181] During the 1850s, the first cotton factories sprang up in Peru, at a time when Great Britain had around 20 million spindles and Germany and France around 4.4 and one million respectively.[182]

The economic backlog that emerged with the late onset of industrialization persisted. Even though the number of *cotton spindles* increased dramatically at the end of the 19th century, around 1914, the two largest Latin American countries, Mexico and Brazil, with 750,000 and 1.4 million spindles, trailed far behind the countries of western and central Europe as well as behind the USA.[183] In Argentina, where industrialization was also sparked by a demand for consumer goods, the apparel industry grew more rapidly, importing most of the necessary yarns.[184]

The *iron and steel industries* developed very slowly. By the time of World War I, only Mexico had a larger iron and steel plant, but its production of raw steel amounted only to a

---

179    For this and the following, see Gómez-Galvarriato (2006), 377-391.

180    See also Donghi (1985), 327 f.

181    Bulmer-Thomas (1994), 135.

182    Mitchell (1977), 510.

183    Mitchell (1998), 376. While Mexico and Brazil had 50 and 60 spindles per 1,000 inhabitants, Great Britain had about 1,300; France and Germany had 170 to 180, and the US around 300. My calculations are based on Mitchell (1998), 376, Mitchell (1977), 489 and 510 and Maddison (Population).

184    Rocchi (2005), 34 f.

fraction of the Canadian production.[185] Due to the lack of a metal-working tradition, most of the materials and equipment necessary for constructing railroads were imported from abroad. The railroads were initially built to ship export goods to international sea ports, but they were later used for the domestic trade as well.[186]

Still, despite the expansion of the export market – mainly products of agriculture and mining[187] – parts of Latin America started to *industrialize* more vigorously in the last quarter of the 19th century.[188] In Argentina, industrial production increased by an average of 8% annually between 1875 and 1913. Right before World War I, Argentina produced 18 times as many industrial goods than it did in 1875.[189] Between 1895 and 1913, the number of industrial enterprises and the number of workers employed by them doubled.[190] The Brazilian industry grew by 6% annually during the first two decades of the 20th century.[191] The number of industrial plants and workers grew just as quickly.[192] The industrialization process occurred more slowly in Chile and Mexico even though the countries' industrial production grew, on average, 3% to 4% annually at the start of the century.[193] As a result of all this, at the beginning of World War I, the domestic

---

185    Moreno-Brid/Ros (2009), 51; Bulmer-Thomas (1994), 137 and 319; Haber (2006), 543; Mitchell (1998), 362.

186    See Haber (2006), 540 f., Clayton/Conniff (1999), 125 f., Summerhill (2006) and Bulmer-Thomas (1994), 107.

187    On the subject of exports, see (among others) Donghi (1985), 330, Roesler (2009), 69 and 231, Clayton-Conniff, 125, Bulmer-Thomas (1994), 273 and 433, Haber (2006), 540 and Thorp (1998), 53, 114-119, 160, 336 f. and 347.

188    Haber (2006), 537 f.

189    Barbero/Rocchi (2003), 267; Rocchi (2005), 17-22; Randall (1977b), 147 f. and 235.

190    Haber (2006), 546.

191    Merrick/Graham (1979), 23; Randall (1977c), 122-125, 135 und 182 f.

192    Between 1889 and 1907, the numbers grew five and threefold, respectively. The number of industrial enterprises doubled again between 1910 und 1915. Randall (1977c), 135 and 183.

193    Thorp (1998), 322; Moreno-Brid/Ros (2009), 57; Fischer (2011), 54 f.; Collier/Sater (2004), 159 f.; Randall (1977 a), 136-141 and 188.

industries in Argentina, Brazil, Chile, Mexico, and Peru met 50% to 80% of the demand for consumer goods.[194]

The new industries clustered in large metropolitan areas, i.e. in Buenos Aires, Montevideo, São Paulo, Rio de Janeiro and along the Atlantic coast, in the central region around Mexico City, in Lima, and in Santiago de Chile on the Pacific.[195] In *Argentina*, more than half of the population lived in the capital and the neighboring provinces of Buenos Aires and Santa Fe. Before the turn of the century, about 70% of the country's industry was located in these areas. Around 1914, no less than 90% of industrial capital was concentrated in the country's middle east and its metropolitan areas: Buenos Aires, with over 1.5 million inhabitants, Córdoba, Rosario, and La Plata, with a combined population of about half a million inhabitants.[196]

In addition to Rio de Janeiro, São Paulo drew an increasingly large amount of the *Brazilian* industry. Thanks to the rapidly expanding coffee production around São Paulo, which attracted numerous European immigrants, the population grew from 65,000 inhabitants around 1890 to 346,000 in 1910.[197] Five years later, 30% of the Brazilian industrial production came from São Paulo.[198] The other big cities – Belém, Recife, Salvador, and Porto Alegre – were much further apart than the Argentinian cities, stimulating much less industrialization. This is why 80% of the Brazilian population, because they lived outside of São Paulo and Rio de Janeiro, were but little affected by the country's early industrialization.[199]

Like in Brazil, Puebla and Monterrey were the only cities in *Mexico*—apart from its capital—that triggered industrialization.[200] Only about 20% of the population lived in the three states in which they were situated,[201] which shows that industrialization in Mexico was also only sporadic.

---

194    Bulmer-Thomas (1994), 145. See Thorp (1998), 4 und Haber (2006), 544 ff.

195    Bulmer-Thomas (1994), 135. Randall (1977d), 136. On the subject of scarce industrialization outside of the large metropolitan areas, see Roesler (2009), 111.

196    Mitchell (1998), 56 f.; Randall (1977 b), 235; Rocchi (2005), 26 and 127 f.

197    Mitchell (1998), 55 und 57.

198    Randall (1977c), 183.

199    Mitchell (1998), 39.

200    Bulmer-Thomas (1994), 135.

201    Around 1921. Mitchell (1998), 33.

As a result, industrialization in Latin America, at least initially, did not have much of a *widespread impact*. There were some large cities whose demand for mass-produced goods stimulated industrialization, but they were too few and too far between. While, around 1920, North America counted twelve cities with more than half a million inhabitants between Montreal, Chicago, St. Louis, and Baltimore, Latin America had only four between Rio de Janeiro, Santiago de Chile, Buenos Aires, and São Paulo, an area of comparable size.[202] In the north, over 16 million people lived in this region; in the south, fewer than four million.[203] While industrialization in Latin America developed around big cities as it did elsewhere, the small number of cities and the great distances between them hampered large-scale industrialization for a long time. Because most of the population lived outside of these far-flung cities, only a relatively small group of people benefitted from the industrialization process.

The above is true for Latin America as a whole and for most of its individual *countries*, excepting those regions where an above-average percentage of the population lived in big cities. In Argentina and Chile in 1920, comparable to the US and Canada, about 18% of the population lived in Buenos Aires and a scant 14% in Santiago de Chile; in Brazil, only 6% lived in Rio de Janeiro and São Paulo; in Mexico, only 4% lived in Mexico City.[204] Accordingly, industrialization affected different countries to a different degree. Around 1914/1920, the number of workers employed in manufacturing amounted to almost 27% and 24% in Argentina and Chile respectively, both fairly small countries; these numbers compare with those of Canada. At about 10%, the numbers were much smaller in Brazil and Mexico, which had much larger populations. In absolute numbers, Brazil had more workers employed in manufacturing enterprises than Argentina, and Mexico had twice as many as Chile.[205] In the

---

202    Mitchell (1998), 50-57.

203    My calculations are based on Mitchell (1998), 50-57.

204    My calculations are based on Mitchell (1998), 50-57 and Maddison (Population). On the subject of different degrees of urbanization, measured by the population in cities over 20,000 inhabitants, see Merrick/Graham (1979), 186 and 188.

205    My calculations are based on Mitchell (1998), 102-109 and Merrick/Graham (1979), 153, 158 f. and 162. A similar picture emerges if we compare industrial production, as calculated by Bulmer-Thom-

small country of Uruguay, where about 30% of the total population lived in Montevideo, the numbers for per-capita industrial production were five times those of Brazil and three times those of Mexico.[206]

The *export economy* affected different countries in similarly uneven ways.[207] The total volume of exported goods was based on abundant natural mineral resources and large areas of agricultural land on the one hand, and on the number of entrepreneurs and landowners who took advantage of available international markets on the other. The economic impact of the export industry thus depended largely on a country's population numbers. If two countries exported a similar amount of goods, the inhabitants of a small country profited more. For example, in 1912, Argentina's per-capita export volume was four times as high as that of Brazil even though the total amount of exported goods was roughly the same in both countries.[208] Chile, Cuba, and Mexico had similar export volumes, but the per-capita numbers differed significantly: Chile's were more than four times higher than Mexico's; Cuba's were about six times higher than Mexico's. And in Uruguay, which exported only about one sixth of Brazil's volume, the per-capita numbers were almost four times higher.[209]

The *national per-capita product* resulted from a growing export economy and/or from city-triggered industrialization on one hand, and from the differences in the population size on the other. In Argentina, Uruguay, Chile, and Cuba, where industrialization and/or a strong export economy coincided with a small population, the numbers for the per-capita gross national product were close to those of some western and central European countries. But in Brazil and Mexico, where industrialization and an export economy coincided with a large population, the numbers compared to those of less developed countries in southern and eastern Europe.[210] In

---

as (1994), 192 for 1928. The numbers in the smaller Argentina were twice as high as they were in Brazil and 2.5 times as high as in Mexico. However, measured by population numbers, Argentina produced almost six and four times as much as the other two countries.

206     My calculations are based on Mitchell (1998), 308 f. and Maddison (Population).

207     See Bértola/Ocampo (2012), 86.

208     My calculations are based on Table 3.5 in Bulmer-Thomas (1994), 69.

209     My calculations are based on Table 3.5 in Bulmer-Thomas (1994), 69.

210     Table 13.9 in Escosura (2006), 500.

other Latin American countries, the numbers remained equally low for the time being: they had neither big cities that stimulated a significant industrialization nor a viable export economy.[211]

During the first decades of the *20th century*, industrialization that had begun before the turn of the century continued and spread to other countries, due to increased population and the number of big cities;[212] external circumstances like the Great Depression and World War II, along with government policies of import substitution, further supported this development.[213] In the course of the 1950s, immigration from Europe slowed down and eventually slowed to a trickle, so the population explosion to about 600 million people at the beginning of the 21st century depended on decreasing mortality rates and consistently high birth rates (See Table 14).[214] At the same time, the push factors of relatively over-populated rural areas, partially due to the uneven distribution of property in favor of large landowners, and the pull factors of non-agrarian jobs beckoning in the large cities caused more people than ever to move from the country into the city. The big cities expanded beyond their administrative borders into metropolitan areas. The number of cities with over a million inhabitants increased from two in 1920 to a still-modest six in 1950, but to 25 by 1980 (See Map 8 and Table 16). At the beginning, only a scant three million people (or 3% of the total population of Latin America) lived in these cities; by 1950, their number had increased to 15 million (9% of the total population) and grew to 86 million (24% of the total population) by 1980.[215]

*Rural flight* continued through the last years of the 20th century and the beginning of the 21st even though a decline in birth rates slowed down the population growth.[216] Still, Latin

---

211    See Maddison (Per Capita GDP).

212    Mitchell (1998), 50-57.

213    Thorp (1998), 161.

214    According to Maddison (Population), the total population of Latin America increased by 84% from 90 million to 165.5 million between 1920 and 1950, and more than doubled to over 360 million during the 30 years that followed. On the subject of decreased immigration, see Thorp (1998), 22 and Bulmer-Thomas (1994), 308.

215    My calculations are based on Table 16 and Maddison (Population).

216    Between 1980 and 2009, the population grew by 62% to 548 million. See Table 14 and Hofman (2000), 52 and Bulmer-Thomas (1994), 6.

America had more than six times the number of inhabitants it had in 1920. The number of cities with over a million inhabitants rose to over 50 by 2010. About 200 million people – a third of the total population of Latin America – lived in them.[217] While most of the economically weak migrants from the countryside lived in urban ghettos, the other social groups constituted a rapidly growing market for industrial goods of all kinds.

In addition to increasing urbanization and the attendant growth of big cities, which expanded and/or triggered industrialization, *external circumstances* such as the Great Depression and the Second World War inspired investments that were increasingly geared to the domestic market. Because the export industry took a hit when foreign demand for traditional export goods decreased drastically, potential entrepreneurs and some state governments decided to invest in the domestic industry to make up the loss.[218]

The reduction of the export industry and especially the demand created by the rapidly growing big cities favored the *progress of industrialization*, which continued to spread through Latin America, albeit at different rates and times. Both the numbers of industrial workers and the industrial product increased even faster than the population and the gross national product.[219] In larger countries, like Brazil, Mexico, Argentina, Colombia, Venezuela, and Chile, which combined around three quarters of the total population of Latin America, manufacturing employed between 26% (in Colombia) and 36% (in Argentina) of all workers.[220] By 1955, for the first time Latin America produced more industrial than agricultural goods[221] and supplied an increasing portion of the domestic demand; the difference was covered by imports. Table 17 in the appendix shows the industrial growth rates of individual countries; the last of the years listed in the table represent the most productive years before 1993.

---

217   My calculations are based on List of cities (Latin American countries).

218   See Merrick/Graham (1979), 16 f. and Bulmer-Thomas (1994), 9.

219   Bulmer-Thomas (1994), 232.

220   Mitchell (1998), 102-110. The percentage of industrial products in the gross national product, which around 1929 was less than 20% (excepting Argentina), increased until the 1970s in all larger countries (excepting Venezuela) to more than 20%, in Argentina and Brazil to over 30%. Bértola/Ocampo (2012), 128 f. und 167; Harberger (1988), 167.

221   Bulmer-Thomas (1994), 9.

Map 8: Cities with Over a Million Inhabitants in Latin America Around 1980

Tirol Atlas – Designed by Klaus Förster based on Table 9.

Map background: World Borders Dataset - http://thematicmapping.org/downloads/world_borders.php

The production of individual *industrial goods* increased in similar fashion; during the second half of the century, the focus of production shifted from consumer goods to investment goods, as it did everywhere else. The per-capita processing of raw cotton increased everywhere, but it never came close to the peak values Europe and North America had attained in the past (see Figure 11; for Europe and North America, see Figure 2, Figure

4, and Table 18). In Argentina, which now had its own cotton spinning mills,[222] cotton production peaked in the 1940s, in Uruguay around 1960, in Brazil and Colombia in 1992.

Figure 11: Processing of Raw Cotton in Latin America, 1948-1992 (Kg Per Capita, Peak Values)

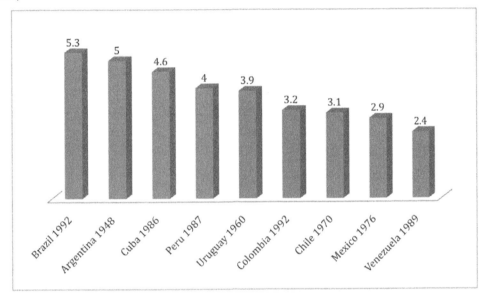

Calculations based on Mitchell (1998), 374 f. and Maddison (Population).

Production of *pig iron* and *crude steel* in Mexico and other Latin American countries increased steadily and peaked in the 1980s and 1990s (see Figure 12 and Table 18). However, like the cotton industry, the iron and steel industries, both of which are fundamental to large-scale industrialization, trailed Europe and North America (see Figure 3, Table 6, and Table 18).

---

222   Rocchi (2006), 39.

Figure 12: Production of Pig Iron in Latin America, 1980-1990 (Kg per Capita, Peak Values)

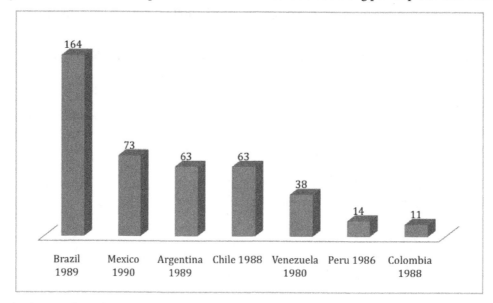

Calculations based on Mitchell (1998), 360 and Maddison (Population).

The Latin American automobile industry, which started after World War II, developed in similar ways, with per-capita numbers never exceeding those of eastern European countries (see Figure 13, Table 7, and Table 18).

After a period of stagnation in the 1980s, the *industrial national product* continued to increase, growing between 2% and 4% annually in individual countries from 1990 to 2008; the total for Latin America was 2.7%.[223] This amounted to an increase of almost 66% while the population grew only by 33% in the same time period. At the same time, because of increasing automatization and capital intensiveness, the industry employed fewer workers; in most countries, employment in manufacturing balanced out at less than 20% (see Figure 14 and Table 20).[224]

---

223    Bértola/Ocampo (2012), 241. For the rise in industrial production in Mexico, see Moreno-Brid/Ros (2009), 193.

224    On the relative decline of the workforce in the secondary sector in Argentina, Brazil, Chile, Columbia, Mexico, and Venezuela since around 1980, see Hofmann (2000), 57; on capital intensiveness in the industry, see Skidmore/Smith (2001), 56.

Figure 13: Production of Passenger Cars in Latin America, 1976-1993 (Peak Values per 1.000 Inhabitants)

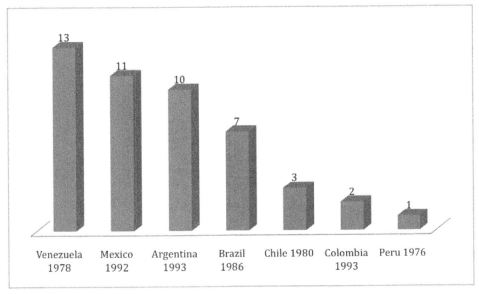

Calculations based on Mitchell (1998), 396 f. and Maddison (Population).

As was the case in eastern and southern Europe, Latin America gradually transitioned to a *service industry*, before ever reaching the production values of western, northern, and central Europe, the US, and Canada. As early as the early 1990s, most wage earners in almost all countries worked in the service industry.[225] Like in Europe and the industrial nations of North America, the Latin American service industry owed its growth to increased industrial productivity, which was interrupted only briefly during the crisis of the 1980s.[226] Increased productivity brought about higher salaries for industrial workers and thus higher tax revenues. More and more, both private income and taxes went to pay for private and public services.[227]

---

225    Skidmore/Smith (2001), 425.

226    See Moreno-Brid/Ros (2009), 114, Thorp (1998), 328 f. and Ros/Bouillon (2002), 362.

227    Bulmer-Thomas (1994), 317.

Figure 14: Employment in Manufacturing in Latin America, 1950-1994 (Percent of Economically Active Population, Peak Values)

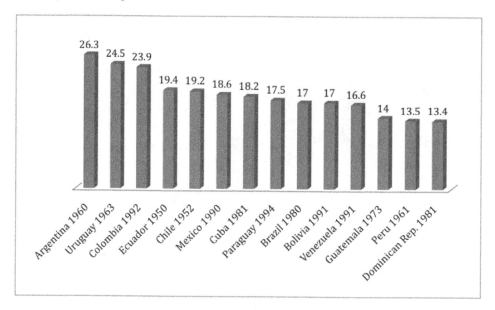

Calculations based on Mitchell (1998), 105-110.

If the *degree of industrialization* in Latin America, despite its progress, continued to trail the traditional industrial nations in Europe and North America before it stagnated,[228] the fault lies with the concentration of big cities in relatively few areas. Because industrialization happens chiefly in and around metropolitan areas, a large part of the population outside of these areas saw little or none of it. At the end of the 1970s, about three quarters of the total industrial production in Latin America came out of only six states and/or three provinces: Buenos Aires and Santa Fe in Argentina (provinces), Rio de Janeiro and São Paulo in Brazil (states), and Mexico and Nuevo León (states) with industrial centers in

---

228    See the declining shares of the secondary sector in the workforce according to Fischer Weltalmanach (2000) and Fischer Weltalmanach (2011).

Mexico City and Monterrey.[229] Less than 20% of the total Latin American population at the time lived in these areas.[230] The remaining quarter of industrial production took place mostly in the metropolitan areas of individual state capitals such as Montevideo, Bogotá, Lima, or Santiago de Chile.[231]

*Brazil* is a good example of the imbalance created by the concentration of industrial production in only a few areas. In 1970, 40% of the population lived on 10% of the land, namely the southeastern states of Rio de Janeiro, São Paulo, Minas Gerais, and Espírito Santo. With two thirds of industrial workers employed in these areas, they produced 80% of industrial goods.[232] The relatively high degree of industrialization in these areas was felt in per-capita incomes as well, which were three to four times higher in the southeast than they were in the north and northeast, and twice as high as they were in the south.[233] In the southeast, almost 30% of the population lived in the metropolitan areas of Rio de Janeiro, São Paulo, and Belo Horizonte; in the northeast, only around 7% of the population lived in Recife and Salvador, cities that had over a million inhabitants at the time.[234]

As was the case in south and eastern Europe, the concentration of *industrial enterprises* in metropolitan centers indicated that they were able, thanks to increased production rates, to meet most of the rising demand for industrial products created by these and other growing cities. At the beginning of the industrialization process, a single city over a million inhabitants could create the demand necessary for a large industrial region to grow up around it. However, from the 1960s and 1970s on, as newer cities grew beyond the one-million

---

229     Thorp (1998), 21 f.

230     My calculations are based on Mitchell (1998), 33 and 38 f. and Maddison (Population).

231     See Reichart (1993), 213 f. and 233. According to Reichart, at the beginning of the 1980s, 53% of industrial workers were employed in Mexico City, where 21% of the population lived. In Argentina, 66% of industrial workers were employed in the industrial centers of Buenos Aires and Rosario. In Columbia, industrial workers were concentrated in the industrial triangle formed by Bogotá, Medellín, and Cali.

232     Merrick/Graham (1979) 10 and Faria (1989), Table 4.9.

233     Merrick/Graham (1979), 10 und 205.

234     My calculations are based on Mitchell (1998), 56 and 57, and Merrick/Graham (1979), 117.

mark, the competition from the established industrial centers was too strong to allow new industrial areas to form around them as they had in the past. These newer cities did not promote industrialization the way older cities had done in the past.

Because the percentage of the population living in industrial regions – both with regard to all of Latin America and individual countries – is smaller than in western, central, and northern Europe, the US, and Canada, the per-capita average national product was smaller as well. Despite significant differences between the individual countries, the per-capita gross domestic product in the larger Latin American countries, by the turn of the millennium, was only 25%-50% that of western and central Europe and roughly equivalent to that of eastern Europe.[235]

If Latin American countries lagged behind older industrial countries with regard to per-capita national product, the explanation is not that industrialization did not happen in these countries but that it happened in only a few regions. As a result, industrial production enabled a small portion of the population to buy the same industrial goods and services people enjoyed in Europe and North America. However, with regard to the total population, the average consumer standard was lower, both qualitatively and quantitatively. Even though Latin American countries made great strides in providing consumer goods for a larger swath of their populations (see Figure 15, Figure 16, and Figure 17), they could never catch up with the standard older industrial countries in North America and Europe had attained (see Figure 7, Figure 8, and Table 19).

And yet, industrialization that is confined to certain regions only partially explains the ongoing backlog; another explanation lies in Latin America's consistently low *industrial productivity*, which also contributed to lower averages in per capita production and per-capita income than those of traditional industrial nations. In 2006, the rates for per-capita industrial production in western, central, and northern Europe, Canada, and the USA were four to five times higher than those in Latin America – individual differences between countries notwithstanding.[236] As the case of eastern and southern Europe demonstrated, the industries in older industrial nations, thanks to new technology and innovations in the production process, were better able to increase and accelerate their productivity, both

235    Maddison (Per Capita GDP).

236    Welt in Zahlen (Industrieproduktion).

quantitatively and qualitatively, to the point where younger industrial nations could follow but never catch up with them.

Figure 15: Television Sets per 1,000 Inhabitants in Latin America, 1960-2006 (Larger Countries)

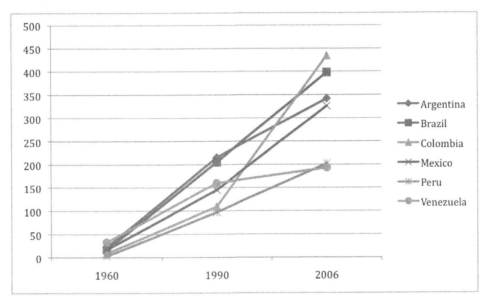

See, also for smaller countries, Table 19.

Figure 16: Passenger Cars per 1,000 Inhabitants in Latin America, 1950-2006 (Larger Countries)

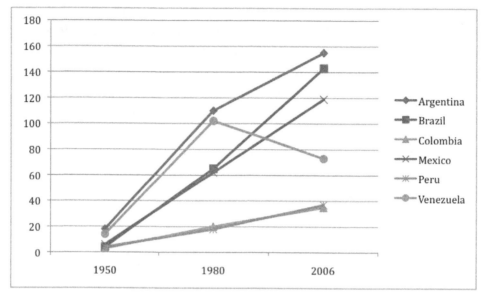

See, also for less populous countries, Table 19.

To sum up, like eastern and southern Europe, Latin America experienced a belated but significant *industrialization process*, which ended rural poverty for millions of people. However, the number of people still living in poverty is much higher than in the industrial nations in North America and western, central, and northern Europe. The fault lies with the belated onset of industrialization on the one hand, and its regional concentration in a few metropolitan centers on the other. In the end, both of these factors were determined by the structure of urbanization. Because Latin America remained sparsely populated for a long time, the large metropolitan centers, whose dense populations created high consumer demand, developed later than those in North America or Europe and were confined to relatively few state capitals and/or international trade centers on the coast. Their expansion and the industrialization they triggered reached only a small segment of the overall population. The rest of the population, which as a whole had increased dramatically since the 1950s, lived in rural areas outside of the big cities and was largely excluded from the industrialization process.

Figure 17: Computers per 1,000 Inhabitants in Latin America, 2006

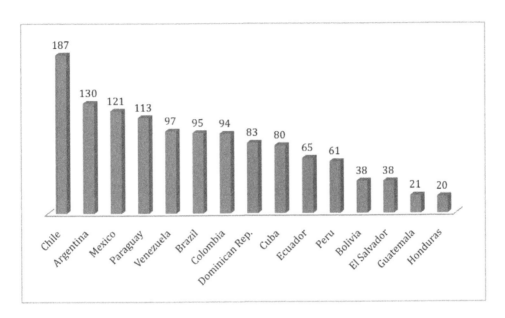

Welt in Zahlen (Computer).

AFRICA

Africa is divided into three *large regions*: the Mediterranean north, tropical, sub-Saharan Africa, and South Africa. Even though, until the more recent centuries, some of the population in all three regions hunted and gathered or lived as nomadic herdsmen, most of the people transitioned to an agricultural economy. As was the case elsewhere, quite a few of them worked as artisans and merchants and lived mostly in urban settlements. However, the towns remained very small for a long time, and they were spread out relatively far. As late as 1900, Africa had only eight cities with over 100,000 inhabitants: Cairo, Alexandria, Tunis, Algiers, and Fez in the north; Cape Town and Johannesburg in the south, and Ibadan in today's Nigeria; none of these cities came even close to a million inhabitants.[237]

The extraordinarily low *degree of urbanization* resulted from the country's *low population density*. While estimates vary considerably, we assume that by 1600, no more than 100 million people lived on the entire continent, which is hardly more than the population of Europe at the time, in an area only one third as large as Africa.[238] Because of the slave trade that started shortly after 1600 and the subsequent abduction of a great number of Africans to America, the population grew very slowly. In fact, according to some estimates, the population shrank[239] and did not grow again until the 19th century – slowly at first, but, from 1950 on, more rapidly than on any other continent.[240] Around 1900, when the population of Europe had grown to more than 400 million, Africa had slightly more than 100 million;[241] by 1950, a scant 230 million.[242]

---

237 Mitchell (2007), 41. See also Zeleza (1993), 75-77.

238 Maddison (Population) estimates 55 million; Mathieu (2011), 87, 113 million.

239 According to Mathieu (2011), 87, to 102 million by 1800.

240 For an in-depth discussion of population development, see Zeleza (1993), 56-77.

241 138 million according to Mathieu (2011), 87; 110 million according to Maddison (Population); between 120 und 141 million according to Zeleza (1993), 60.

242 228 million according to Maddison (Population).

During the following decades, Africa saw a *population* explosion: In only 50 years, the number of inhabitants grew to around 800 million,[243] and by 2009, to almost a billion (see Table 21). The rapid population growth resulted almost exclusively from declining mortality rates and pre-modern – i.e. consistently high – birth rates.[244] Immigrants from Europe, who at first settled primarily in South Africa and Algeria but who had been expanding to the rest of Africa since the end of the 19th century, did not contribute to the population growth in any significant way; compared to America, only a small number of immigrants went to Africa.[245]

Until the 20th century, Africa experienced very little urbanization, which is why *industrialization* remained very modest as a result.[246] The export trade, in particular, created a market economy on a larger scale that went beyond mere subsistence farming. As was the case in South America, the export economy was based on satisfying the European demand for products from agriculture and the mining industry; in turn, European industrial products were imported to Africa.[247] Industrial production in North and South Africa, which had the highest population density, happened on a slightly larger scale. By 1950, five of the 30 African cities with over 100,000 inhabitants were located in South Africa – Cape Town, Johannesburg, Durban, Pretoria, and Port Elizabeth – even though only 5% of the total population lived there. Twelve additional cities of similar size were located in the Mediterranean countries, i.e. in Morocco, Algeria, Tunisia, Libya, and Egypt, with Cairo as the only city in Africa with over a million inhabitants at the time.

However, even in the urbanized south and north of the continent, industrialization remained modest and rarely amounted to more than larger manufactures. After a strong uptick in the mining of precious metals during the last quarter of the 19th century, entrepreneurs

---

243   Less than 800 according to Mathieu (2011), 87; over 800 million according to Maddison (Population).

244   See Bairoch (1975), 5-12.

245   See Zeleza (1993), 73 f.

246   For a detailed discussion of the development of industry and manufacture, see Zeleza (1993), 175-251 and – to a lesser degree – Austen (1987).

247   For a detailed discussion, see Albertini (1985).

in *South Africa* invested some of their profits in industrial production,[248] which, along with construction and energy production, grew more than ten-fold during the first half of the 20th century; the number or workers in these industries increased more than five-fold.[249] After some early – but fleeting – attempts at government-initiated industrialization around the middle of the 19th century, *Egypt* took another hundred years to establish a successful cotton industry that processed domestic supplies of raw cotton.[250] As part of an import-substitution program, some of the locally grown raw cotton – which up to this point had all been exported – was processed in domestic cotton mills. In 1960, Egypt processed 4.3 kg cotton per capita into yarns and materials, an amount that approached the production of continental Europe. No other African country could come close: South Africa produced 1.2 kg, neighboring Southern Rhodesia (today's Zimbabwe) 2 kg per capita.[251] The Egyptian industry, much of which was government-owned and grew six-fold between 1945 and 1970, clustered in the metropolitan areas of Cairo, Alexandria, and the canal zone around Suez and Port Said.[252]

At the behest of their governments, South Africa and Zimbabwe were the first countries to establish significant *iron and steel industries*, which took advantage of domestic ore resources and supplied some of the domestic market; Egypt, Algeria, and Tunisia followed their example, albeit to a lesser extent.[253] In this regard, the South African production of pig iron – in both absolute numbers or per capita – far outstripped those of the other countries, excepting Zimbabwe. In 1961, the per-capita production in South Africa amounted to about 140 kg and that of the much-smaller Zimbabwe – which had fewer than 2 million inhabitants at the time – around 122 kg. By comparison, the North African countries produced barely 10 kg.[254] According to these numbers, South Africa and Zimbabwe did not

---

248    For a detailed discussion, see Feinstein (2005).

249    Feinstein (2005), 122 and Lal (1988), 201.

250    Mabro/Radwan (1978), 10-26; Albertini (1985), 187.

251    My calculations are based on Mitchell (2007), 466 and Maddison (Population).

252    Mabro/Radwan (1978), 84 and 93-97.

253    Cooper (2002), 100; Feinstein (2005), 121.

254    My calculations are based on Mitchell (2007), 440 and Maddison (Population).

come up to the standard of western European countries before World War I but clearly exceeded the standard of eastern and southern Europe (see Figure 3).

Because they were more *industrialized*, South Africa and Egypt were the only countries at the time where manufacturing – measured by employment statistics – amounted to more than 10% of the national economy. The share of agriculture in South Africa had shrunk to 30%; everywhere else, however – excepting smaller countries like Libya and the island of Mauritius – agriculture still employed more than half of the workforce.[255] The South African per-capita gross domestic product reflected the country's advanced degree of industrialization. With the exception of Algeria and Libya (and a few smaller, atypical countries like Gabon, Mauritius, Namibia, the island of Réunion, and the Seychelles, which, together, had a total population of only 2 million), the South-African numbers, according to Angus Maddison, exceeded those of other countries by more than twice – most of them even by three to five times the amount.[256] By mid-20th century, the South African economy produced approximately as much as Spain, Portugal, Greece in the south of Europe, or Bulgaria and Poland in the east.[257]

During the second half of the 20th century, other countries (now independent nations) adopted the *industrial policies* of South African governments, which favored import substitution and the establishment of state-owned iron and steel industries.[258] However, because they lacked the infrastructure, they did not achieve the same results as South Africa. Their attempts to process domestic natural resources industrially remained limited. Instead, they mostly exported them in the form of (iron) ore, crude oil, and, occasionally, crude metal.[259] Apparently, the domestic market was not large enough to make the processing of raw materials profitable. Thanks to the rapid increase in population, urbanization continued to spread through the rest of the continent – the number of cities with over one million inhabitants increased from 11 to over 50 between 1980 and 2014

---

255   My calculations are based on Mitchell (2007), 96-102 and Maddison (Population).

256   Many countries were even further behind. Maddison (Per Capita GDP) and Maddison (Population).

257   Maddison (Per Capita GDP).

258   See Cooper (2002), 100 f.

259   Helmschrott (1990), 16 and 135-160.

(see Map 9 and Table 22) – but it was mostly only one and especially the capital city of each country.[260]

Map 9: Cities with Over a Million Inhabitants in Africa Around 1980

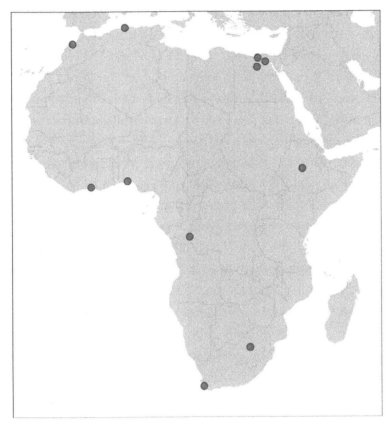

Tirol Atlas – Designed by Klaus Förster based on Table 9.
Map background: World Borders Dataset - http://thematicmapping.org/downloads/ world_borders.php

---

260    Lions (2010), 18 and List of metropolitan areas in Africa.

The *momentum for industrialization* that emanated from the big cities rarely went beyond their metropolitan areas and thus remained largely isolated. The much larger, widely scattered, and rapidly growing rural population saw very little of it. Despite massive rural flight, which swelled the urban population between North and South Africa by 3% annually,[261] the rural population continued to grow rapidly, from approximately 200 to 600 million between 1950 and 2010.[262] In addition, much of the urban population – especially in sub-Saharan Africa – consisted of people who lived in slums and had very little purchasing power, which diminished the cities' positive influence on economic development. While, according to UNO calculations, the slum population decreased in North Africa from 38% to 14.5% of urban population between 1900 and 2005, around 200 million people or 62% in sub-Saharan Africa still lived in urban slums, even though their numbers were going down.[263] Although they settled in and around the big cities, economically they were still a part of the under-developed rural population.

This is why *industrial production* and *industrial employment* grew in all countries – and especially around big cities – but the impact of industrialization, because of a vast rural population and large numbers of people living in slums, remained rather modest. In most of the 30 countries for which Brian Mitchell produced statistics, the percentage of workers employed in manufacturing amounted to only 10% or less at the turn of the century.[264] In other countries, only 11% to 22% of the workforce (in Ghana and Morocco, respectively) was employed in manufacturing at the height of industrialization (see Figure 18).[265]

From the 1980s and 1990s on, the percentage of industrial workers has been sinking even though it was still far away from the peak values of the industrial nations in Europe and North America. As in these, the relative decline of industrial employment was paralleled by a rapid expansion of the service economy.[266]

---

261   Urbanisierung (2011), 4.

262   My calculations are based on Urbanisierung (2011), 3 and Maddison (Population).

263   Urbanisierung (2011), 4.

264   My calculations are based on Mitchell (2007), 96-102.

265   Only on the small and atypical island of Mauritius, where, at last count, about half of its million inhabitants lived in the metropolitan area of Port Louis, 43% of the population worked in industrial jobs in 1995, a considerably higher percentage.

266   Mitchell (2007), 96-102.

Figure 18: Employment in Manufacturing in Africa, 1980-1996
(Percent of Economically Active Population, Peak Values)

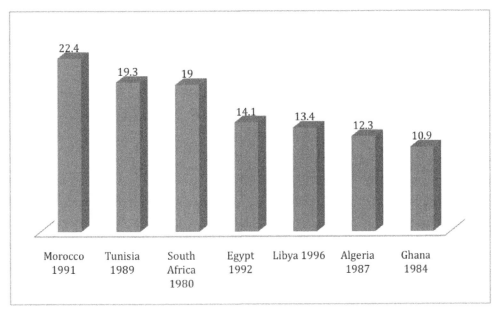

Calculations based on Mitchell (2007), 96-102.

*Industrial production* developed along with industrial employment, albeit not at the same rate in all countries. In the wake of overall industrialization, production increased more quickly than the population until the 1970s.[267] Soon, however, import substitution reached its limits. While industrial production in sub-Saharan Africa increased by an annual average of 10% between 1965 and 1973, it decreased to 8% during the remainder of the 1970s and shrank to less than 1% between 1980 and 1987.[268] Industrial production trailed population growth and did not increase until fairly recently. In South Africa, for example, per-capita industrial production, after a decline during the 1980s and 1990s, started

---

267    This conclusion is based on the data for 12 countries, but I assume it is the same or similar for the other countries. My calculations are based on Mitchell (2007), 365 f. and Maddison (Population).

268    Sub-Saharan Africa (1989), 223.

to increase at the turn of the century. Production in Ghana, which saw a brief but heavy decline in the 1970s, started to increase in 1983. From at least the 1980s on, population growth in Senegal, Zimbabwe, and Zaire outstripped industrial production; in Algeria and Malawi, this happened a littler later. However, in Egypt, per-capita industrial production continued strong until the turn of the century, and it lasted even longer in Morocco and Tunisia.[269]

The development of individual economic sectors reflected the *discontinuous industrialization process* in African countries. Even though other countries had by now established cotton industries, Egypt remained at the top until the very last; however, its per-capita processing of *raw cotton* declined from a record 8 kg in 1981 to about 6 kg by the end of the century. Zimbabwe had similar values in 1995 while South Africa had remained steady between 2 kg and 3 kg since the mid-1960s, followed by Algeria, Morocco, and Nigeria with 1.5 kg. The values for Zaire, Ethiopia, and Sudan were even lower during the 1970s and 1980s.[270]

Around 1980, with a per-capita production of 302 kg, South Africa had the strongest *production of pig iron* in all of Africa, both in absolute and relative terms, followed by Zimbabwe with a little over 100 kg (1982), Algeria with approximately 60 kg (1988), Tunisia with 20 kg (2000), and Egypt with only 12 kg (1973).[271] The lack of an independent African *automobile industry* constituted a significant factor in her late and undistinguished industrial development. Workers merely assembled imported automobile parts, which resulted in an irregular and modest production. South Africa was an exception in this regard: The number of assembled passenger cars rose from a scant 40,000 during the 1950s to over 300,000 by the turn of the century. Morocco, in second place, produced fewer than 100,000 during the 1990s. This amounted to seven (South Africa) and three (Morocco) cars per 1,000 inhabitants; during their peak years, Germany, France, and Canada produced over 50 (see Table 7 and Table 18).[272]

---

269   My calculations are based on Mitchell (2007), 365 f. and Maddison (Population).

270   My calculations are based on Mitchell (2007), 466 and Maddison (Population).

271   My calculations are based on Mitchell (2007), 440 and Maddison (Population).

272   My calculations are based on Mitchell (2007), 501 and Maddison (Population).

Apart from the share of industrial production in the gross national product, African *industrial productivity* remained far behind the highly developed industrial countries in Europe and North America. Based on production in the secondary economic sector and the number of workers it employed, we can calculate that in 2000, the productivity of most African countries compared to that of the poorer countries of eastern Europe; the productivity of slightly more developed countries – Algeria, Libya, Gabon, and South Africa – compared to that of the more productive countries of eastern Europe.[273]

But why did the modest *industrialization process*, despite progressive urbanization, falter before it could expand? There are three possible answers: For one, industrial productivity increased in Africa despite its relative backwardness, which meant that fewer workers were necessary to meet the largely urban demand for industrial products. Second, imported goods satisfied most of the demand of the big cities, which diminished the market for domestic products. Third, a majority of urban customers, whose demand for industrial products had been satisfied, demanded more and more services, as was the case in the highly industrialized countries.

We can trace the importance of imported goods to meet urban demand in the growing and well-documented *numbers of passenger cars* in individual countries, especially since only South Africa, Morocco, and Egypt had a viable automobile industry of their own. Passenger-car density increased in the wake of economic development, especially in the metropolises, but with regard to the entire country, remained very modest (see Figure 19 and Table 23). Even in more developed countries like Libya, Algeria, Tunisia, and Morocco in the north, and South Africa and Zimbabwe in the south, car-density never exceeded that of the poorer countries in eastern Europe (See Table 8).

---

273   My calculations are based on Welt in Zahlen (Industrieproduktion) and Mitchell (2007), 96-102. Limited industrialization impeded the fight against hunger as well. While, according to FAO, the number of malnourished people, despite rapid population growth, has declined world-wide from one billion to about 800 million since 1992, it rose from 182 to 227 million in Africa. "Die Zeit," 29 Apr. 2015, 24.

Figure 19: Passenger Cars per 1,000 Inhabitants in Africa, 2006 (Larger Countries, Over 20 Cars)

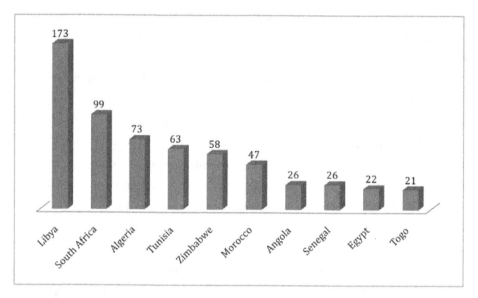

Welt in Zahlen (PKW).

The explanation for the low passenger-car density lay not only in the little statistical weight of urban populations but also in the fact that only few city dwellers could afford a car. Still, the numbers of imported cars could keep pace with the population growth in most countries and even exceeded it in some others.

The distribution of *less expensive consumer goods,* such as televisions or – more recently – computers, presented a similar picture. Apart from a few exceptions, the numbers in Figures 20 and 21 and in Table 23 confirm yet again that South Africa and the countries in North Africa enjoyed a higher degree of economic development. Among the smaller countries, Libya, Gabon, Swaziland, Djibouti, and Togo reached similar standards; with regard to computers, the list includes Namibia and Gambia. As was the case with cars, all of these countries had fewer televisions and just about as many computers per capita as the poorest European countries (see Table 9).[274] Typically for little developed countries, there were significant differences between them with regard to these three consumer goods, differences that lessened as economic development continued.

Figure 20: Television Sets per 1,000 Inhabitants in Africa, 2006 (Larger Countries, Over 100 TVs)

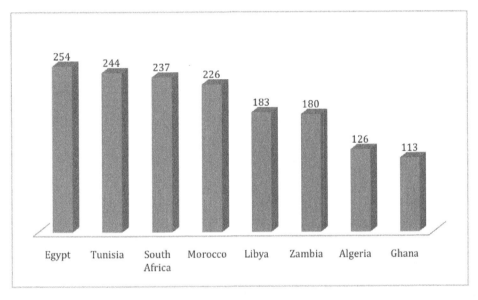

Welt in Zahlen (Fernsehgeräte).

---

274    Welt in Zahlen (Fernsehgeräte).

Figure 21: Computers per 1,000 Inhabitants in Africa, 2006 (Larger Countries, Over 20 Computers)

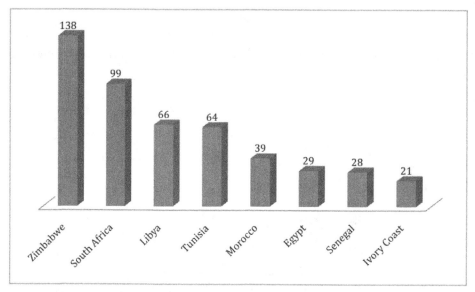

Welt in Zahlen (Computer).

In the face of only spotty industrialization, *other sources of income* – such as the export of agricultural products or mineral commodities (including crude oil) or government loans and development aid – became more important, even though their significance differed from country to country.[275] Not only private entrepreneurs profited from export-oriented agricultural production, mining, and foreign trade; these sources of income also boosted government revenue significantly, either through direct involvement in mining enterprises or through taxes and tariffs. Government revenue created a large, public employment sector and facilitated investments in infrastructure; this created public income and purchasing power in addition to the profits of private business enterprises.[276]

---

275    Moyo (2001), 114.

276    See Helmschrott (1990), 17, who rates government expenses rather negatively.

This *purchasing power* facilitated not only the import of industrial consumer goods; it also created increasing demand for private and public services in metropolitan areas. As a result, despite a relatively small degree of industrialization, the tertiary economic sector in Africa expanded especially in big cities and contributed more to the overall gross national product than the other two economic sectors (see Table 24).

According to a study of 15 countries that, together, constituted 80% of the total African product, manufacturing made up only 9% of the total economic growth between 2002 and 2007; services, on the other hand, amounted to 50%. An additional 36% came from raw materials and agricultural products, 5% from the construction industry.[277] The same trend was manifest in the employment structure: In six of the seven countries for which we have data,[278] the service sector increased more rapidly during the first years of the 21st century than the secondary sector.[279]

In this way, an *urban service economy* developed away from the rural population that was largely untouched by industrialization. A dualistic economic structure developed, which consisted of a relatively narrow urban segment on the one hand, which compared to the urban centers in industrial nations, and the rural population on the other, which remained large despite continued urban flight. At the turn of the century, the latter still comprised between 80% and 90% of the total population in individual countries like Burundi, Rwanda, Botswana.[280] City dwellers enjoyed a large amount of services while the majority of the population in rural areas still lived in pre-industrial conditions.

Despite Africa's progress toward a modern economy, the lesser-developed parts of the population weighed so heavily that the *average* per-capita *national product* was significantly lower than it was in countries with large-scale industrialization, which, on the whole, indicated that African countries had achieved only a very low degree of development. In 2008, the per-capita gross domestic product even in the most developed countries – Tunisia, South Africa, Namibia, and Botswana – amounted to only a fourth to a fifth of the western

---

277   Lions (2010), 2.

278   Burkina Faso, Ethiopia, Mozambique, Rwanda, Tanzania, Uganda, Nigeria.

279   Outlook (2013), 37.

280   My calculations are based on Mitchell (2007), 96-102 and Maddison (Population).

and central European average.[281] The 18 poorest countries on the continent, which together made up about a third of the total African population, were even further behind.[282] Their per-capita gross domestic product comprised only 25% or less of the gross domestic product of the poorest countries in the Balkans and the farthest eastern parts of Europe.

To conclude, the significant *backlog in* Africa's *economic development* did not primarily result from an industrialization process that happened too slowly or not at all; rather, it came about because industrialization in Africa was restricted to a few "islands," i.e. large metropolitan centers. Combined with lagging industrial productivity, Africa's small-scale industrialization was the reason that the per-capita domestic product – despite much lower basal levels and an attendant need to catch up – only doubled between 1950 and 2008;[283] during the same time period, the per-capita gross national product in central and northern Europe increased more than four-fold.  In the USA and Canada, it increased 3.5-fold. However, the growing income gap – as reflected in national averages – affected the African people in different ways. The contrast was most keenly felt in the population that lived in rural and urban poverty, while the small minority of an affluent urban middle and upper class enjoyed a lifestyle that, meanwhile, had come up to the standard of developed nations.

---

281    The significantly larger numbers in Equatorial Guinea and Mauritius, two small countries, constitute exceptions and are thus not representative.

282    Burundi, Chad, Niger, Ethiopia, Guinea, Guinea Bissau, Malawi, Tanzania, Liberia, Madagascar, Sierra Leone, Eritrea, Somalia, Zambia, Zimbabwe, Togo, the Central African Republic, the Democratic Republic of Congo, all of which had a per capita gross domestic product of less than $1,000. Maddison (Per Capita GDP).

283    Among the larger countries, the gross domestic product increased significantly faster only in Tunisia and Egypt. Maddison (Per Capita GDP).

# ASIA

Given the size of Asia, whose 45 million square km occupy almost one third of the continental land mass and whose 4 billion inhabitants make up more than half of the world's population, we will divide the continent into *large regions* and analyze their economic development separately. With regard to geography and population size, we can distinguish five such regions:

North and central Asia, with a population of about 100 million people, who live in the Asian part of Russia east of the Ural Mountains and in Mongolia, Kazakhstan, and the region between Turkmenistan and Kyrgyzstan.

West Asia, with a population of a scant 300 million people, who live between the Mediterranean, the Caucasus, and the Arabian Sea.

South Asia, with a population of almost 1.5 billion people, who live mostly in Afghanistan, Pakistan, India, and Bangladesh.

Southeast Asia, with a population of over half a billion people, who live between Myanmar, Indonesia, and the Philippines.

East Asia, including the People's Republic of China, Japan, North and South Korea, and Taiwan, with a combined population of about 1.5 billion.

During the 19th century, as was the case in other parts of the world, many Asians lived as hunters and gatherers like their ancestors. Most of them, however, had settled down to an agrarian lifestyle sooner than other populations. In addition, several thousand years ago, some regions saw the development of urban settlements, whose inhabitants worked in non-agrarian occupations as artisans and tradesmen. However, the degree of urbanization and population density varied between regions both large and small.

## NORTH AND CENTRAL ASIA

Until recently, north and central Asia was sparsely populated. Around 100 million people, which amounted to less than 3% of the population (see Table 25), lived on 18.7 million square km, about 40% of the total area of Asia.[284] The *population density* in this area was about one-fourteenth of the population density in Europe and one-sixth to that of Africa. The degree of urbanization, as a result, was low as well. Until fairly recently, most of the people in northern and central Asia lived as nomadic or half-nomadic herdsmen, who moved seasonally in search of pasture. Some still do to this day. In Mongolia in the 1980s, nomads made up 35% of the scant two million inhabitants;[285] in the territories of the former Soviet Union in northern and central Asia, their numbers decreased from 20 million to between 2 and 2.5 million as a result of government-ordained collectivization.[286] Because most of the remaining population lived as sedentary peasants, only a few larger urban settlements developed, and they were located at great distances from each other.

By the turn of the 20th century, there was not a single *city* with over 100,000 inhabitants in the entire enormous territory. Not surprisingly, the output of local manufactures was modest as well. In 1908, the per-capita manufacturing production in the Asian part of the Russian Empire amounted to only a quarter of the Russian average, which was low to begin with.[287] In 1926, fewer than 15% of the people living in the Soviet part of the region east of the Ural Mountains were city dwellers; by 1939, a scant 30% of the population lived in cities and by 1959, their numbers had grown to over 40%.[288]

---

284   Wikipedia (Asia).

285   Wikipedia (Mongolia).

286   See Köllmann (1965), 220.

287   Wagener (1972), 8.

288   We assume that the numbers for Siberia and the Far East, for which we do not have any 1959 data, were a little higher than in the Soviet republics in central Asia. Köllmann (1965), 222 and 229.

As the *population* continued to *grow* and the Soviet government developed the region economically, the number of big cities increased. In 1956, northern and central Asia – including the Urals region – had around 20 cities with over 200,000 inhabitants,[289] but only four of them – Novosibirsk, Sverdlovsk/Ekaterinburg, Chelyabinsk, and Omsk – had passed the half-million mark. These cities were predominantly located in the mid and southern Urals region and in south-west Siberia, where, since the 1930s, they had profited from the mining of important raw materials and from their position on the Trans-Siberian railroad line, which was built in 1891.[290] The share of the eastern regions[291] in Russian/Soviet coal mining increased from 12% to over 50% between 1913 and 1970; their share in power production increased from 10% to 38%.[292] In addition, 25% of all crude oil produced in the Soviet Union came from the eastern part of the country. Between 1940 and 1956, west Siberia and the Urals region – and for a period of time Kazakhstan as well – belonged to the Soviet territories where industrial production increased the most.[293]

Cities like Novosibirsk, Ekaterinburg, Omsk, and Chelyabinsk – as well as Alma Ata and Tashkent, the rapidly growing capitals of Kazakhstan and Uzbekistan – grew into cities with over a million inhabitants by the end of the Soviet Union (see Map 11);[294] and yet, the region industrialized not so much because of the demand for consumer goods but because of Soviet *economic planning*, which championed the iron and steel industries. The combination of valuable iron ore deposits in the Ural Mountains and the coal resources in the Kuznetsk basin enabled the Soviet Union to establish the Ural-Kuznetsk-Combine, which became one of the most important iron and steel production centers in the world.[295] By 1970, about 40% of Soviet-produced pig iron and crude steel, 20% of tractors and 12% of power tools came from the eastern part of the country. Despite the fact that most of Soviet raw cotton

---

289    Including Omsk and Bishkek, which are not mentioned in Köllmann (1965), 229.

290    See Mauro (1984), 173-176 and Köllmann (1965), 221.

291    The Urals region, west and east Siberia, the Far East, middle Asia, and Kazakhstan.

292    Merl (1987), 697.

293    Hutchings (1971), 220.

294    List of cities (individual countries).

295    Raupach (1964), 93.

was grown in Uzbekistan and Turkmenistan, only a scant 10% of cotton textiles came from this area.[296] Considering that, at the time, about 30% of the total Soviet population lived in this area, the regional per-capita production of pig iron and crude steel exceeded the Soviet average but the region fell considerably short in the other three production groups. The Urals region alone produced about three quarters of all Soviet iron ore and crude steel, but the production of cotton textiles took place almost entirely outside of this region.

During the 20 years before the dissolution of the Soviet Union, economic planning for the Asian regions supported the production of power and raw materials at the expense of the manufacturing industry. Between 1970 and 1985, the per-capita *production of electrical power* increased in the Russian part of the Soviet Union, which included the European and the north-Asian part of the country, by 86%; in central Asian Kazakhstan and Uzbekistan, it increased by 92% and 72% respectively; in Kyrgyzstan, Tajikistan, and Turkmenistan, it multiplied more than two, three, and four times.[297] A large portion of Soviet crude steel also came from the Urals and the eastern regions of the Russian republic; in Kazakhstan in central Asia, per-capita production approached western European values. However, the crude steel production of Uzbekistan trailed that of the other regions. The rest of central Asia never had a steel industry to speak of.[298]

As far as the *consumer goods industry* is concerned, by the end of the 1980s, only Uzbekistan, the most important producer of raw cotton, managed to come up to the Soviet – and thus the western and central European – averages in the production of cotton textiles. Per-capita production in the rest of central Asia was only half as high;[299] the data for north Asia (which are based on conjecture) indicate that the cotton industry played only a minor

---

296    Merl (1987), 697, Hutchings (1971), 225 and Pomfret (1996), 4.

297    Pockney (1991), 157.

298    My calculations are based on Mitchell (1992), 460, Sowjetunion (1992), 78 and Pockney (1991), Table 3.

299    My calculations are based on Mitchell (1992), 505, Sowjetunion (1992), 78 and Pockney (1991), Table 3.

part until the end.[300] A domestic television industry existed only in the European part of the Russian Republic.[301]

All in all, despite some strong local impulses, these industries could not spark *large-scale industrialization* in north and central Asia. As a result, we assume that, in 1970, only in the Urals region about 40% of workers worked in the second economic sector, a number that approached western and central European values.[302] The percentage in Siberia and the Far East was lower – in Kazakhstan and the rest of the central-Asian republics it ranged between 21% and 30% – and this would not change significantly in the near future.[303] As a result, the average per-capita income was low in central Asia: In 1965, it came to about 60% of the Soviet average; in 1989, it ranged between 50% (Tajikistan) and 75% (Kazakhstan).[304] In Mongolia, which was focused on the Soviet model of development, the numbers were even lower, despite the fact that production in the secondary sector (which had started at very low initial values) multiplied between 1950 and 1989.[305]

The *dissolution of the Soviet Union* in 1990 ended the fledgling industrialization in north and central Asia. The region's government-regulated planned economy was replaced by a market economy, which not only interrupted long-standing trade relationships between the former Soviet republics but also put industrial enterprises in competition with each other, for which few of them were adequately prepared.[306] The crisis hit the Asian parts of the former Soviet Union especially hard. Between 1990 and 1994, industrial production

---

300    In the absence of separate data for the European and Asian part of the Russian Soviet Republic, we can only surmise the latter by comparing the central-Asian and the total Soviet values of 1970 and 1989. Merl (1987), 697 and Sowjetunion (1992), 78.

301    Sowjetunion (1992), 78.

302    Wagener does not provide separate data for the Urals region, but we can deduce them from the 39.7% he gives for the Russian Soviet Republic because its per-capita production was slightly below that of the Urals region. Wagener (1972), 96 and 136.

303    Wagener (1972), 96 and 136.

304    Wagener (1972), 86 and Fischer Weltalmanach (1992), 547.

305    Pomfret (1996), 2 and 77 and Mitchell (2007), 367 und 370.

306    Andrejew (1993), 19 and 23.

in the new Russian Federation, which still included the north Asian region, declined by at least 25% (over 33% by some accounts) before it started to grow again.[307] The production of crude steel was cut in half; by 1996, the fabrication of cotton yarns had shrunk to one-eighth of its 1990 volume. Central Asia saw similar drops in production: Between 1990 and 1993, manufacturing production in Turkmenistan and Uzbekistan shrank by 12%, in Kazakhstan by almost 30%, in Tajikistan by almost 40%, and in Kyrgyzstan by almost 45%.[308]

During the second half of the 1990s, industrial production started to *grow again*, a trend that continued into the new century. Between 2000 and 2004, annual growth rates in the secondary sector ranged between 3.2% in Uzbekistan and 11.8% in Kazakhstan. Even in Mongolia, which was struggling with similar problems as the Asian parts of the Soviet Union, the secondary sector grew annually by an average of 7.4%. Still, the actual gross national product in 2002 was (in some areas significantly) below the 1989 standard.[309]

Because productivity increased, *employment rates* during the early growth period trailed those of earlier decades. As happened elsewhere, the number of workers employed in the secondary sector declined to less than 20% (see Figure 22 and Table 26). The decline of employment in industrial production, however, was not only accompanied by rising employment rates in the service industry. With the exception of Uzbekistan and Mongolia, the agricultural sector employed more workers at the beginning of the new century than before. We assume that the same was true for the Asian part of the Russian Federation, where the share of agriculture in the economy increased before it decreased again after the turn of the century. In addition, a varying number of people worked in low-paying jobs in the informal sector, which is not represented in Figure 22 and Table 26.[310]

---

307    My calculations are based on Andrejew (1993), 88, Fischer Weltalmanach (1995), 519 and Commander (1995), 148.

308    My calculations are based on Fischer Weltalmanach (1995), 519. See also Growth Amid Change (2007), 49, which includes data for the growth in the 1980s and the recession in the 1990s.

309    Transition report (2003), 56 and Growth Amid Change (2007), 49.

310    Johnson/Kaufmann (2001), 215.

Figure 22: Employment in the Secondary Sector in North and Central Asia, 1990-2004 (Percent of Economically Active Population, Annual Averages)

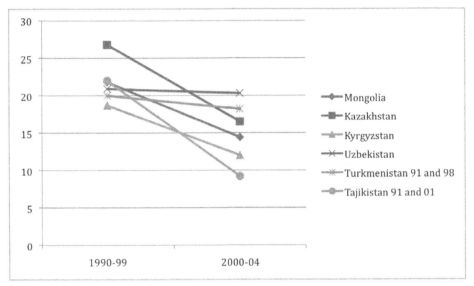

See Table 26

As was the case in Africa, north and central Asia was a long way from the kind of large-scale industrialization that the industrial nations of Europe and North America had attained long before. At the beginning of the new century, per-capita production in the secondary economic sector in the Russian Federation and in Kazakhstan ranged between one-sixth and one-fifth of the production rates in western, central, and northern Europe.[311] Mongolia and other central-Asian nations had even lower values. Only a small percentage of the population profited from the development of relatively isolated industries, which showed in the very low average per-capita incomes of individual countries. The 2008 gross domestic product trailed the highly-developed industrial nations by a wide margin, despite the fact that, since the crisis of the 1990s, it had been growing vigorously everywhere

311    Welt in Zahlen (Industrieproduktion).

– except in Mongolia and Kyrgyzstan – thanks to increased exports of raw materials.[312] In essence, the low number of long-lasting consumer goods indicated the lack of economic development in north and central Asia, which put them on a level with the poorer (and poorest) countries in the east and south-east of Europe.[313]

Figure 23: Television Sets per 1,000 Inhabitants in North and Central Asia, 2006.

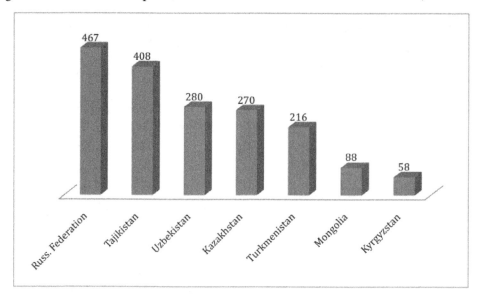

Welt in Zahlen (Fernsehgeräte).

---

312    Maddison (Per Capita GDP).

313    See Table 8 und Table 9, as well as Welt in Zahlen (Fernsehgeräte).

Figure 24: Passenger Cars per 1,000 Inhabitants in North and Central Asia, 2006.

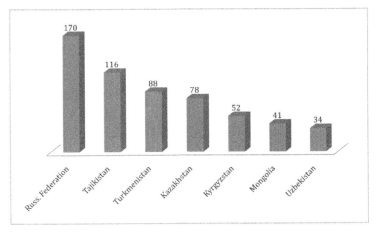

Welt in Zahlen (PKW).

Figure 25: Computers per 1,000 Inhabitants in North and Central Asia, 2006.

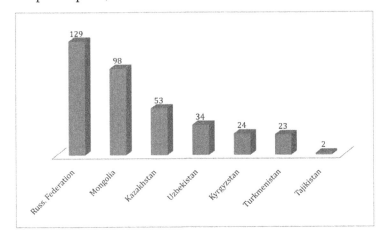

Welt in Zahlen (Computer).

# WEST ASIA

If the age of *urban settlements* were the main criterion, modern industrialization would have started in western Asia rather than in western and central Europe. The inhabitants of the Fertile Crescent, which stretches from the eastern Mediterranean through today's Syria and north Iraq to west Persia, were the first to settle down to an agrarian lifestyle over 10,000 years ago, and they built the first urban settlements not long after. At the same time, in other parts of west Asia, people lived as nomadic herdsmen far into the 20th century.[314] Urban settlements remained relatively small for thousands of years. For the longest time, west Asia did not have any big cities over 100,000 inhabitants, the kind that had emerged on both sides of the Atlantic since the late 18th and (especially) the 19th century.

As late as 1920, West Asia had 12 cities with over 100,000 inhabitants; by 1950, the number had gone up to a mere 25, with a total population of only a scant 70 million.[315] Istanbul was the only city that had passed the one-million mark by the turn of the century, while Baku, Tiflis, and Teheran reached a half-million inhabitants by the 1930s. All others were far below these numbers until the mid-20th century.

Accordingly, *manufacturing* was under-developed. The percentage of workers employed in manufacturing varied from country to country, but according to existing data, it ranged between 14% in Iraq (1956) and 7% in Turkey (1960), by far the two largest countries in the region, which between them combined more than half of the west-Asian population (see Table 27). Only in Israel, which profited from immigration and whose three big cities – Tel Aviv, Jerusalem, and Haifa – indicated an above-average degree of urbanization, 25% of wage earners worked in manufacturing.[316] Thanks to their planned economy, the Soviet republics Azerbaijan, Armenia, and Georgia achieved similar values.[317]

With a production of 2 kg per capita, the *cotton industry*, a much-consulted indicator for the beginning of mechanized industrial production, performed clearly below the standard of western and central Europe before World War I – at least as much as we can tell from

---

314    Köllmann (1965), 246 and 249 and Schuster (1979), 56 and 61-63.

315    Mitchell (2007), 42-46 und Köllmann (1965), 224 f. and 247-251.

316    My calculations are based on Mitchell (2007), 105 and 112 and Wolffsohn (1991), 382

317    Wagener (1972), 136.

existing data.[318] With 5 kg of *pig iron* per capita, Turkey amounted to only a fraction of the production of western and central Europe at the beginning of the century.[319] The other west-Asian countries showed similarly modest beginnings of industrialization during the first half of the century.[320]

During the first decades after World War II, the region saw more robust *spurts of industrialization*. Along with growing markets and government-regulated industrialization, *oil production* had begun on a large scale. The largest oil-producing country in the region, Iran stepped up its oil exports from 1.3 billion barrels (1969/70) to 21 billion barrels (1974/75) in only a few years.[321] Oil production not only spawned some oil-processing plants but also increased government revenues, which could be invested in economic development. As a result, the revenues paid by oil companies to governments in the Near East increased from $1.5 billion in 1961 to $135.6 billion in 1979,[322] which made possible a gigantic increase in government expenses, which, in Iran, multiplied almost five-fold between 1968 and 1974. Private expenses, on the other hand, did not even double in the same time period.[323] By 1980, a number of oil-processing plants had sprung up in Saudi Arabia, Qatar, Kuwait, Iraq, Iran, and the United Arab Emirates: 39 refineries and 16 plants that produced nitrogen fertilizer. However, the production of hard commodities was restricted to only four iron and steel plants and five aluminium plants.[324]

In addition to the direct and indirect incentives for industrialization that came from the oil industry, the rapidly growing *domestic market* spawned a large number of industrial enterprises in west Asia. As was the case elsewhere, these were concentrated in the metropolitan areas of big cities and capitals, which were growing both in size and population. As the result of a population explosion – the number of people living in west Asia more than

---

318   My calculations are based on Mitchell (2007), 467 f.

319   My calculations are based on Mitchell (2007), 441-443.

320   Issawi (1982), 150-203.

321   Looney (1977), 4.

322   Issawi (1982), 203.

323   Looney (1977), 16.

324   Ochel (1978), 45.

quadrupled between 1950 and 2009 – and accelerated rural flight, the number of cities in the region with over a million inhabitants increased from 11 in 1980 to more than 20 at the turn of the century (see Map 11 and Table 28). The influence of big cities on industrialization can be illustrated with several examples: In 1964, almost 70% of industrial enterprises in Lebanon were located in the Beirut metropolitan area. In Iraq at the same time, the same percentage of all factory workers were employed in Baghdad. In 1980s Turkey, the majority of industries were located in the western part of the country, in the areas surrounding Istanbul, Bursa, and Izmir, as well as in Ankara and on the Black Sea Coast.[325] At the beginning of the 21st century, almost 75% of the revenues of the 500 largest Turkish businesses came from Istanbul and the neighbouring Kocaeli Province; an additional 14% came from Ankara, Bursa, and Izmir.[326] In Saudi Arabia, industrial plants clustered around the largest cities: Dammam, Riyadh, and Jeddah initially, followed by Mecca, Medina and Al-Khobar.[327] In Israel in the 1970s and 1980s, more than half of industry workers were employed in and around Tel Aviv and in the central region around Rishon LeZion.[328]

Figure 26 and Table 29 illustrate how much *industrial production* grew in some of the larger countries – and probably in the other countries as well. Between 1960 and 1980, industrial production in Iran, Turkey, Syria, and Israel increased five to seven-fold, and doubled and then tripled again during the next 20 years.

---

325    Lechleitner (1972), 87, Issawi (1982), 166 and Weitz (1987), 25.

326    Bronger/Trettin (2011), 278 f.

327    Schuster (1979), 87.

328    Wolffsohn (1991), 395.

Figure 26: Manufacturing Production in West Asia, 1960-1999
(1980 = 100, Select Countries)

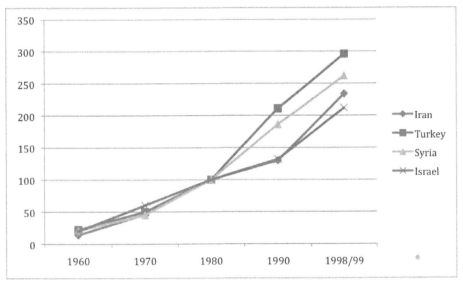

See Table 29.

However, industrialization was not a continuous process; it fluctuated annually and en-countered occasional setbacks. During the revolutionary year of 1978/79, for instance, and again in the late 1980s, Iran saw a decline in production. The same happened in Syria and Israel half-way through and at the end of the 1980s, and it happened in Turkey at the end of the 1980s, the middle of the 1990s, and at the turn of the century.[329]

We can see even bigger annual fluctuations if we look at individual types of industries, such as the *cotton* or the *pig iron industry*. By the end of the century, the processing of raw cotton in Iran had increased to 2 kg per capita, to about 5 kg in Syria, to 10 kg in Turkey, but in Israel it decreased to 6 kg after a high of 10 kg in 1960.[330] These values came close to what countries in west and central Europe had attained several decades before. Industrial

---

329    Mitchell (2007), 367-370 and OECD Turkey (1990/91), 13, (1996), 6 and (2002), 30.

330    My calculations are based on Mitchell (2007), 467 f. and Maddison (Population).

production beyond consumer goods existed only sporadically. By the turn of the century, pig-iron production, which only Iran and Turkey had developed to any noteworthy degree, ranged between 25 kg and 80 kg per capita, a value much below the production in western and central Europe a century earlier (see Figure 3).[331]

However, both countries had been developing their own *automobile production* since the 1960s, and it expanded considerably. Between 1990 and 2011, Iran's production of passenger cars, busses, and trucks increased from fewer than 50,000 to 1.6 million units. Turkey's automotive industry grew from about 30,000 to over 600,000 automobiles between 1980 and 2007.[332] The automobile industry satisfied a growing – and predominantly urban – domestic demand on one hand, and a demand for inexpensive cars from lesser developed countries on the other. Measured by population numbers, the automobile industry in Iran and Turkey came close to that in other lesser developed countries like Russia, Romania, Mexico, Brazil, Argentina, or South Africa, which produced between 10 and 20 cars per 1,000 inhabitants.[333]

The effect of industrial production in Turkey and Iran, which lasted into the new century, was felt in the country's employment structure. However, thanks to growing productivity, production increased significantly faster than the percentage of wage earners working in manufacturing, which, at the turn of the century, was less than 20%.[334] The majority of wage earners, at this point, worked in the service industry, and 40% still worked in agriculture. We have yet to see if Iran and Turkey will industrialize further or, like other developed and lesser developed countries, if they will move toward a service industry.

It seems as if the process of *industrialization* – as measured by the percentage of people working in industrial jobs – had already peaked in the former Soviet republics Armenia, Georgia, and Azerbaijan, as well as in the countries between the Mediterranean and the Persian Gulf. The dissolution of the Soviet economy and the transition from a planned to a market economy had brought about a quasi-return to an agricultural economy: The percentage of workers employed in this sector went back up to over 40% during the first

---

331   My calculations are based on Mitchell (2007), 442 and Maddison (Population).

332   Mitchell (2007), 502 f. and Wirtschaftszahlen zum Automobil.

333   My calculations are based on Wirtschaftszahlen zum Automobil and Maddison (Population).

334   OECD Turkey (2002) and Mitchell (2007), 112.

decade of the new century.[335] In the other countries, more and more workers found employment in the service industry, which owed its expansion largely to the export of crude oil and natural gas. Israel and, to a degree, Lebanon followed the European model and expanded the service industry on the base of large-scale industrialization. Population-dense Yemen had neither much industrial production nor a service industry that could compare to other countries; at 50%, the share of agriculture in the national economy was much higher than it was in other countries in the region at the time.[336]

Overall, average *per-capita income* rose in all larger countries, albeit at different rates and with setbacks and interruptions.[337] Iraq, where the gross national product declined drastically during the late 1980s, constitutes an exception. Both the economic growth and the regional differences are reflected in the distribution of long-lasting consumer goods (see Figure 27-29 and Table 30).

Figure 27: Television Sets per 1,000 Inhabitants in West Asia, 1980-2006 (Larger Countries)

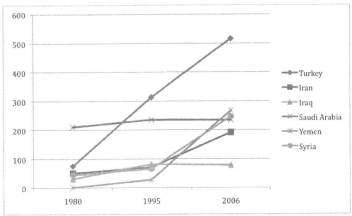

See Table 30.

---

335    Fischer Weltalmanach (2011). In Azerbaijan, fewer than 6% of the workforce was employed in manufacturing at the turn of the century. Growth Amid Change (2007), 52.

336    Fischer Weltalmanach (2005), 238.

337    Maddison (Per Capita GDP).

Figure 28: Passenger Cars per 1,000 Inhabitants in West Asia, 1970-2006 (Larger Countries)

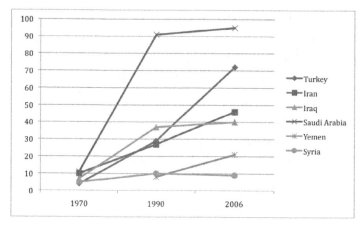

See Table 30.

Figure 29: Computers per 1 000 Inhabitants in West Asia, 2006

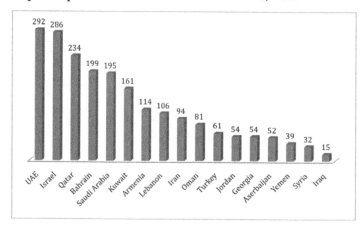

Welt in Zahlen (Computer).

Because they represent mathematical averages, the different revenues gained from exporting crude oil and natural gas and the size of the population account for the differences in the degree of industrialization in individual countries. Even though the automobile and computer density in all countries trailed those of the highly developed industrial nations, the smaller countries –Israel, Lebanon, Kuwait, Bahrain, Qatar, the United Emirates, and, to a degree, Oman – did slightly better than the larger ones (see Table 30). In the bigger counties, a larger percentage of the population did not profit from either industrial production or the export trade and continued to live in pre-industrial conditions. Still, even the more affluent countries could, at best, reach the status of eastern and some of the southern European countries with regard to per-capita incomes and the distribution of consumer goods. Granted, west Asia industrialized in parts thanks to the rapid growth of big cities since the 1950s, but to this day, only a minority of the population is able to attain the kind of prosperity seen in the highly industrialized countries in western, central, and northern Europe.

## SOUTH ASIA

In South Asia, between Afghanistan and Sri Lanka, on the densely populated Indian sub-continent, *urban settlements* developed early, at a time when most people lived off subsistence farming. However, their size remained small. In 1900, with a total population of around 300 million, the region had only 25 cities with over 100,000 inhabitants. Five of these – the port cities of Calcutta, Bombay, Madras, and Karachi, as well as Lahore – a center of administration and an important railroad junction—had passed the one-million mark by 1950.[338] These trade and administrative centers had grown faster than the cities in the countries' interior thanks to international trade, which was dominated by the British (see Map 10 and Table 32).

---

338   Köllmann (1965), 114-116 und Mitchell (2007), 42-46.

Map 10: Cities in Asia with Over a Million Inhabitants Around 1950

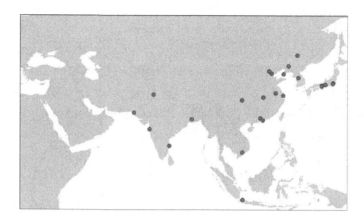

Tirol Atlas – Designed by Klaus Förster based on Table 9.

Map background: World Borders Dataset - http://thematicmapping.org/downloads/world_borders.php

The first *industries* developed around the big cities. After the traditional cotton manufacture had been put out of business by imports from Great Britain, where cotton was fabricated by machines and thus cheaper, Indian entrepreneurs, in the second half of the 19th century, launched a modern *cotton industry* in and around Bombay that processed the domestic supply of raw cotton. By 1914, India had become the biggest cotton-producing country in Asia and the fourth-biggest in the world, supplying domestic and foreign markets. Other centers of cotton production developed later in Ahmedabad and in Kanpur in northern India, and to a lesser degree in Madras, Madurai, and Solapur.[339]

From its very beginning, the *jute industry* in and around Calcutta had been focused on the export trade. On the initiative of British entrepreneurs, it developed in the jute-growing regions and quickly became a fast-growing franchise of the Scottish jute-goods industry. In 1914, the Indian jute industry ranked second among all jute-producing countries. Factories in other industrial branches sprang up in addition to the two main industries, including the

---

339   Rothermund (1985), 69-72.

first larger iron and steel plant in 1907.[340] Overall, the industrial national product increased by no less than 10% annually between 1868 and 1900, by 6% between 1900 and 1913, and by almost 4% between 1919 and 1939.[341] In 1946, Indian industrial production (minus artisanal manufacture) had increased almost seven-fold since the beginning of the century. The number of industry workers increased a little more slowly.[342]

Still, only a small part of the Indian population – 360 million by mid-century – had experienced any *industrialization* because of the large distances between big cities and the resulting lack of demand for consumer goods outside of metropolitan areas (See Table 31 and Map 10). Calcutta, especially, was a kind of "industrial island" in the middle of an agricultural region that produced goods mostly for the export trade. Similarly, in proportion with the total population of India, the cotton industry, which by this point had spread to several regions, had little economic impact despite its impressive production volume.[343] Right before World War I, British India processed only 1.2 kg raw cotton per-capita; in 1950, now-independent India processed 2 kg. The few iron and steel plants in the country were even more isolated, producing less than 1kg and 5 kg per capita, respectively. By mid-century, only about 10% of wage earners worked in the secondary sector.[344]

The *other countries* in south Asia fared similarly, both the larger countries – Pakistan and Bangladesh – and the smaller ones – Sri Lanka, Afghanistan, and Nepal. In the latter two, especially, many people lived as nomadic and semi-nomadic herdsmen;[345] no other big cities with over a million inhabitants developed besides Karachi and Lahore.

---

340  During the first decade of the 20th century, 44% of the industrial workforce was employed in the cotton and jute industries, but by the 1940s, their number had decreased to 30%. Sivasubramonian (2002), 109 f. See also Rothermund (1985), 74 and Lal (1988), 200.

341  Lal (1988), 196.

342  Sivasubramonian (2002), 106 and 109, Lal (1988), 196 and 200).

343  Rothermund (1985), 72-83.

344  My calculations are based on Mitchell (2007), 442, 467, 103 f. und Maddison (Population).

345  In Afghanistan, about two million at the end of the 1960s and six million later on, according to estimates of UNO and the Afghanistan government respectively. Noor (1974), 28 and Kuchis (Afghanistan).

During the second half of the 20th century, thanks to declining death rates, population numbers exploded and the number of *big cities* increased (see Table 31 and Table 32). In India, whose population had passed the one-billion mark by the turn of the millennium, the number of cities with over a million inhabitants rose from 10 in 1980 to 25 in 2000; Mumbai (formerly Bombay) and Calcutta had over 10 million inhabitants each. However, the big cities were not evenly distributed across the country: About two thirds of them and especially the bigger ones were located west of the line between Delhi and Chennai (formerly Madras) (see Map 11).

Map 11: Cities with Over a Million Inhabitants in Asia Around 1980

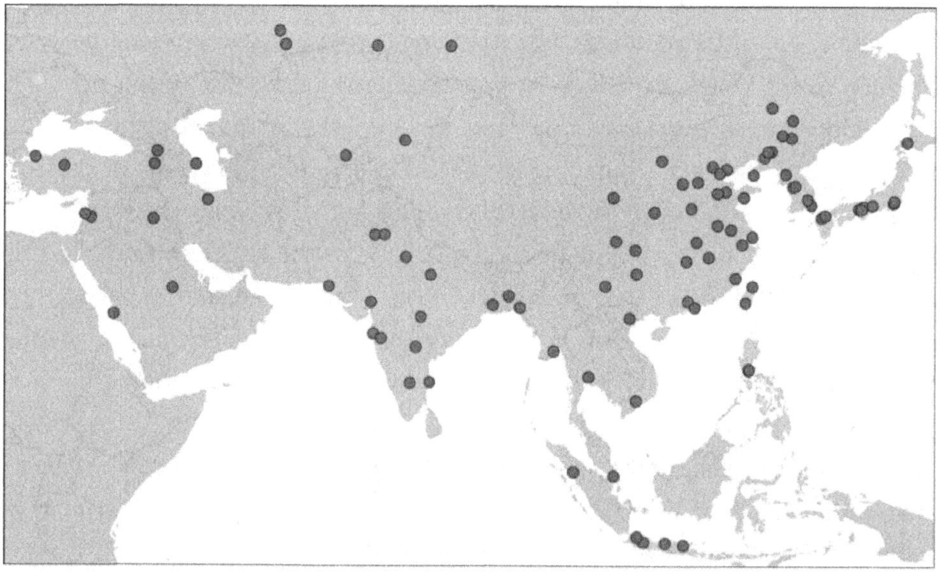

Tirol Atlas – Designed by Klaus Förster based on Table 9.

Map background: World Borders Dataset - http://thematicmapping.org/downloads/world_borders.php

As a result, the *process of industrialization*, which the Indian government supported much more than the British ever did, went off more dynamically in the western than in the eastern part of the country. The state of Tamil Nadu, which included Madras and the industrial city of Bangalore in the south, developed into one of the most important industrial areas, along with the region between Ahmedabad and Pune, which included the Bombay metropolitan area, and the Punjab including the country's capital Delhi. Although less than 25% of the total population lived in these regions, they produced far more than half of the country's industrial goods by the mid-1970s. Another 25% of industrial production was produced in the eastern states of West-Bengal, Bihar, and Orissa (today's Odisha).[346] Here, besides the old industrial city of Calcutta, the centers of the heavy industry sprang up as a result of the region's large ore and coal deposits. Unlike the relatively well industrialized regions in the west, these centers remained "enclaves of industrial progress" in the midst of their predominantly agrarian surroundings.[347]

Bombay illustrates how the *big cities*, in particular, attracted industrial enterprises in India. In 1961, almost two thirds of the industrial workforce of Maharashtra, the second-largest state, were employed in Bombay; combined, the metropolitan areas of Bombay and nearby Pune employed 89% of industrial workers. The rest of the country was virtually industry-free, with the exception of Nagpur further to the east, a big city and industrial center.[348] Although some smaller and mid-size industrial enterprises sprang up later in other parts of the state, in 1998, almost a third of all industrial workers were employed in Bombay, home to only 10% of the inhabitants of Maharashtra.[349]

Industrial development in India increased significantly during the second half of the century; in addition to the traditional textile industry, other industrial branches – and especially the capital goods industry – played a more important role. Between 1947 and 1997, manufacturing production increased more than 15-fold while agrarian production merely tripled.[350] Given the population increase, agricultural per-capita values had practically

---

346    Tischner (1981), 192. See also Schmidt (1974), 89.

347    Rothermund (1985), 194-199.

348    Bronger (2004), 108.

349    See also Bronger/Trettin (2011), 287.

350    Sivasubramonian (2002), 117.

stagnated while manufacturing production had increased five-fold.[351] Measured by the national product per wage earner, no other economic branch increased productivity – and thus income – as quickly as the industrial sector.[352]

Not only did the industrialization process accelerate during this half of the century, it also expanded to other branches of production. Between 1960 and 1980, production of pig iron, crude steel, and automobiles increased two to three-fold, the manufacture of bicycles and radios four to six-fold, the production of nitrogen and phosphate fertilizers even 20-fold; however, the production of jute and cotton goods increased only by about 25%.[353] As a result, the relative percentages of individual branches of the total industrial production evened out. Between 1951 and 1994, the percentage of the textile industry decreased from 40% to 10% while the percentage of the chemical and metal industries and of machine construction increased from about 20% to about 69%.[354] While the per-capita processing of raw cotton increased only slightly to 2.6 kg by the end of the century, pig-iron production increased seven-fold between 1950 and 2011.[355] Yet, applied to population numbers, India's per-capita production of 32 kg trailed behind the values of the highly developed industrial countries although, in terms of total volume, it ranked among the world's five biggest producers of pig iron.[356]

Thus, we can draw similar conclusions about industrialization in India as for other lesser developed countries. Despite significant accomplishments in the last few decades, industrialization in India remained confined to a relatively small part of the population, especially those living in large metropolitan areas. Because big cities in India were fewer and further apart than they were in industrial nations, industrialization did not spread to all parts of the country. As they had in the past,[357] only about 11% of wage earners worked in manufac-

---

351　My calculations are based on Sivasubramonian (2002), 117 and Maddison (Population).

352　Sivasubramonian (2001), 120.

353　Rothermund (1985), 170.

354　Sivasubramonian (2002), 126.

355　My calculations are based on Mitchell (2007),442, 467 und Maddison (Population).

356　World Pig Iron Producing countries.

357　Mitchell (2007), 103 f.

turing at the turn of the century.[358] Because industrial production raised the gross national product, millions of upper and middle-class people who lived in the larger cities were able to make the kind of money people made in industrial countries, but people who lived in rural areas and in urban slums, where many had migrated from the countryside, did not enjoy this kind of prosperity. In 2003, almost 60% of the workforce were employed in agriculture;[359] according to government statistics for the Mumbai metropolitan area, 50% of the people lived in the city's slums.[360]

Figure 30: Employment in Manufacturing in South Asia, 1981-2002
(Percent of Economically Active Population, Peak Values)

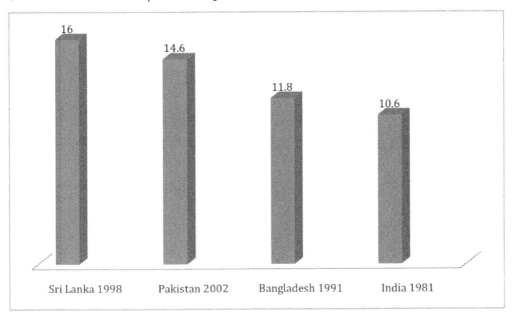

Calculations based on Mitchell (2007), 103 f. und 109 f.

---

358    Growth Amid Change (2007), 52.

359    Fischer Weltalmanach (2008), 218.

360    Bronger (2004), 163.

As a measuring stick for a country's *economic prosperity*, the distribution of televisions, passenger cars, and computers followed similar patterns (see Figure 31-33). Regional differences notwithstanding, in 2006, with a scant 98 televisions, 10 passenger cars, and 14 computers per 1,000 inhabitants, India ranked among the poorest countries in the world – despite the fact that it had, by this point, become one of the world's biggest producers of passenger cars.[361] Almost one third of all passenger cars were owned by people who lived in one of the four mega cities Mumbai, Calcutta, Delhi, and Chennai, which, together, housed only 5% of the population.[362] The average domestic product per inhabitant was just as dramatic: In 2008, it amounted to less than one-seventh of western, central, and northern European industrial countries. However, insufficient economic development did not cause these differences as much as the concentration of industries in relatively few metropolitan areas, which excluded many other regions whose inhabitants remained stuck in pre-industrial poverty.[363]

Figure 31: Television Sets per 1,000 Inhabitants in South Asia, 1985-2006

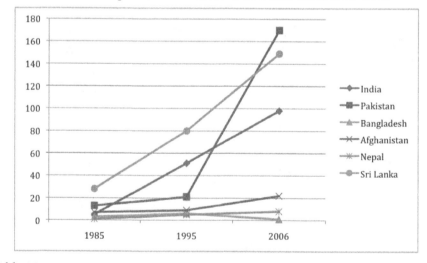

See Table 33.

---

361    Wirtschaftszahlen zum Automobil.

362    Bronger/Trettin (2011), 281.

363    See Lal (1988), 216.

Figure 32: Passenger Cars per 1,000 Inhabitants in South Asia, 1970-2006.

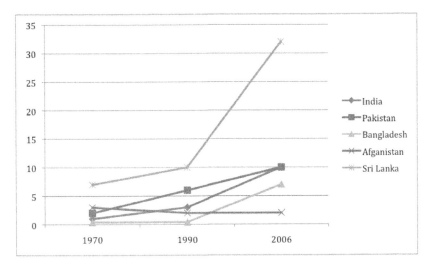

See Table 33.

Figure 33: Computers per 1,000 Inhabitants in South Asia, 2006

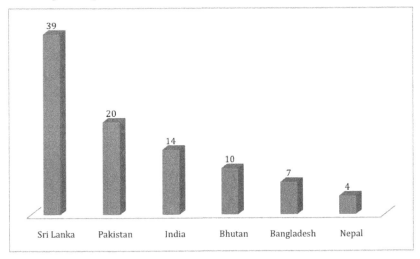

Welt in Zahlen (Computer).

The industrialization process accelerated markedly in other successor states of British India as well: By 2000, Pakistan had seven cities with more than a million inhabitants, and Bangladesh, which had separated from Pakistan in 1971, had three cities that size.[364] By the turn of the millennium, the entire secondary sector in *Pakistan* produced 24 times the amount it produced in 1955, which translates into a seven-fold increase per inhabitant.[365] A disproportionately large share fell to the cotton industry, which profited from an abundance of raw materials. Despite its relatively late start – it was developed by private entrepreneurs after 1947 – the cotton industry grew rapidly and made Pakistan the world's third-largest producer of cotton, after China and India. By 2000, Pakistan produced 14 kg of cotton per capita, which exceeded most of the European countries with the exception of Great Britain.[366] The new (if temporary) capital of Karachi became a center of industry, followed by Punjab, with Lahore, an industrial city with over a million inhabitants, Faisalabad, Multan, Gujranwala, and Rawalpindi, as well as the southern industrial city of Hyderabad. On the other hand, rural and sparsely populated Baluchistan, the northwestern border province, and the mountainous regions in the north had very little industry, which meant that at the turn of the millennium, over 40% of the population worked in agriculture and only a scant 15% in manufacturing (see Figure 30).[367]

With its high percentage of agriculture and the towering importance of the textile industry, Pakistan resembled *Bangladesh*, which advanced to being the world's second-largest textile producer after China.[368] However, the country's economic success depended less on the processing of raw cotton (of which Bangladesh had only produced about one kg per capita around 2000)[369] but on the clothing industry. Domestic demand, however, did

---

364    On the subject of the concentration of industrialization on big cities see Zingel (1979), 279 and Heimat and Welt (Südasien – Wirtschaft).

365    My calculations are based on Mitchell (2007), 368 and 370 and Maddison (Population).

366    My calculations are based on Mitchell (2007), 468 and Maddison (Population), and Fischer (1987), 135.

367    Zingel (1979), 233-248, 290-297 and 374-523; Hübner-Schmid (2004), 11; Mitchell (2007), 109.

368    Textilindustrie in Bangladesch.

369    My calculations are based on Mitchell (2007), 467 and Maddison (Population).

not play much of a role in the expansion of the cotton industry in either country. Foreign demand for yarns and cloths from Pakistan and for clothing from Bangladesh was much more important.[370] Like crude oil and other mineral raw materials in other countries, textiles were the primary export goods in Pakistan and Bangladesh. Because they imported many industrial goods, the two countries never had many businesses that were focused on the domestic market. In 1991, at the peak of industrialization, only 12% of the Bangladesh workforce was employed in manufacturing (see Figure 30).[371]

The low *degree of industrialization* had negative consequences on the average national values. Pakistan did a little better in this regard than Bangladesh, whose 2008 per-capita gross national product amounted to half of Pakistan's and a good third of India's.[372] Both countries had modest averages with regard to long-lasting consumer goods as well (see Figure 31-33).

Industrial development in Afghanistan, Nepal, and the small country of Bhutan, all of which had a largely agricultural economy, remained equally modest. As late as 2000, 70% of workers in Afghanistan – some of whom were nomads – and over 90% of registered workers in both states lived off subsistence farming.[373] Kabul was the only city with over a million inhabitants; Kathmandu had almost a million. The armed conflicts since the late 1970s interrupted whatever industrial beginnings Afghanistan might have had in the manufacture of cotton cloths since the 1950s.[374]

Sri Lanka (formerly Ceylon) industrialized much more successfully. Besides its export-oriented agriculture, which made the relatively small country the world's third biggest tea exporter, manufacturing developed in the metropolitan area of Colombo, the de-facto capital, which employed 16% of the workforce by the end of the century.[375] The share of agriculture decreased to less than 40% in the end. According to Maddison's calculations,

---

370   Wikipedia (Pakistan) und Wikipedia (Bangladesh).

371   Mitchell (2007), 103 and Growth Amid Change (2007), 50.

372   Maddison (Per Capita GDP).

373   Fischer Weltalmanach (2008), 44, 79 and 345 as well as Kafle (2007), 1-9.

374   See Fischer (1968), 20.

375   Mitchell (2007), 110, Wikipedia (Sri Lanka) and Sri Lanka Industry Country Studies.

Sri Lanka's 2008 gross domestic product per capita amounted to more than twice that of Pakistan's and to more than four times that of Nepal, a value that approached those of the poorer countries in southeastern Europe.[376]

# SOUTH EAST ASIA

While the countries in south east Asia and south Asia have a lot in common when it comes to urbanization and industrialization, *Singapore* is a notable exception. Singapore managed to catch up to the highest-developed industrial nations thanks to its structure as a small city state: In 2008, its per-capita domestic product was as high as Norway's and only surpassed by the US.[377] A conveniently placed entrepôt and commercial city on the sea route between Europe and China, Singapore crossed the one-million population mark in the 1950s; by 2000, it had over four million inhabitants.[378]

Thus, Singapore had all the prerequisites for industrialization, and it made good use of them. While other big cities were surrounded by large – and frequently rural – areas, Singapore was both a *city* and a *state* in one, which increased its national averages in its degree of industrialization, its national product, and its distribution of long-lasting consumer goods. In addition, its national borders prevented unrestrained immigration from the surrounding countryside and thus the formation of city slums. In this fashion, Singapore became an industrial city as well as an industrial country whose inhabitants, almost without exception, had considerable spending power: In 1957, a scant 10% and, in 1987, only 1 % of the people worked in agriculture.[379]

Initially, besides the service industry typically found in a commercial city, the *urban domestic market* had spawned manufacturing, which employed around 17% of the workforce in 1959, when Singapore broke free from British dominion.[380] The global market sparked

---

376    Maddison (Per Capita GDP).

377    Maddison (Per Capita GDP).

378    Mitchell (2007), 45.

379    Mitchell (2007), 110 and Pascha (1990), 99.

380    Mitchell (2007), 110.

further industrial investments, which took advantage of the city's location, its commercial structure, and its favorable economic and political environment.[381] Numerous companies from highly-developed industrial nations – among them the US, Great Britain, the Netherlands, Japan, Hong Kong, and neighboring Malaysia – established branch offices in Singapore. In conjunction with the domestic enterprises, they increased the national product of manufacturing by an average of 10% annually between 1960 and 1989.[382] Although industrial employment did not increase at the same rate because of increased productivity, manufacturing employed almost 30% of the work force in 1990 (see Figure 34).

Figure 34: Employment in Manufacturing in South East Asia, 1989-2004
(Percent of Economically Active Population, Peak Values)

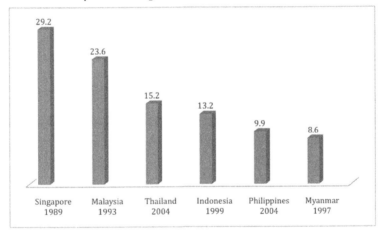

Calculations based on Mitchell (2007), 105 and 109-111.

---

381    Kim (1990), 178, Woronoff (1992), 129 and Agrawal (1995), 56.

382    In 2005, the secondary economic sector was 20 times more productive than it had been 40 years before. My calculations are based on Mitchell (2007), 368 and 370. The share of manufacturing in the domestic product increased from 12% to 26% between 1960 and 1982. Harberger (1988), 167.

After 1990, the number of industrial workers decreased while employment in the service industry increased: In 2003, 18% of wage earners worked in manufacturing.[383] As a result of economic development, the number of households living in abject poverty shrank from 19.2% to a mere 0.3% between the early 1950s and the early 1980s. The fact that in 2006, only the USA, Australia, Sweden, Luxemburg, and Switzerland had more computers per capita serves as an indication of the city state's prosperity.[384]

Apart from Singapore, the majority of countries in south east Asia present the same picture as most other less industrialized developing countries:

A largely agrarian economy and population and relatively little trade or manufacture in small-to-mid-sized cities, which persisted well into the 20th century;

Rapid population explosion in the second half of the 20th century;

An even more rapid urban population growth, especially in big cities;

Industrial production – stimulated by urban growth – that did not spread beyond the metropolitan areas and a fledgling service industry;

A consistently large rural population that was only marginally touched by industrialization and big-city slums swelled by rural flight;

Subsequently, a dualistic society whose per-capita incomes do not accurately reflect the gap between a small, affluent upper class and the rest of the population that continued to live in poverty.


Relatively speaking, *Malaysia* industrialized the furthest (see Figure 34). Especially in the western part of the Malaysian peninsula, where the majority of the population lived on 20% of the land, a large number of smaller and mid-sized cities had sprung up in addition to the capital Kuala Lumpur, which created a city density that stimulated industrialization. Both, urban and total population continued to grow (see Table 34); as a result, in 2000, no fewer than 32 big cities had over 100,000 inhabitants while Kuala Lumpur had over a million.[385] Two thirds of them were located on the only 700 km long and narrow strip of land in the west that stretches from the state of Perlis in

---

383    Agrawal (1995), 98, Mitchell (2007), 210 and Growth Amid Change (2007), 52.

384    Welt in Zahlen (Computer).

385    List of cities (Malaysia).

the north to Johor in the south. Those located close to Kuala Lumpur had fused into the capital's metropolitan area, which, meanwhile, counted around six million inhabitants.

This is where the first *industrial settlements* sprang up. Thanks to private and government initiatives, the first industrial area developed in Petaling Jaya – close to Kuala Lumpur – in 1952, while the country was still under British colonial rule. By the 1970s, similar industrial parks had developed, especially in the larger cities on the western coach like Butterworth and Ipoh in the north or Johor Bahru in the south.[386] Later, the government subsidized industrial zones in smaller cities and the lesser developed regions in the east where oil and natural gas resources had been discovered. Unlike earlier enterprises, which processed domestic supplies of tin ore and India rubber, these new industrial parks initially supplied the domestic market, which they continued to do after the establishment of free industrial zones that produced for both the domestic and the international markets.[387] As is typical for economies with an increasing degree of industrialization, traditional consumer goods – such as food, drink, and tobacco – lost their primary importance to the electrical, machine-building and automobile industries, the latter of which had transitioned from assembly of imported parts to a full-scale production of domestic vehicles.[388]

Even if the numbers do not always agree, they reflect a rapid and steady increase in both *industrial production* and *employment*. And since industrial enterprises were largely located in areas, where the majority of total population lived, industrial production in Malaysia boosted the national averages. The share of manufacturing in the national product increased from 15% to 40% between 1970 and 1993.[389] Per capita, the Malaysian industry produced twice as much as Thailand, five times as much as Indonesia, and almost ten times as much as the Philippines. Almost 25% of all wage earners were by now employed in manufacturing at this point – compared to a mere 7% in 1957, when Malaysia declared its independence.[390] With the exception of Singapore and the small and atypical oil state of Brunei, Malaysia had

---

386    See Vorlaufer (2009), 186 and Fessen/Kubitschek (1984), 174-177.

387    Kratoska (1998), 20-22.

388    Tucher (1999), 52 und 82-89.

389    Chowdhury (1997), 49.

390    My calculations are based on Mitchell (2007), 109; see Growth Amid Change (2007), 52.

the lowest agricultural employment rates (see Table 36).[391] As a result of wide-spread industrialization, Malaysia's per-capita domestic product – even though it could not match western, central, and southern European countries – exceeded several eastern European countries and the other larger countries in the region.[392] The same is true for the distribution of television sets and other long-lasting consumer goods (see Figure 35-37). As a further consequence of economic development, markedly fewer people lived in big-city slums in Malaysia than in other countries in south east Asia – with the exception of Thailand.[393]

Figure 35: Television Sets per 1,000 Inhabitants in South East Asia, 1985-2006 (Larger Countries)

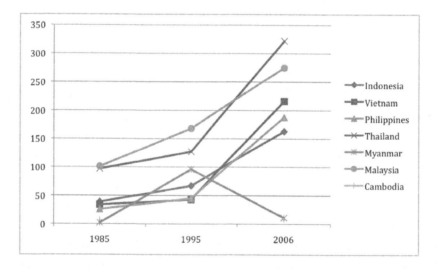

See Table 37

---

391     The small sultanate of Brunei constitutes a special case as it focused on producing crude oil and natural gas, like the small emirates on the Persian Gulf, which made the small population (a scant 400,000 in 2009) relatively affluent. Maddison (Population) and Siddiqui (1997), 1-3.

392     Maddison (Per Capita GDP).

393     According to Vorhofer, only 2% of the urban population lived in slums in 2000. Vorlaufer (2009), 106. On the positive development of Malaysia, see also Chowdhury (1997), 43-50.

Figure 36: Passenger Cars per 1,000 Inhabitants in South East Asia, 1970-2006 (Larger Countries)

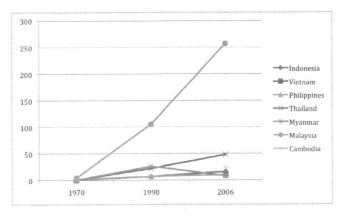

See Table 37.

Figure 37: Computers per 1,000 Inhabitants in South East Asia, 2006

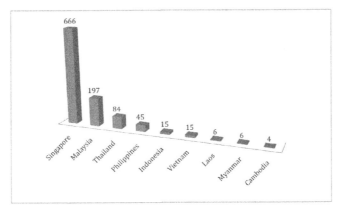

Welt in Zahlen (Computer)

During the second half of the 20th century, *Thailand*'s industrialization process was as robust as Malaysia's. However, the country's economic development clustered in the Bangkok metropolitan area and did not spread to benefit the rural population. While Malaysia, in 2000, had three big cities with over half a million inhabitants in addition to Kuala Lumpur, which had over a million, the largest cities in Thailand after Bangkok were Samut Prakan and Nonthaburi, with fewer than 400,000 inhabitants each.[394]

*Industrialization* in Thailand, which started from smaller enterprises that had produced paper, textiles, sugar, or alcoholic beverages since the 1930s, took an upturn with the establishment of Bangkok Cotton Mills, the first larger cotton-spinning factory that employed about 1,000 workers by 1950.[395] Other similar enterprises followed and eventually made Thailand one of the largest producers of cotton goods. However, the iron and steel industries, which did not start in earnest until 1965, was not quite as successful; in 2015, it produced only about half as much steel as, for instance, the much smaller Austria.[396] The Thai automobile industry, which started in the 1970s, initially assembled imported parts but eventually manufactured these components locally.[397] Overall, industrial production – initially for the domestic market but, starting in the 1980s, for the export trade as well – grew faster than all other economic sectors; in 2005, the secondary sector accounted for almost half of the total economic product of the country.[398]

However, as mentioned above, Thailand's industry clustered in the metropolitan area of its *capital* city. Industrial parks, which started to spring up in the 1970s, were initially located close to Bangkok and started to spread to the surrounding areas in 1989. Especially in Eastern Seaboard, an industrial zone in south-east of the Bangkok metropolitan area, many large and efficient enterprises developed, many of them government-subsidized and owned by international companies. Others were established further south in the Rayong Province, which became Thailand's dominant industrial region. However, most of the rest of the country remained untouched by these developments.[399] In 1980, more than half of Thailand's industrial products came from Bangkok and the neighboring provinces, and more than 75% from the entire central region, which comprised only about a third of the

---

394     List of cities (Malaysia) and List of cities (Thailand).

395     Ingram (1971), 121.

396     List of countries (Steel).

397     Buchmann (1980a), 443-445.

398     Buchmann (1980a), 442 and Schmid (2013), 92.

399     Vorlaufer (2009), 186.

total population.[400] Toward the end of the 20th century, over 40% of the industrial workforce was employed in Bangkok, home to only 10% of the population.[401] The total national product reflected this concentration: it rose significantly faster in Bangkok and its environs than anywhere else in the country. In 2005, the Bangkok metropolitan area and the neighboring provinces Ayutthaya, Chachoengsao, Chon Buri, and Rayong had a significantly higher per-capita domestic product than the rest of the country.[402] In the greater region of Bangkok a good 20% of the population produced almost two thirds of the country's economic output.[403] Thanks to the region's dynamic development, relatively few people lived in slums.[404]

The downside of this one-sided concentration of the Thai industry in the *Bangkok metropolitan area* was that the large majority of the population did not profit from it. The number of workers in manufacturing grew to only 15% by 2004 while still over 40% of the workforce was employed in agriculture.[405] As was the case in other developing countries, industrialization in Thailand remained sporadic and benefited only a small percentage of the population.[406]

The same holds true for the *remaining countries* on the south-eastern peninsula, where, in 2000, two thirds of the population still lived in rural areas. In 1950, Saigon (Ho-Chi-Minh City today) was the only city with more than a million inhabitants in all of Indochina (see Map 10).[407] Since the 17th century, it had grown into a commercial city of international importance, which the French colonial regime had elevated to the status of regional capital. Conversely, Yangon and Phnom Penh, the capitals of Myanmar and Cambodia, and Hanoi in divided Vietnam, crossed the one-million mark at some point during the following

---

400    Buchmann (1980a), 443. In the 1980s, the Bangkok metropolitan area contributed almost 70% of the industrial national product. Amin (1997), 118. See also Schmid (2013), 74.

401    Bronger/Trettin (2011), 306.

402    Bronger/Trettin (2011), 215.

403    Bronger/Trettin (2011), 278, 310 und 428.

404    According to Vorlaufer (2009), 106 they amounted to only 2% of the urban population.

405    My calculations are based on Mitchell (2007), 112; see Growth Amid Change (2007), 52.

406    See Bronger/Trettin (2011), 321.

407    Mitchell (2007), 42-46.

decades. Vientiane, the capital of Laos, never did.[408] In addition, Indochina's economic development was hampered by years of war; only recently did the country step up its industrial production.[409]

Since the 1980s, industrial zones had developed particularly in *Vietnam*, whose two parts had only modest and often inefficient industries in the years before. The first and largest of these were located in the metropolitan areas of Ho-Chi-Minh City, Hanoi, Haiphong, and Da Nang and their environs.[410] They developed thanks to several factors: the mass demand of the urban populations, an infrastructure that included large sea- and airports, and the presence of international corporations that focused on export trade. Between 1991 and 2003 alone, foreign corporations established 1,600 businesses in Vietnam, as compared to 1,300 domestic ones, many of which were state-owned.[411] In 2007, a good two thirds of industrial products came from the metropolitan areas of Ho-Chi-Minh City, Hanoi, and Haiphong, even though less than 25% of the total population lived in these regions.[412] Despite a strong increase during the last few years, industrialization in Vietnam – like Myanmar, Laos, and Cambodia – did not expand beyond certain regions. The large majority of the population – both in rural areas and in the urban slums of the big cities – benefitted only marginally or not at all from industrial development. Despite the prosperity in its urban centers, Vietnam overall remained one of the world's poorest countries.[413] According to the Asian Development Bank, 47% to 72% of the urban population in Vietnam, Laos, and Cambodia lived in slums at the beginning of the century.[414]

The Philippines and Indonesia, the two big *island states*, presented a similar picture: respectively, 44% and 23% of their urban populations lived in slums.[415] The two countries' in-

408    Mitchell (2007), 42-46.

409    See Vorlaufer (2009), 9 f., 84-88 und 96.

410    Schmid (2013), 76-80.

411    Vorlaufer (2009), 187 and Pomfret (1996), 63.

412    Bronger/Trettin (2011), 312.

413    Maddison (Per Capita GDP). Vgl. Pomfret (1996), 2 and 70.

414    Vorlaufer (2009), 106.

415    Vorlaufer (2009), 106.

dustrial production was restricted to the metropolitan areas of their capitals as well. In the Philippines, this meant Metro Manila and the regions north and south of it, Central Luzon and Calabarzon, which, in the 1980s, employed almost 75% of the industrial workforce.[416] The region of Metro Manila, which included Quezon City and Caloocan City, both of which had over one million inhabitants, had employed half and more of the industrial workforce since the 1960s even though only one eighth of the total population lived there in 2007.[417]

Under Spanish colonial rule, *Manila* had been an important entrepôt for America and Asia, where Mexican silver was traded for Chinese silk and spices.[418] However, the city's exceptional growth resulted from its position as the capital under Spanish and, later, American rule. Although Quezon City was the official capital from 1948 to 1976, Manila crossed the one-million-inhabitants mark in 1950 and attracted the majority of industrial production that had developed – albeit modestly – in other parts of the country.[419] The businesses that had processed agricultural products declined in importance as the new industrial enterprises developed vigorously around the capital cities (especially during the 1950s).

After an initial phase of *import substitution*, industrial production served the export trade as well and spread to the more urbanized regions of the Visayas and the island of Mindanao, where Davao City had soon over one million inhabitants.[420] Most of the workforce was still employed in the food, liquor, and tobacco industries, as well as in textile and leather production, but many worked in the electrical industry; the iron, steel, and hardware industries and the enterprises that built machines and vehicles employed significantly fewer workers. Overall, industrialization in the Philippines was sporadic. In 2000, almost 40% of wage earners still worked in agriculture, and only about 10% worked in manufacturing.[421]

In *Indonesia*, the island that had by far the largest population in the region, urbanization and industrialization were restricted to only a few areas as well. In 1930, Java, the most

---

416    Bauer (1988), 110.

417    Bronger/Trettin (2011), 306, Bauer (1988), 43 and 100 and Vorlaufer (2009), 89 f. und 96.

418    Kim (1990), 123.

419    Bauer (1988), 30 f. und Mitchell (2007), 44.

420    Bauer (1988), 44 und 110, and Vorlaufer (2009), 188.

421    My calculations are based on Mitchell (2007), 110. See Growth Amid Change (2009), 52.

densely populated island, had six of the country's seven big cities with over 100,000 inhabitants. Although Indonesia had begun to process agricultural goods for the export trade relatively early,[422] the big cities created the mass market that triggered industrialization on a larger scale. Thanks to their rapidly growing populations, five of them had over one million inhabitants by 1980: Jakarta, Surabaya, Bandung, and Semarang on Java and Medan on Sumatra (see Map 11 and Table 35), followed by Palembang on Sumatra, Bekasi and Tangerang close to Jakarta, and Makassar on Sulawesi (formerly Celebes) by 2000.[423]

By 1970, about 78% of the country's mid-size and large businesses were located on Java, which included the capital; another 11% were located on Sumatra.[424] By 2000, almost all branches of industrial production could be found in the large urban centers of Jakarta, Surabaya, Semarang, and Bandung on Java and in Medan, Palembang, and Padang on Sumatra, where a specialized food and consumer-goods industry had developed. Industrial production was less vigorous on the more lightly populated and less urbanized islands, where enterprises took advantage of existing raw materials. As was the case in the Philippines, significantly more workers in Indonesia were employed in the food, liquor, and tobacco industries and in businesses producing textiles and wooden articles; fewer worked in the iron and steel industries, the machine-building industry, and the oil and gas industries – although the latter contributed significantly to the total industrial product.[425] And despite the fact that manufacturing in Indonesia grew more quickly than other branches of the economy, it employed only 13% of the workforce in 2000. Over 40% still worked in agriculture.[426]

---

422    In 1930, Java and Madura had 180 sugar factories. Röpke (1982), 185.

423    Mitchell (2007), 42-46 and List of cities (Indonesia). See Zimmermann (2003), 90-266 und Vorlaufer (2009), 88 f. und 96.

424    Zimmermann (2003), 397. Vgl. Kötter (1979), 448-452. On the subject of the significance of the domestic market, see Vorlaufer (2009), 189 and 213-215 and Hossain (1997), 71.

425    Zimmermann (2003), 400-402, Mishra (1995), 103 and Röpke (1982), 267.

426    My calculations are based on Mitchell (2007), 105. See Zimmermann (2003), 268 and Growth Amid Change (200), 52.

# EAST ASIA

*Japan* started to industrialize much sooner than most non-European countries. As happened in Europe, Canada, and the US, the country's early and dense urban development and the attendant mass demand stimulated the process.[427] The big cities resulted from Japan's particularly dense population, particularly in two regions: In the Kantō region in the south and in the Kinki region in the northwest, a large part of the total Japanese population lived on a mere 7.5% of the land, over 40% live there today.[428]

As early as 1900, Tokyo, the former Edo, and Osaka – cities that were only about 400 km apart from each other – grew to over a million inhabitants. They were surrounded by Yokohama, Kyoto, and Kōbe, which had about 400,000 inhabitants each. Nagoya, situated between Tokyo and Osaka, was about the same size.[429]

Figure 38: Processing of Raw Cotton in Japan and the US, 1900-1969 (Kg per Capita, Annual Averages)

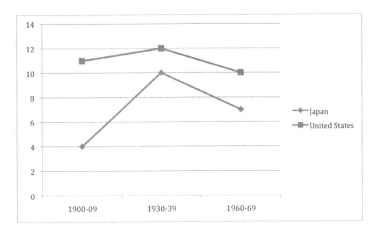

Calculations based on Mitchell (2007), 467 f. und Mitchell (1998), 374 f.

---

427    See Mathis (2006), 228-233.

428    Calculated for the Tokio, Kanagawa, Saitama, and Chiba Prefectures in Kantō and the Osaka, Kyoto, and Hyōgo Prefectures in Kinki. Japan (Präfekturen).

429    Mitchell (2007), 44-46.

As happened elsewhere, *industrialization* in Japan started with the mechanization of the textile industry, which was based on a long proto-industrial tradition. Unlike the export-oriented silk industry, the cotton industry was focused on the domestic market and expanded greatly in only a few years.[430] Yarn production multiplied fourteen-fold between 1886 and 1897 after the founding of the Osaka Spinning Company (1880) and other cotton mills.[431] Right before World War I, the cotton spinning plants employed more than 100,000 workers instead of only 6,000.[432] At the beginning of the 20th century, they processed around 4 kg raw cotton per capita, production values that could not eclipse Great Britain or the US but that came very close to those of other western and central European countries (see Figure 2 and 38).

Figure 39: Production of Pig Iron in Japan and the US, 1912-1979 (Kg per Capita, Annual Averages)

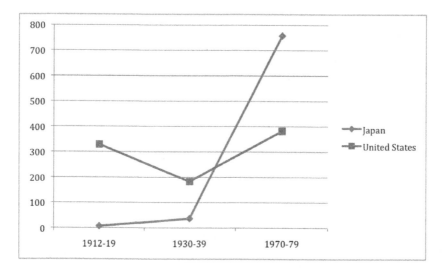

Calculations based on Mitchell (2007), 441 f. und Mitchell (1998), 359 f.

---

430    Kim (1990), 140.

431    Mathis (2006), 228. The number of mechanized cotton spindles increased from a modest 72,000 to almost 6.7 million between 1887 and 1929. Kim (1990), 138.

432    Hentschel (1986), I, 134.

Japan's domestic iron and steel industries developed more slowly, and with them the machine and ship-building industry, which up to this point had almost exclusively relied on imports. Because it got off to a slow start, Japan produced 7 kg of pig iron per capita, which was significantly less than the US or Europe, but considerably more than all other Asian, African, or Latin American countries (see Figure 3 and 39). In 1910, 14% of wage earners worked in manufacturing.[433]

Over the following decades, the *urban population* and *industrial production* continued to increase. Although the total population grew by only 50% between 1910 and 1940, 14 million people lived in six cities with over a million inhabitants, which was more than four times the population of Tokyo and Osaka 30 years prior (see Map 10 and Table 40). The percentage of people living in these cities had increased three-fold to include almost 20% of the total population.[434] The production values of manufacturing increased more than five-fold between 1913 and the beginning of World War II, the number of industrial workers doubled.[435] In the 1930s, the processing of raw cotton, which was now also exported to other Asian countries, amounted to about 10 kg per capita, which is higher than the values of western and central Europe (see Figure 4). The production of pig iron, however, remained behind the values of these countries and the US even despite an increase to almost 40 kg per capita (see Figure 39).[436]

The *destruction* of World War II only temporarily stopped industrial production in Japan; it decreased to 10% of the volume recorded in the mid-1930s, but by 1950, it had regained 84% of its pre-war values, and by 1954, it exceeded them with 167%.[437] By 1991, industrial production had increased more than seventeen-fold.[438] As was the case in other industrial

---

433    Mitchell (2007), 107.

434    Apart from Tokyo, Osaka, Nagoya, and Kyoto, which had over a million inhabitants, Yokohama and Kōbe had almost 970,000 inhabitants in 1940. Mitchell (2007), 44-46.

435    Lal (1988), 201for production and Mitchell (2007), 107 for employment (calculated for 1910 and 1940).

436    For western and central Europe, my calculations are based on Mitchel (1992), 450 f. and Maddison (Population).

437    Kim (1990), 147-149.

438    My calculations are based on Mitchell (2007), 368 f.

countries, the importance of the traditional industrial branches like the textile industry gave way to machine construction, the automobile and electrical industries, and the iron and steel industries on which they were based. Although it had virtually no iron ore or coal resources, Japan had started to produce more crude steel in the 1970s than the US. And while it did not establish a more expansive automobile industry until after the war, from the 1980s on, Japan produced more cars than the US (see Figure 40).[439] Japan surpassed the US in the production of television sets even sooner.[440] Overall, starting in the 1970s, over 25% of the workforce was employed in manufacturing (see Figure 41) before the percentages dropped to below 20% as the country –like other highly developed industrial nations – transitioned to a service economy. In the end, less than 5% of the people worked in agriculture, a significant reduction from almost 50% in 1950.[441]

Figure 40: Production of Automobiles in Japan and the US, 1950-1989 (Annual Averages per 1,000 Inhabitants)

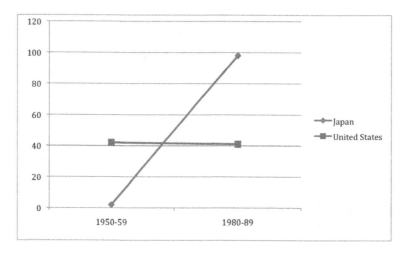

Calculations based on Mitchell (2007), 503 and Mitchell (1998), 395 f.

---

439    Stahl (Tabellen und Grafiken) and Wirtschaftszahlen zum Automobil.

440    Statistisches Jahrbuch (2003), 571.

441    Mitchell (2007), 107.

Figure 41: Employment in Manufacturing in East Asia, 1970-1993 (Percent of Economically Active Population, Peak Values)

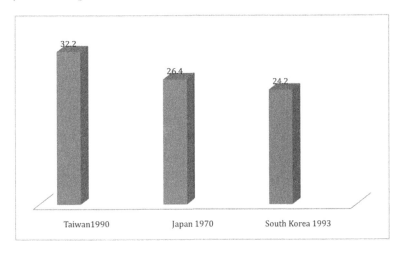

Calculations based on Mitchell (2007), 107 und 111.

Japan's successful, broad-scale *industrialization* coincided with the continued growth of its big cities and their population. By 2000, Japan had 13 cities with over a million inhabitants.[442] Combined, the agglomerations of Tokyo, Osaka, and Nagoya had around 63 million inhabitants in 2006, which amounted to about half of the total population. Another 7 million lived in the metropolitan areas of Fukuoka and Kitakyushu in the southwest and Sapporo in the north.[443] Japan's industry clustered in these areas.[444] Because the total population, thanks to declining birth rates, grew more slowly than it did in other non-European countries (see Table 38), more people profited from the growth of the big cities and the industry they stimulated. As a result, Japan took a leading position not only in its per-capita domestic product but also in its distribution of long-lasting consumer goods. Among the larger countries, Japan's 2008 per-capita gross domestic product came in fifth behind the

442   Mitchell (2007), 42-46.

443   List of cities (Japan).

444   Japan-Perspektiven (1990), 98.

US, Australia, Canada, and Great Britain.[445] The distribution of passenger cars and computers presents a similar picture, although South Korea and Taiwan have meanwhile surpassed Japan with regard to the latter (see Figure 42-44).

Figure 42: Television Sets per 1,000 Inhabitants in East Asia, 1985-2006

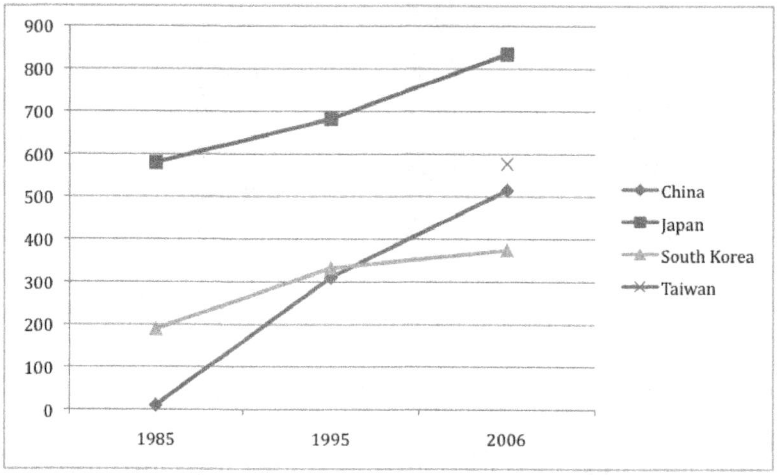

See Table 39.

---

445    Maddison (Per Capita GDP).

Figure 43: Passenger Cars per 1,000 Inhabitants in East Asia, 1970-2006

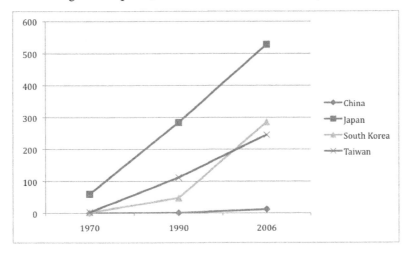

See Table 39.

Table 44: Computers per 1,000 Inhabitants in East Asia, 2006

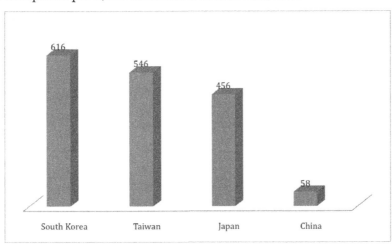

Welt in Zahlen (Computer).

*Korea* experienced a modest degree of industrialization during the first half of the 20th century while still under Japanese colonial rule. Although most of the traditional small businesses processed agricultural products, an increasing number of enterprises in manufacturing already employed over 100 workers.[446] The south produced largely consumer goods, food, and textiles, but the north had developed a significant heavy industry as a result of Japanese armament policies in the 1930s. This industry, along with a thriving chemical industry, was based on abundant resources of mineral raw materials and water power for the production of hydroelectricity.[447] In 1940, about 86% of textiles and 65% of food products came from the south; 80% to 90% of chemical and metal products, as well as natural gas and electricity, came from the north.[448]

In each of the two parts of the country, World War II, along with the war between the north and south that followed, destroyed much of Korea's industrial production and infrastructure.[449] Afterwards, the governments of more-industrialized *North Korea* followed the Soviet example and adopted a planned economy that privileged the heavy industries, which was a great success at first.[450] However, the plan neglected agriculture and the consumer goods industry. As opposed to the heavy industries, whose production grew 21-fold between 1953 and 1965, the textile industries only increased seven-fold.[451] Along with the country's increasing political isolation from the 1960s on, North Korea's economic strategies and the attendant decline in production rates caused the country to fall further and further behind other nations.[452] By 2000, almost 30% of North Korean wage earners still worked in agriculture while South Korea was down to only 8%.[453] According to Angus Maddison's calculations, North Korea's 2008 per-capita gross domestic product constituted only one-18th of the South Korean value.[454]

---

446    Suh (1978), 109 and 139-141.

447    Reichart (1993), 187-189 and Frank (2005a), 235.

448    Wontroba/Menzel (1978), 213.

449    Bronger/Trettin (2011), 173 and Hughes (1988), 27.

450    Frank (2005a), 238 and Frey (1986), 51.

451    Frey (1986), 54.

452    Engelhard (2004), 343.

453    Fischer Weltalmanach (2008), 289 and 293.

454    Maddison (Per Capita GDP)

By contrast, *South Korea*, whose population grew from 25 to around 50 million inhabitants between 1960 and 2010, developed from a poor agricultural country – over half of the work force was employed in agriculture in 1965 – into one of the world's leading industrial nations in only a few decades.[455] Between the end of the 1950s, when the annual economic output had returned to the status of the 1940s, and 2008, South Korea's per-capita domestic product increased sixteen-fold.[456] Production in the secondary economic sector grew faster than production in all other sectors; by 2005, it had increased 100-fold since 1965.[457] In 1990, around 27% of wage earners worked in manufacturing instead of less than 10%.[458] This percentage later declined to a scant 20% in favor of the service sector, similar to other highly developed industrial nations.[459]

Figure 45: Processing of Raw Cotton in East Asia, 1937-1998
(Kg per Capita, Peak Values)

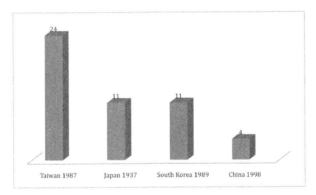

Calculations based on Mitchell (2007), 467 f.

---

455    Engelhard (2004), 21.

456    Bronger/Trettin (2001), 173 and Maddison (Per Capita GDP).

457    Kim (2001), 19; my calculations are based on Mitchell (2007), 368 f.

458    Kim (2001), 127; my calculations are based on Mitchell (2007), 107f.

459    My calculations are based on Mitchell (2007), 107 f.

As was the case in traditional industrial countries, the focus of *industrial production* soon shifted from the initially dominant, labor-intensive lighter industries such as the cotton industry to the more capital-intensive heavy industries such as car manufacture.[460] The cotton industry peaked in 1989, when the country processed almost 11 kg raw cotton per capita, which partially exceeded the western and central European peak values (see Figure 2, Figure 4, and Figure 45). The automotive industry had started in 1967 with an assembly plant serving the local market, but it grew to develop its own models and, in the end, produced over 4 million cars, a volume only eclipsed by China, the US, Japan, and Germany (see Figure 46).[461] The iron and steel industries, which began in the 1970s, developed along similar lines; by 2005, South Korean steel production ranked fifth behind China, Japan, the US, and the Russian Federation (see Figure 47).[462]

Figure 46: Production of Automobiles in East Asia, 1990-2003 (per 1,000 Inhabitants, Peak Values)

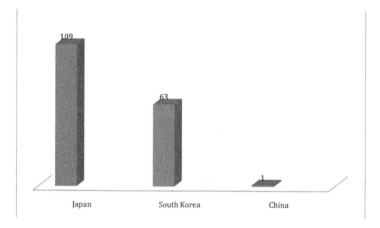

Calculations based on Mitchell (2007), 502 f.

---

460   See Kim (1990), 180 f. und Gokarn (1995), 27.

461   Kim (2001), 74 and Wirtschaftszahlen zum Automobil.

462   Stahl (Tabellen und Grafiken).

Although South Korea's rapid industrialization was largely due to a significant increase of the country's exports, closer inspection reveals that it was initially triggered off by the growing demand of its *domestic market*.[463] In 1917, Korea's first cotton factory was founded to meet the domestic demand for cotton products.[464] In 1968, when production exceeded the domestic demand, less than 20% of cotton yarns and only 50% of cotton cloths were exported, but this changed rapidly due to the limited domestic market. The production of electrical appliances, too, began in the late 1950s with radios and other electronics for the domestic market before it started exporting on a larger scale.[465]

Figure 47: Production of Pig Iron in East Asia, 1974-2003
(Kg per Capita, Peak Values)

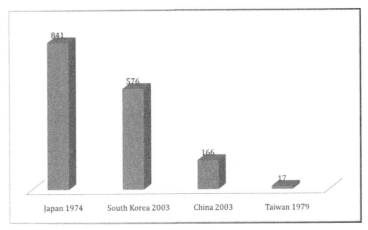

Calculations based on Mitchell (2007), 441 f.

As in Japan, two urban centers with a high *population density* developed not far away from each other in populous and urbanized South Korea. In 1960, Seoul, the long-time capital in the northwest, had 2.4 million inhabitants, and Busan, a port city 300 km to the

---

463   Kim (1990), 180.

464   Suh (1978), 99-103.

465   Hasan (1976), 169 und 177.

south east, had 1.2 million. By 1980, Incheon, a port city connected to Seoul, and Daegu, a city located on the increasingly important axis between Seoul and Busan, crossed the one-million mark (see Map 10, Map 11, and Table 40). By 2005, the country had seven cities with over a million inhabitants and another nine big cities with over half a million.[466]

As happened elsewhere, Korea's *big cities* became industrial centers as a result of their concentrated purchasing power; their impact soon extended beyond the city limits to include the surrounding provinces. Between 1963 and 1986, over 40% of the country's industrial products came from Seoul and the surrounding Gyeonggi-do Province, including Incheon, and around 27% came from Busan and the surrounding Gyeongsangnam-do Province. Together with the Gyeongsangbuk-do Province in the east, which included the big city of Daegu, they combined 80% of the country's total production by 1980.[467]

And since around 60% of the South Korean *population* lived in these areas,[468] more people benefited from industrial production here and in a few other big cities, which drove up the national averages.[469] The gross domestic product per capita was almost that of western and central European values and notably above those of other lesser developed countries in the world.[470] In its per-capita industrial production, South Korea ranked tenth behind the larger countries (over 20 million inhabitants) in 2006, eleventh in the distribution of passenger cars, and third in the distribution of computers.[471] Increasingly fewer people lived in abject poverty: Since 1980, their number had shrunk to less than 10%.[472]

Industrialization in *Taiwan* took a similar route. Here, too, the industry got off to a modest start under Japanese colonial rule, initially processing agricultural products like rice and

---

466    Mitchell (2007), 43-46 und List of cities (South Korea).

467    Reichart (1993), 307 f. See Engelhard (2004), 22 und 149.

468    Engelhard (2004), 91 and Maddison (Population).

469    The percentage of people living in cities increased from 18% in 1950 to 89% in 2002. Engelhard (2004), 79-92.

470    Maddison (Per Capita GDP).

471    Welt in Zahlen (Industrieproduktion), Welt in Zahlen (PKW) und Welt in Zahlen (Computer).

472    Kim (2001), 20.

sugar for the Japanese market.[473] After World War II, Taiwan became a modern industrial country. Despite massive destruction during the war, the secondary sector had regained its pre-war values by 1955, after which industrial production expanded significantly, first to meet domestic demand, but as of the 1960s, it focused more and more on the export trade.[474] In 1993, the secondary sector of Taiwan's economy produced 60 times more than it had 40 years before.[475]

Because the population numbered only about 7.5 million in 1950, the country did at first not have any cities with over a million inhabitants, but the *big cities* of Taipei in the north and Kaohsiung in the south, which were only about 300 km apart from each other, grew rapidly. The first of these passed the one-million mark in the late 1960s, the second in the 1980s, followed shortly by Taichung and Tainan, which were located between them. In the end, around 14 million people – of the 23-million total population – lived in these cities and in New Taipei, which emerged from the Taipei Province to become another of the country's big cities with over a million inhabitants.[476]

Domestic industrial enterprises were soon able to meet the demand for *industrial goods* created by these cities. In 1937, Taiwan imported almost two thirds of its textiles and cloth-ing; by 1954, the number had shrunk to less than 10%.[477] By the end of the 1950s, domestic businesses supplied over 90% of consumer goods.[478] On the other hand, exports – then still mostly agricultural products – amounted to less than 5% of the gross national product; only later on, in the 1980s, exports increased to around 40%.[479] Thus, domestic demand carried Taiwan's industrial production at the beginning, before it shifted to foreign markets.[480] By 1970, a third of all manufacturing businesses was located in the big cities listed above, where

---

473    Woronoff (1992), 81. See Menzel (1985), 156.

474    Frey (1986), 28 f., Kim (2001), 13 and Hughes (1988), 27.

475    My calculations are based on Mitchell (2007), 367 f. and 370.

476    Mitchell (2007), 44-46, List of cities (Taiwan) und Maddison (Population).

477    Ranis (1979), 210.

478    Ranis (1979), 211.

479    Menzel (1985), 64 und 200.

480    Kim (1990), 180.

about a fifth of the total population lived at that time.[481] Additional enterprises had sprung up in large numbers all over the country to meet domestic demand.

Eventually, 60% of Taiwanese people lived in the five big cities, which meant that a much larger percentage of the population benefitted from the *industrialization* they inspired,[482] which resulted in correspondingly higher national averages. At 24 kg per capita in 1987, Taiwan processed more raw cotton than any other Asian country and even more than the leading European industrial nations before World War I (see Figure 2 and Figure 45). The domestic iron and steel industries did not develop quite as successfully despite their shift toward the heavy and the capital goods industries in recent decades (see Figure 47).[483] Overall, in 1970, the percentage of Taiwanese workers employed in manufacturing was almost the same as in Singapore. The number rose to 35% in the 1980s before it decreased to slightly below 30%.[484] In 2008, the per-capita gross domestic product exceeded that of South Korea and brought Taiwan up to par with Germany.[485] The country ranked only a few places behind South Korea in the distribution of computers and passenger cars (see Figure 43 and Figure 44).

Unlike Taiwan and South Korea, where a majority of the population lived in cities and thus profited from industrialization, industrial production in *China* initially benefitted only an urban minority and excluded the rural majority. However, with a total population of over a billion, this minority – as in India – consisted of several million people. As was the case in India, China remained an *agricultural country* for a long time. During the 1880s, manufacturing accounted for an estimated 4% of the gross domestic product.[486] After a modest start, industrial production in China, which initially supplied the country's armament efforts, numerous factories were founded after the turn of the century, especially in

---

481    Ranis (1979) 223; my calculations are based on Mitchell (2007), 44-46 und Maddison (Population).

482    See Myers (1986), 22.

483    See Cheng (2002), 9 f.

484    Mitchell (2007), 110 f.

485    Maddison (Per Capita GDP).

486    Goswin (1996), 19.

the far-flung port cities of Shanghai, Tientsin, Canton, and Wuhan, which the Yangtze river connected to the ocean.[487] These were the largest of China's 25 big cities with over 100,000 inhabitants in 1900, at a time when the total population numbered 400 million. Over time, Shanghai grew particularly fast – to over five million inhabitants by 1950 – followed by (then British) Hong Kong with over two million and another nine cities with between one and two million inhabitants (see Map 10 and Table 40).[488]

At first, the Chinese industry focused on producing consumer goods, which progressively replaced the cotton goods and yarns that had been imported before.[489] In the 1930s, China's absolute volume of processed raw cotton – albeit not its per-capita values – approached those of India and Japan.[490] However, the domestic iron and steel industries trailed behind those of both countries. On average during the 1930s, China's production of pig iron amounted to less than half of British India's and to about a third of Japan's.[491]

The Chinese-Japanese war and the Chinese civil war interrupted the country's *industrialization process*.[492] After the formation of the People's Republic of China in 1949, industrial production resumed, driven not so much by market impulses but by a planned economy. Following the Soviet model, the Chinese government favored the heavy industries, which fluctuated significantly in accordance with changing political agendas, such as the so-called Cultural Revolution in the late 1960s.[493] The industry was partly based on metal-working and chemical enterprises created during the Japanese occupation in southern Manchuria.

Despite diverging information in scholarly sources, researchers agree that the *light industry* declined significantly in favor of the *heavy industry*.[494] Between 1950 and 1978, the

---

487    Goswin (1996), 23.

488    In addition to the big cities listed, Beijing, Shenyang, Harbin, Dalian, Chongqing, and Nanking. See Table 40.

489    Goswin (1996), 35.

490    Mitchell (2007), 467.

491    Mitchell (2007), 441.

492    Kraus (1979), 31 and Goswin (1996), 28.

493    Goswin (1996), 40-55.

494    Goswin (1996), 40 and Wu (2002), 92.

per-capita production of the cotton industry increased by a factor of 3.5; the production of pig iron increased more than twenty-fold.[495] The latter exceeded Indian values by more than double, but it amounted to only a fraction of the rapidly increasing per-capita production in Japan (see Figure 45 and Figure 47). The same is true for television sets, a relatively recent consumer product: Japan, although much smaller, produced about five times as many television sets as China.[496] After the economic and political reforms of the late 1970s and China's opening up to the outside world, the country gradually transitioned to a market economy, which enabled the rapidly-growing big cities to stimulate industrial production on a larger scale.[497]

Industrial production around the big cities resulted in rapid *economic growth*, which was at first concentrated in metropolitan areas close to the coast and did not spread much to the rural areas in the country's interior.[498] The per-capita domestic product, which more than doubled between 1950 and 1978, increased seven-fold by 2008.[499] The gross national product grew annually by often more than 10%. Industrial production, which more than doubled between 1960 and 1978, increased more than four-fold by the 1990s and then multiplied again by six between 2000 and 2014.[500] Its thriving automobile industry made China the world's largest automobile producer in absolute numbers – albeit not in per-capita production.[501] The Chinese steel industry had already reached this goal by 2000,[502] and the country manufactured 20 times more television sets than it did two decades before – more than any other country in the world.[503]

---

495    My calculations are based on Mitchell (2007), 442 and 467.

496    Statistisches Jahrbuch (2003), 571.

497    Goswin (1996), 56-74.

498    As early as 1952, three quarters of the industrial product were based on the seven coastal provinces. Kraus (1979), 101.

499    Maddison (Per Capita GDP).

500    Wu (2002), 89 and Quest Trend Magazin.

501    Wirtschaftszahlen zum Automobil.

502    Stahl (Tabellen und Grafiken).

503    Statistisches Jahrbuch (2003), 571.

However, the rapid *economic development* in China did not apply to the entire country in equal measure. It was restricted to a few – predominantly coastal – regions, each of which, however, had more inhabitants than some countries as a whole.[504] These regions include the Liaoning Province (including Shenyang, Anshan, and Dalian, all of which had over a million inhabitants), the capital Beijing and nearby Tientsin, the Yangtze Delta around Shanghai, Nanking, Hangzhou, the Pearl River Delta around Hong Kong, Shenzhen, and Canton. In recent decades, they have become China's most dynamic economic regions and the world's biggest industrial zones, each of them with an economic product that was definitely on par with South Korea's.[505] In 1980, half of China's 34 cities with over a million inhabitants were located in the four large coastal areas; 30 years later, the same areas contained seven of China's ten largest metropolitan areas – in addition to Chongqing, Xi'an, and Harbin, big cities in the country's interior.[506]

The 1993 per-capita regional product in the seven provinces to which these big cities belonged was notably higher than it was in China's other 23 provinces, which showed how much these regions had become the centers of the country's modern *economic development*.[507] In 2012, they contributed almost 40% of China's gross domestic product – even though only 25% of the total population, which had by now grown to 1.3 billion, lived in these areas.[508] Included in these values were numerous smaller businesses in rural areas, which had been growing rapidly since the late 1970s, especially in the vicinity of the big cities on the coast between Beijing and Tientsin to Hong Kong and Macau.[509]

As a result of the geographical imbalance in its industrial development, China's national averages remain relatively low despite the country's spectacular economic growth. Angus Maddison calculated that the 2008 per-capita domestic product exceeded India's and that of many lesser developed countries, but it amounted to between a third and a quarter of the

---

504    See Bronger (2004), 92 f.

505    Brink (2013), 13 and Bronger/Trettin (2011), 293 f.

506    Mitchell (2007), 42-46 and List of cities (China).

507    Herrmann-Pillath (1995), 29.

508    My calculations are based on China (2012a) and China (2012b).

509    Pomfret (1996), 16.

values attained by the industrial nations in western, northern, and central Europe, Canada, the US, Japan, South Korea, and Taiwan.[510] The numbers for China's per-capita industrial production in 2000 tell a similar story: On average, they amounted to one-eighth to one-tenth of the industrial nations' values.[511] Despite some notably higher values in some regions, the overall distribution of computers and cars lagged behind as well (see Figure 43 and Figure 44). Even though these parameters put China ahead of India, we cannot explain the difference by looking at the overall performance in industrialization, which has happened in both countries; the answer lies rather in the fact that, compared to India, a larger percentage of the Chinese population lives in the highly developed regions as opposed to rural areas.

---

510    Maddison (Per Capita GDP).

511    Welt in Zahlen (Industrieproduktion).

# OCEANIA

Apart from Australia and New Zealand, the size of the population and the degree of urbanization of the Pacific islands were too small to trigger industrial production on a larger scale.[512] The same goes for Papua New Guinea and its seven million inhabitants: Only the country's capital has over 100,000 inhabitants, and the majority of the widely-scattered population live as subsistence farmers.[513]

## AUSTRALIA AND NEW ZEALAND

The situation looked very different in *Australia* and *New Zealand* although both of them had remained sparsely populated for a long time.[514] When the former British colonies united to become an independent nation in 1901, Australia had 3.7 million inhabitants and New Zealand less than a million.[515] Even then, about a third of the population – mostly immigrants and their descendants and a small minority of indigenous Aborigines – lived in big cities.[516]

*Australian* "port capitals"[517] grew because they served both as ports and as administrative centers under their respective colonial – and later provincial – governments. Two of them – Sydney in New South Wales and Melbourne in Victoria – grew particularly fast and passed

512   Kreisel (2009), 256.

513   Wikipedia (Papua New Guinea).

514   See Fitzpatrick (1969).

515   Maddison (Population).

516   Mitchell (2007), 47.

517   Hofmeister (2002), 24.

the one-million mark between the two World Wars. Brisbane, Adelaide, and Perth, the capitals of Queensland, South Australia, and Western Australia, followed suit in the 1980s (see Map 12 and Table 41).[518]

Map 12: Cities with Over 100,000 Inhabitants in Australia and New Zealand Around 1950

Tirol Atlas – Designed by Klaus Förster based on Table 5
Map background: World Borders Dataset - http://thematicmapping.org/downloads/world_borders.php

From the very beginning, *industrialization* in Australia was concentrated in these big cities. Industrial production started out slowly but gained momentum from the first half of the 20th century on.[519] In the 1960s, when manufacturing employed about 30% of the

---

518    Mitchell (2007), 47. By 1950, Newcastle had over 100,000 inhabitants as well.

519    Between 1913 and 1938, manufacturing production almost doubled. Lal (1988), 201. See Hofmeister (2002), 24.

workforce – which was far more than agriculture and mining – almost 75% of factory workers lived in one of the five big cities, most of them in Sydney and Melbourne.[520] Thirty years later, after employment rates in manufacturing had gone down to 15% as they did in all industrial countries, the five big cities were still home to almost 70% of the industrial workforce.[521]

Unlike agriculture and mining, which had been producing for the export trade from the very start, industrial production supplied the *domestic market* in the big cities. Between 1927/28 and 1936/37, Australia exported less than 4% of its total industrial production. Textiles and apparel, in particular, almost exclusively supplied the domestic market.[522] Later, after the industry had further expanded, it exported more of its industrial products.[523]

Thanks to the mass market of the big cities, Australia developed into a highly-industrialized country and, like other industrial nations, it has become a *service society* in the last few decades. From the mid-1970s on, as industrial productivity continued to increase unabated and resulted in ever-increasing incomes, and as the demand for industrial goods diminished, industrial employment decreased in favor of high-quality employment in the service industry. In 1960, more than 50% of the Australian population lived in one of the five biggest cities, which increased to 60% by 2000. The high percentage of urban population resulted in a per capita gross domestic product, which, since 1960 on, has been at par with that of Canada and the western, central, and northern European countries.[524]

*New Zealand*, a much smaller country with about 4 million inhabitants, developed in like fashion. For a long time, its economy had supplied the export trade with agricultural products, especially wool, meat, and dairy products.[525] Auckland, its biggest city, had over half a million inhabitants in the 1960s and passed the one-million mark toward the end

---

520    My calculations are based on Mitchell (2007), 113 and Boehm (1971), 140.

521    My calculations are based on Braun/Grotz (2002), 185 and Mitchell (2007), 113.

522    Fitzpatrick (1969), 287 und 311.

523    See OECD Australia (2001).

524    My calculations are based on Maddison (Population) and Mitchell (2007), 47. See Maddison (Per Capita GDP).

525    Fellmeth/Rohde (1999), 26.

of the century (see Map 12 and Table 41).[526] Likewise, manufacturing grew rapidly during the decades after World War II; in the 1960s and 1970s, it employed more than 25% of the workforce and contributed significantly to the growing domestic product.[527] New Zealand's per capita gross domestic product was the same as Australia's for a long time and only fell behind in the course of its transition to a service economy, which grew more slowly than Australia's.[528] Still, New Zealand takes its place among the world's more affluent countries, which is also reflected in its distribution of more than 500 passenger cars and computers per 1,000 inhabitants.[529]

---

526    Mitchell (2007), 47. In 1950, Wellington and Christchurch joined the list of cities with over 100,000 inhabitants.

527    Mitchell (2007), 114 und Kreisel (2009), 255.

528    Maddison (Per Capita GDP). On the subject of low industrial production per capita see Welt in Zahlen (Industrieproduktion).

529    Welt in Zahlen (PKW) und Welt in Zahlen (Computer).

# CONCLUSIONS

We can summarize the insights gained from our economic-historical tour of the world in 30 points:

For thousands of years, the world was so lightly populated that people – both hunters and gatherers and settled peasants – supplied their daily needs on their own. They had no real use for trade, which, if it existed at all, was very rare.

Around 10,000 years ago, people started to settle down in a region known to us as the Middle East – a process that would eventually occur at different times in almost all parts of the world – which increased their numbers, albeit very slowly by modern standards.

As population density increased, the number and size of settlements increased as well. People now profited from producing goods for others, which stimulated local, regional, and trans-regional trade.

The larger these settlements became, the more people were engaged in the division of labor. These settlements grew as birth rates surpassed death rates and/ or when people from other places moved there.

Settlements that were located along trade routes – on water or land – attracted more migrants than others, as did places that were suitable as government or administrative centers; some of them combined both of these advantages.

These settlements – whose legal status identified them as cities – sprang up everywhere in the world, albeit at different times and frequencies.

The increasingly specific division of labor created a market for goods and thus for local and trans-regional trade: Individual suppliers produced goods that could compete in the market, and traders distributed their products.

In order to stay competitive in the markets, producers had to step up productivity quantitatively and/or qualitatively.

Increased productivity resulted in higher individual profits and an improved standard of living for both the townspeople and for the peasants that supplied them with goods. Their standard of living was generally higher than that of mere subsistence farmers.

Productivity increased drastically with the advent of mass production, which was accomplished through machines, powered by new forms of energy derived from coal, oil, or electricity.

On account of its magnitude, this shift in production was called the Industrial Revolution, and the changes it introduced came to be known as industrialization.

In order for mass production to be profitable, there had to be an adequate demand for goods – preferably concentrated in certain areas, which reduced transportation costs.

Big cities of several 100,000 and over a million inhabitants were more likely to produce this concentrated demand than smaller cities.

London was the first city to cross the one-million mark around 1800, followed by other cities in continental Europe and in the eastern part of north America.

Around the end of the 19th and especially in the second half of the 20th century, as populations grew rapidly, many other cities joined their ranks.

All of these cities triggered industrial production in their vicinities, which first supplied consumer goods and then, to a larger or smaller degree, branched out into the capital goods and heavy industries.

In recent decades, especially in highly-industrialized countries, industrial production partially outstripped the demand for industrial goods.

Industrial productivity increased faster than the demand for industrial goods, which continued to grow but more slowly than in the past.

Wherever this happened, industrial employment rates decreased, first in relative but eventually in absolute terms as well.

Along with increased productivity, individual incomes and tax revenues continued to grow.

As a result of all this, the private and public demand for services increased, which, if there was sufficient buying power, created high-level jobs in the service industry.

The metropolitan areas of big cities, which supported and often triggered this process, developed not because of political decisions and circumstances but because of a region's population density, trade infrastructure, and migration patterns. More often than not, big cities developed because of human needs and motives, not because of government economic politics.

Because metropolitan areas, for the most part, developed independent of state borders, their number, distribution, and relative importance was not the same in every part of every country.

As a result, the numerical distribution of a country's population between more-developed big cities and less-developed rural areas determined its national production averages.

As a result, it does not make sense to speak of highly-developed/rich and under-developed/poor countries as a whole. The difference lies not in whether a country experienced industrialization or not but in the balance (or lack thereof) between higher and less developed regions.

Instead of looking for specific differences between countries, it makes more sense to divide countries into higher and less industrialized regions, which developed independent of national characteristics.

Industrialization is a neither a European nor a non-European phenomenon. It happened in both the First and the Third World and on all continents.

Industrialization does not depend on a country's wealth of raw materials, its religion, or cultural history.

A few short-lived attempts at planned economies notwithstanding, industrialization is fueled by market demand and the people's desire to improve their economic situation.

Governments in individual countries were able to support the process with import-substitution policies or the establishment of industry zones, but they could never trigger industrialization nor spread it beyond the existing industrial regions.

Instead, industrialization occurred wherever people's desire for improving their lives led to the formation of big cities, whose concentrated demand for goods of all kinds rendered industrial enterprises worthwhile and profitable.[530]

In the end, we must ask what history can teach us about future developments and what it recommends that we do. As rural flight continues unabated in almost all parts of the world, we can expect the process of urbanization and the growth of big cities to continue. With regard to development policy, there are short and long-term consequences: In the short term, we have to enable as many people as possible, in both urban and rural areas, to free themselves from abject poverty. In the long run, we not only have to sustain urban buying power, which in the past has triggered economic development, but also expand it to include more people. Besides supporting private investments, we must invest public funds in big-city infrastructure and social services in the widest sense of the term. Both of these measures boost a population's buying power, which, in turn, would increase the demand for industrial goods and services. This, in turn, could inspire further investments, thus creating more jobs for all the people flocking to the big cities.

---

530    Michael D. Mehta, a Canadian geographer cited by Dirk Bronger, is one of the very few scholars that share the view that big cities support economic development. The metropolis, he says, "has the advantage of a large and concentrated labour and consumer market; it is the focus of transportation routes; it has the economics of scale and juxtaposition of industries and specialists; it is a fertile ground for social and cultural change necessary for development; it is a centre from which these innovations or new adoptions, artefacts and technologies ... diffuse into the country side, and it is an area that receives migrants from the country side thus relieving the farming areas of the burden excess population." Bronger (2004), 107. My study confirms how much this is also true for the industrialization process in different parts of the world and at different periods of time.

# TABLES

Table 1: Cities with Over 20,000 Inhabitants in Europe Around 1300

| Western and Central Europe | | | Eastern and Southern Europe | | |
|---|---|---|---|---|---|
| London | Cologne | Aachen | Novgorod | Pskov | Tver |
| Bruges | Ghent | Louvain | Vladimir | Moscow | Smolensk |
| Tournai | Ypres | Saint-Omer | Polotsk | Vilnius | Bolghar |
| Lille | Valenciennes | Douai | Sudak | Feodosiya | Suceava |
| Arras | Amiens | Rouen | Preslav | Plovdiv | Belgrade |
| Laon | Paris | Troyes | Sofia | Vel. Tarnovo | |
| Metz | Mainz | Speyer | Durres | | |
| Worms | | | | | |

| | | | | | |
|---|---|---|---|---|---|
| Tours | Angers | Bordeaux | Thessaloniki | Corinth | Athens |
| Lyon | Toulouse | Narbonne | Naples | Messina | Palermo |
| Montpellier | Marseille | | | | |

| | | | | | |
|---|---|---|---|---|---|
| Erfurt | Prague | Vienna | | | |
| Augsburg | Lübeck | | | | |

| | | | | | |
|---|---|---|---|---|---|
| Genoa | Pavia | Milan | Barcelona | Burgos | León |
| Brescia | Cremona | Piacenza | Valladolid | Valencia | Córdoba |
| Parma | Mantua | Verona | Toledo | Granada | Málaga |
| Vicenca | Padua | Venice | Seville | Medina d. C. | |
| Ferrara | Bologna | Pisa | Lisbon | | |
| Florence | Arezzo | Siena | | | |
| Perugia | L'Aquila | Rome | | | |

Bairoch/Batou/Chèvre (1988).

Table 2: Cities with Over 20,000 Inhabitants in Europe Around 1750

| France | Spain | Italy | Germany | Russia |
|---|---|---|---|---|
| Aix-en-Provence | Antequera | Bergamo | Aachen | Feodosiya |
| Amiens | Barcelona | Bologna | Augsburg | Kaliningrad |
| Angers | Cádiz | Brescia | Berlin | Kazan |
| Arles | Cartagena | Cagliari | Braunschweig | Kiev |
| Avignon | Córdoba | Catania | Bremen | Lviv |
| Besançon | Écija | Cremona | Dresden | Moscow |
| Bordeaux | Granada | Ferrara | Frankfurt/Main | St. Petersburg |
| Brest | Jaén | Florence | Hamburg | **Poland** |
| Caen | Jerez de la Front. | Genoa | Cologne | Wroclaw |
| Clermont-Ferrand | Lorca | Livorno | Leipzig | Krakow |
| Dijon | Madrid | Lucca | Lübeck | Poznan |
| Douai | Málaga | Milan | Mainz | Warsaw |
| Grenoble | Murcia | Mantua | Mannheim | **Lithuania** |
| Lille | Palma de Mall. | Messina | Munich | Vilnius |
| Lyon | Santiago de C. | Modena | Nuremberg | **Czech Republic** |
| Marseille | Saragossa | Modica | Regensburg | Prague |
| Metz | Sevilla | Naples | **Great Britain** | **Slovakia** |
| Montpellier | Toledo | Padua | Birmingham | Bratislava |
| Nancy | Valencia | Palermo | Bristol | **Hungary** |
| Nantes | **Portugal** | Parma | Edinburgh | Debrecen |
| Nîmes | Lisbon | Pavia | Glasgow | Budapest |
| Orléans | Porto | Piacenza | Liverpool | **Serbia** |
| Paris | **Greece** | Rome | London | Belgrade |
| Reims | Thessaloniki | Turin | Newcastle/Tyne | **Romania** |
| Rennes | **Malta** | Venice | Norwich | Bucharest |
| Rouen | La Valletta | Verona | **Ireland** | Yassy |
| Saint-Étienne | **Switzerland** | Vicenza | Downpatrick | **Bulgaria** |
| Strasbourg | Geneva | | Dublin | Shumen |
| Toulon | **Belgium** | **Austria** | **Denmark** | Plovdiv |
| Toulouse | Antwerp | Graz | Copenhagen | Ruse |
| Versailles | Bruges | Vienna | **Sweden** | Silistra |

| **Netherlands** | Brussels | **Albania** | Stockholm | Sofia |
|---|---|---|---|---|
| Amsterdam | Ghent | Shkoder | | |
| Gouda | Liège | **Kosovo** | | |
| Groningen | Tournai | Prizren | | |
| Haarlem | | | | |
| Leiden | | | | |
| Middelburg | | | | |
| Rotterdam | | | | |
| The Hague | | | | |
| Utrecht | | | | |

Bairoch/Batou/Chèvre (1988).

Table 3: Population of Europe, 1820-1950 (Borders of 1950, Millions)

| | 1820 | 1850 | 1900 | 1950 |
|---|---|---|---|---|
| **Soviet Union** | 54.8 | 73.8 | 124.5 | 179.6 |
| **Germany** | 24.9 | 33.7 | 54.4 | 68.4 |
| **United Kingdom** | 14.1 | 20.3 | 36.7 | 50.1 |
| **Italy** | 20.2 | 24.5 | 33.7 | 47.1 |
| **France** | 31.1 | 36.4 | 40.6 | 42.5 |
| **Spain** | 12.2 | 14.9 | 18.6 | 28.1 |
| **Poland** | 10.4 | 13.0 | 24.8 | 24.8 |
| **Romania** | 6.4 | 8.0 | 11.0 | 16.3 |
| **Yugoslavia** | 5.2 | 6.0 | 11.2 | 16.3 |
| **Czechoslovakia** | 7.7 | 9.3 | 12.1 | 12.4 |
| **Netherlands** | 2.3 | 3.1 | 5.1 | 10.1 |
| **Hungary** | 4.1 | 5.2 | 7.1 | 9.3 |
| **Belgium** | 3.4 | 4.4 | 6.7 | 8.6 |
| **Portugal** | 3.3 | 3.8 | 5.4 | 8.4 |
| **Greece** | 2.3 | 3.0 | 5.0 | 7.6 |
| **Bulgaria** | 2.2 | 2.5 | 4.0 | 7.3 |
| **Sweden** | 2.6 | 3.5 | 5.1 | 7.0 |
| **Austria** | 3.4 | 4.0 | 6.0 | 6.9 |
| **Switzerland** | 2.0 | 2.4 | 3.3 | 4.7 |
| **Denmark** | 1.2 | 1.5 | 2.6 | 4.3 |
| **Finland** | 1.2 | 1.6 | 2.6 | 4.0 |
| **Norway** | 1.0 | 1.4 | 2.2 | 3.3 |
| **Ireland** | 7.1 | 6.9 | 4.5 | 3.0 |
| **Albania** | 0.4 | 0.5 | 0.8 | 1.2 |

Maddison (Population).

Table 4: Cities with Over 100,000 Inhabitants in Europe, 1800 and 1850 (Thousands)

| | 1800 | 1850 | | 1800 | 1850 |
|---|---|---|---|---|---|
| London | 948 | 2 236 | Paris | 550 | 1 053 |
| St. Petersburg | 220 | 524 | Moscow | 300 | 440 |
| Berlin | 172 | 437 | Vienna | 247 | 431 |
| Naples | 430 | 409 | Glasgow | 70 | 345 |
| Manchester | 84 | 303 | Madrid | 168 | 281 |
| Dublin | 200 | 262 | Lisbon | 195 | 240 |
| Birmingham | 71 | 233 | Amsterdam | 217 | 225 |
| Barcelona | 100 | 220 | Milan | 135 | 209 |
| Marseille | 101 | 195 | Edinburgh | 83 | 194 |
| Lyon | 109 | 177 | Rome | 153 | 175 |
| Leeds | 53 | 172 | Palermo | 139 | 168 |
| Warsaw | 63 | 167 | Budapest | 50 | 161 |
| Hamburg | 130 | 149 | Bristol | 64 | 137 |
| Turin | 82 | 137 | Sheffield | 46 | 135 |
| Brussels | 66 | 132 | Bordeaux | 96 | 130 |
| Copenhagen | 101 | 130 | Genoa | 90 | 128 |
| Venice | 138 | 127 | Prague | 76 | 118 |
| Wroclaw | 60 | 114 | Seville | 96 | 113 |
| Cologne | 41 | 110 | Bradford | 13 | 110 |
| Ghent | 55 | 107 | Bucharest | 50 | 104 |
| Rouen | 80 | 101 | Odessa | 15 | 100 |

Bairoch/Batou/Chèvre (1988).

Table 5: Cities with Over a Million Inhabitants in Europe, 1910/11 and 1950/51 (Thousands)

|  | 1910/11 | 1950/51 |  | 1910/11 | 1950/51 |
|---|---|---|---|---|---|
| London | 7 256 | 8 348 | Moscow | 1 533 | 5 600 |
| Paris | 2 888 | 4 823 (1954) | Berlin | 2 071 | 3 337 |
| Leningrad | 1 962 | 3 000 | Vienna | 2 031 | 1 766 |
| Rome | 542 | 1 652 | Madrid | 600 | 1 618 |
| Hamburg | 931 | 1606 | Budapest | 880 | 1 571 |
| Athens | 167 (1907) | 1 379 | Barcelona | 587 | 1 280 |
| Milan | 579 | 1 260 | Copenhagen | 559 | 1 168 |
| Birmingham | 840 | 1 113 | Glasgow | 1 000 | 1 090 |
| Naples | 723 | 1 011 |  |  |  |

Mitchell (1975), 78, for Leningrad and Moscow Fischer (1987), 52.

Table 6: Production of Crude Steel in Europe, 1920-1998
(Kg per Capita, Annual Averages)

|  | 1920-29 | 1950-59 | 1960-69 | 1970-79 | 1980-88 | 1989-98 |
|---|---|---|---|---|---|---|
| Western and Central Europe | 147 | 284 | 453 | 545 | 473 | 429 |
| Northern Europe | 32 | 137 | 278 | 380 | 375 | 393 |
| Soviet Union | 13 | 220 | 388 | 538 | 561 | 442 (89-93) |
| Russian Federation |  |  |  |  |  | 327 (94-98) |
| Remaining Eastern Europe | 20 | 93 | 194 | 339 | 407 | 237 |
| Southern Europe | 16 | 27 | 79 | 214 | 250 | 279 |

**Western and Central Europe:** Austria, Belgium, Czechoslovakia, Germany, France, Ireland, Italy, Luxemburg, Netherlands, Switzerland, United Kingdom.
**Northern Europe:** Denmark, Finland, Norway, Sweden.
**Remaining Eastern Europe:** Bulgaria, Hungary, Poland, Romania, Yugoslavia.
**Southern Europe:** Greece, Portugal, Spain.
Calculations based on Fischer (1987), 12 f. and 124, Mitchell (1992), 460, Mitchell (2003), 471-473 and Maddison (Population).

Table 7: Production of Automobiles (Passenger Cars and Commercial Vehicles) in Europe, 1950-2009 (Annual Averages per 1,000 Inhabitants)

|  | 1950-59 | 1960-69 | 1970-79 | 1980-88 | 1989-98 | 2007-09 |
|---|---|---|---|---|---|---|
| **Germany (FRG)** | 17 | 49 | 62 | 68 | 59 | 71 |
| **France** | 17 | 37 | 68 | 64 | 60 | 40 |
| **UK** | 20 | 37 | 34 | 23 | 28 | 25 |
| **Italy** | 6 | 23 | 31 | 30 | 28 | 18 |
| **Sweden** | 7 | 24 | 43 | 51 | 27 |  |
| **Spain** | 1 | 7 | 24 | 35 | 55 | 63 |
| **Germany (GDR)** | 2 | 6 | 11 | 15 |  |  |
| **Czechosl.** | 3 | 7 | 13 | 15 | Ca. 11 (89/92) | 95 |
| **Poland** | 1 | 2 | 8 | 9 | 10 | 23 |
| **Romania** | 0.3 | 1 | 5 | 6 | 4 | 14 |
| **Yugosl.** | 0.3 | 2 | 8 | 10 | 3 |  |
| **Soviet Union./ Russian Fed.** | 2 | 4 | 7 | 8 | 10 | 10 |

My calculations are based on Fischer (1987), 12 f. and 128, Mitchell (1992), 537, Mitchell (2003), 552 f., Wirtschaftszahlen zum Automobil and Maddison (Population).

Table 8: Passenger Cars per 1,000 Inhabitants in Europe, 1949-2006

|  | 1949 | 1969 | 1988 | 2006 |
|---|---|---|---|---|
| Italy | 6 | 166 | 428 | 605 |
| Austria | 6 | 151 | 366 | 573 |
| Switzerland | 27 | 208 | 421 | 526 |
| Belgium | 26 | 196 | 366 | 517 |
| Spain | 3 | 50 | 276 | 516 |
| Sweden | 28 | 274 | 413 | 514 |
| Germany (FRG) | 7 | 207 | 418 | 510 |
| France | 37 | 235 | 393 | 500 |
| Portugal | 7 | 54 | 196 | 497 |
| Finland | 6 | 137 | 363 | 472 |
| Slovenia |  |  |  | 466 |
| United Kingdom | 42 | 208 | 322 | 465 |
| Netherlands | 11 | 178 | 356 | 458 |
| Norway | 18 | 181 | 385 | 448 |
| Greece | 1 | 22 | 150 | 441 |
| Ireland | 24 | 122 | 212 | 416 |
| Denmark | 26 | 209 | 311 | 411 |
| Czechoslovakia | 10 | 49 | 193 | 395/253 |
| Estonia |  |  |  | 393 |
| Croatia |  |  |  | 353 |
| Bulgaria |  |  |  | 337 |
| Lithuania |  |  |  | 334 |
| Poland | 2 | 45 | 118 | 318 |
| Hungary | 1 | 19 | 171 | 313 |
| Latvia |  |  |  | 267 |
| Serbia-Montenegro |  |  |  | 195 |
| Belarus |  |  |  | 185 |
| Soviet Union/ Russian Federation |  | 5 | 40(1983) | 170 |
| Romania |  | 2 |  | 170 |
| Macedonia |  |  |  | 162 |
| Ukraine |  |  |  | 118 |
| Moldavia |  |  |  | 71 |
| Yugoslavia | 0.4 | 28 | 137 |  |
| Germany (GDR) | 4 | 54 |  |  |

Mitchell (1992), 718-721; Fischer (1987); Statistisches Jahrbuch (2013), 614; Welt in Zahlen (PKW).

Table 9: Computers per 1,000 Inhabitants in Europe, 2006

| | | | | | |
|---|---|---|---|---|---|
| Switzerland | 757 | Luxembourg | 737 | Sweden | 710 |
| Iceland | 637 | Denmark | 616 | Germany | 602 |
| Norway | 602 | Ireland | 548 | Finland | 533 |
| Netherlands | 529 | Austria | 502 | Great Britain | 495 |
| Slovenia | 417 | Slovakia | 417 | Croatia | 402 |
| Malta | 399 | France | 385 | Cyprus | 344 |
| Belgium | 336 | Italy | 313 | Spain | 312 |
| Czech Republic | 307 | Estonia | 305 | Latvia | 250 |
| Portugal | 203 | Belarus | 102 | Romania | 184 |
| Poland | 168 | Lithuania | 161 | Hungary | 156 |
| Russian Fed. | 129 | Macedonia | 126 | Bulgaria | 111 |
| Greece | 107 | Bosnia-Herceg. | 57 | Serbia-Monten. | 46 |
| Ukraine | 35 | Albania | 28 | Moldavia | 27 |

Welt in Zahlen (Computer).

Table 10: Cities with Over 100,000 Inhabitants in the United States, 1850 and 1900 (Thousands)

|  | 1850 | 1900 |  | 1850 | 1900 |
|---|---|---|---|---|---|
| New York City | 696 | 3 437 | Chicago | 30 | 1 699 |
| Philadelphia | 340 | 1 294 | St. Louis | 78 | 575 |
| Boston | 137 | 561 | Baltimore | 169 | 509 |
| Pittsburgh | 68 | 452 | Cleveland | 17 | 382 |
| Buffalo | 42 | 352 | San Francisco | 35 | 343 |
| Cincinnati | 115 | 326 | New Orleans | 116 | 287 |
| Detroit | 21 | 286 | Milwaukee | 20 | 285 |
| Washington | 40 | 279 | Newark | 39 | 246 |
| Jersey City | 7 | 206 | Louisville | 43 | 205 |
| Minneapolis |  | 203 | Providence | 42 | 176 |
| Indianapolis | 8 | 169 | Kansas City |  | 164 |
| Rochester | 36 | 163 | St. Paul | 1 | 163 |
| Denver |  | 134 | Toledo | 4 | 132 |
| Columbus | 18 | 126 | Worcester | 17 | 118 |
| Syracuse | 22 | 108 | Fall River | 12 | 105 |
| Paterson | 11 | 105 | Omaha |  | 103 |
| Memphis | 9 | 102 | Los Angeles | 2 | 102 |

Mitchell (1998), 46-53.

Table 11: Population and Urbanization in the United States, 1900 and 1990

| | Population (Millions and Percent of Total) | | | | Urban Population (Percent of Total) | |
|---|---|---|---|---|---|---|
| | **1900** | **Percent** | **1990** | **Percent** | **1900** | **1990** |
| **Northeast** | 21.0 | 27.6 | 50.8 | 20.4 | 66.1 | 78.9 |
| **Midwest** | 26.3 | 34.6 | 59.7 | 24.0 | 38.6 | 71.1 |
| **South** | 24.5 | 32.2 | 85.4 | 34.4 | 18.0 | 68.6 |
| **Pacific** | 2.6 | 3.5 | 39.1 | 15.7 | 44.7 | 88.6 |
| **USA** | **76.2** | **100.0** | **248.7** | **100.0** | **39.6** | **75.2** |

Heim (2000), 101 and 141.

Table 12: Cities with Over a Million Inhabitants in the United States, 1950 and 1980 (Thousands)

|  | 1950 | 1980 |  | 1950 | 1980 |
|---|---|---|---|---|---|
| New York | 9 556 | 8 275 | Los Angeles | 4 368 | 7 478 |
| Chicago | 5 495 | 6 060 | Philadelphia | 3 671 | 4 717 |
| Detroit | 3.016 | 4 488 | San Francisco | 2 241 | 3 251 |
| Washington | 1 464 | 3 251 | Dallas | 615 | 2 931 |
| Boston | 2 370 | 2 806 | Houston | 807 | 2 736 |
| St. Louis | 1 681 | 2 377 | Baltimore | 1 337 | 2 200 |
| Pittsburgh | 2 213 | 2 219 | Atlanta | 672 | 2 138 |
| Minneapolis | 1 117 | 2 137 | Anaheim | 15 | 1 933 |
| Cleveland | 1 466 | 1 899 | Newark | 439 | 1 879 |
| San Diego | 557 | 1 862 | Miami | 495 | 1 626 |
| Denver | 564 | 1 618 | Tampa | 409 | 1 614 |
| Seattle | 733 | 1 607 | San Bernardino | 282 | 1 558 |
| Phoenix | 332 | 1 509 | Kansas City | 814 | 1 433 |
| Cincinnati | 904 | 1 401 | Milwaukee | 871 | 1 397 |
| Portland | 705 | 1 298 | San José | 291 | 1 295 |
| New Orleans | 685 | 1 256 | Columbus | 503 | 1 244 |
| Buffalo | 1 089 | 1 243 | Indianapolis | 552 | 1 167 |
| Norfolk | 446 | 1 160 | Sacramento | 277 | 1 100 |
| San Antonio | 500 | 1 072 | Fort Lauderdale | 36 | 1 018 |

Mitchell (1998), 50-53.

Table 13: Employment in Manufacturing in the United States, 1900-1990
(Percent of Economically Active Population)

|  | 1900 | 1940 | 1950 | 1960 | 1970 | 1980 | 1990 |
|---|---|---|---|---|---|---|---|
| **New England** | 34.6 | 38.8 | 38.4 | 37.2 | 30.9 | 28.0 | 19.3 |
| **Mideast** | 22.9 | 30.3 | 31.9 | 32.2 | 27.2 | 22.7 | 15.8 |
| **Great Lakes** | 15.2 | 31.9 | 35.5 | 36.2 | 33.4 | 28.7 | 22.8 |
| **Plains** | 6.9 | 12.5 | 15.6 | 18.9 | 19.2 | 18.8 | 16.7 |
| **Southeast** | 6.9 | 17.3 | 19.5 | 22.9 | 24.4 | 21.8 | 18.0 |
| **Southwest** | 3.4 | 9.3 | 11.9 | 14.8 | 16.4 | 16.3 | 13.6 |
| **Rocky Mountains** | 7.6 | 9.0 | 10.4 | 13.9 | 13.0 | 12.8 | 12.4 |
| **Far West** | 11.8 | 17.4 | 19.0 | 23.2 | 19.9 | 18.7 | 15.9 |
| **USA** | **14.6** | **23.7** | **25.7** | **27.4** | **25.2** | **22.1** | **17.4** |

Heim (2000), 106-112.

Table 14: Population of Latin America, 1820-2009 (Millions)

|  | 1820 | 1900 | 1950 | 2009 |
|---|---|---|---|---|
| Brazil | 4.5 | 18.0 | 53.4 | 198.7 |
| Mexico | 6.6 | 13.6 | 28.5 | 111.2 |
| Colombia | 1.2 | 4.0 | 11.6 | 43.7 |
| Argentina | 0.5 | 4.7 | 17.2 | 40.9 |
| Peru | 1.3 | 3.6 | 7.6 | 29.5 |
| Venezuela | 0.7 | 2.5 | 5.0 | 26.8 |
| Chile | 0.8 | 3.0 | 6.1 | 16.6 |
| Ecuador | 0.5 | 1.4 | 3.4 | 14.6 |
| Bolivia | 1.1 | 1.7 | 2.8 | 9.8 |
| Paraguay | 0.1 | 0.4 | 1.5 | 6.3 |
| Uruguay | 0.1 | 0.9 | 2.2 | 3.5 |
| Central America | 1.2 | 3.6 | 9.2 | 40.8 |
| Caribbean | 2.1 | 5.7 | 15,7 | 38.2 |
| Latin America | 21.6 | 64.6 | 165.5 | 584.0 |

Central America: Guatemala, El Salvador, Honduras, Costa Rica, Nicaragua, Panama.
Caribbean: Cuba, Puerto Rico, Haiti, Dominican Republic, Jamaica, Trinidad and Tobago.
Maddison (Population)

Table 15: Cities with Over 100,000 Inhabitants in Latin America, 1900 and 1920 (Thousands)

| | 1900 | 1920 | | 1900 | 1920 |
|---|---|---|---|---|---|
| **Buenos Aires** | 664 | 1 663 | **Rio de Janeiro** | 811 | 1 158 |
| **Mexico City** | 345 | 615 | **São Paulo** | 240 | 579 |
| **Santiago de Chile** | 256 | 507 | **Montevideo** | 268 | 385 |
| **Havanna** | 236 | 364 | **Salvador** | 206 | 283 |
| **Rosario** | 92 | 250 | **Recife** | 113 | 239 |
| **Belém** | 97 | 236 | **Valparaiso** | 122 | 182 |
| **Porto Alegre** | 73 | 180 | **Lima** | 130 | 176 |
| **La Plata** | 45 | 151 | **Bogotá** | 100 | 144 |
| **Guadalajara** | 101 | 143 | **Córdoba** | 48 | 140 |
| **Guatemala City** | 74 | 116 | **Campinas** | 45 | 116 |
| **La Paz** | 53 | 107 | **Santos** | 30 | 103 |

Mitchell (1998), 50-57.

Table 16: Cities with Over a Million Inhabitants in Latin America, 1950 and 1980
(Thousands, *Agglomeration)

|  | 1950 | 1980 |  | 1950 | 1980 |
|---|---|---|---|---|---|
| **Mexico City** | 3 050* | 12 932* | **São Paulo** | 2 109 | 12 273* |
| **Buenos Aires** | 4 722 | 9 948* | **Rio de Janeiro** | 2 377 | 9.619* |
| **Lima** | 835 | 4 699* | **Bogotá** | 648 | 4 177 |
| **Santiago de Chile** | 1 348* | 3 899* | **Caracas** | 694* | 2 944* |
| **Recife** | 525 | 2 307* | **Belo Horizonte** | 353 | 2 279* |
| **Guadalajara** | 377 | 2 245* | **Porto Alegre** | 394 | 2 133* |
| **Havanna** | 1 218* | 1 929* | **Monterrey** | 333 | 1 916* |
| **Salvador** | 417 | 1 563* | **Medellín** | 358 | 1 452* |
| **Cali** | 284 | 1 369* | **Fortaleza** | 270 | 1 340* |
| **Santo Domingo** | 182 | 1 313 | **Montevideo** | 784 | 1 252 |
| **Guayaquil** | 250 | 1 199 | **Brasília** |  | 1 177 |
| **Nova Iguaçu** | 59 | 1 095 | **Curitiba** | 181 | 1 093* |
| **San Juan** | 466* | 1 086 |  |  |  |

Mitchell (1998), 50-57.

Table 17: Manufacturing Production in Latin America in the 20th Century
(Multiplication per Inhabitant)

| | Factor | | Factor |
|---|---|---|---|
| **Argentina 1935-1979** | 3.2 | **Nicaragua 1953-1976** | 3.7 |
| **Brazil 1920-1981** | 5.1 | **Panama 1958-1987** | 3.3 |
| **Chile 1927-1993** | 1.6 | **Peru 1945-1980** | 3.7 |
| **Ecuador 1953-1993** | 7.1 | **Uruguay 1953-1980** | 1.3 |
| **Colombia 1948-1993** | 3.5 | **Venezuela 1948-1987** | 18.5 |
| **Mexico 1920-1981** | 3.2 | | |

Calculations based on Mitchell (1998), 307-310 and Maddison (Population).

Table 18: Processing of Raw Cotton, Production of Crude Steel and Automobiles in America, 1940-1993 (Kg per Capita and Units per 1,000 Inhabitants, Peak Values)

|  | Raw Cotton | Crude Steel | Automobiles |
|---|---|---|---|
| **Argentina** | 5.0 (1948) | 120 (1989) | 8 (1993) |
| **Brazil** | 5.3 (1992) | 159 (1993) | 6 (1986) |
| **Chile** | 3.1 (1970) | 77 (1993) | 2 (1980) |
| **Colombia** | 3.2 (1992) | 24 (1988) | 2 (1993) |
| **Cuba** | 4.6 (1986) | 41 (1986) | |
| **Mexico** | 2.9 (1976) | 97 (1990) | 9 (1993) |
| **Peru** | 4.0 (1987) | 25 (1987) | 1 (1976) |
| **Uruguay** | 3.9 (1960) | 17 (1993) | |
| **Venezuela** | 2.4 (1989) | 208 (1987) | 7 (1978) |

| | | | |
|---|---|---|---|
| **USA** | 20.4 (1942) | 645 (1973) | 45 (1973) |
| **Canada** | 9.8 (1940) | 662 (1979) | 54 (1973) |

Calculations based on Mitchell (1998), 362 f., 374 f., 395-397 and Maddison (Population)

Table 19: Consumer Durables per 1,000 Inhabitants in America, 1950-2006

| | Television Sets | | | Passenger Cars | | | Computers |
|---|---|---|---|---|---|---|---|
| | 1960 | 1990 | 2006 | 1950 | 1980 | 2006 | 2006 |
| Brazil | 17 | 205 | 398 | 4 | 65 | 143 | 95 |
| Mexico | 17 | 145 | 326 | 6 | 62 | 119 | 121 |
| Colombia | 9 | 109 | 434 | 3 | 20 | 35 | 94 |
| Argentina | 22 | 215 | 342 | 18 | 110 | 155 | 130 |
| Peru | 3 | 97 | 202 | 4 | 18 | 37 | 61 |
| Venezuela | 33 | 160 | 193 | 14 | 102 | 73 | 97 |
| Chile | 1 | 205 | 281 | 6 | 40 | 89 | 187 |
| Ecuador | 1 | 85 | 263 | 1 | 12 | 30 | 65 |
| Guatemala | 8 | 53 | 65 | 3 | 25 | 57 | 21 |
| Cuba | 71 | 168 | 409 | 1 | 16 | 27 | 80 |
| Bolivia | | 111 | 126 | 1 | 9 | 33 | 38 |
| Dominican Rep. | 5 | 85 | 99 | 2 | 16 | 82 | 83 |
| Haiti | 0.5 | 5 | 6.5 | 1 | 4 | 6.5 | |
| Honduras | 0.7 | 77 | 166 | 1 | 8 | 60 | 20 |
| Paraguay | | 71 | 226 | 1 | 18 | 58 | 113 |
| El Salvador | 8 | 93 | 252 | 3 | 16 | 31 | 38 |
| Nicaragua | 3 | 65 | 84 | 1 | 14 | 21 | 39.5 |
| Costa Rica | 3 | 139 | 233 | 5 | 38 | 101 | 289 |
| Puerto Rico | 71 | 263 | 354 | 17 | 296 | 302 | 211 |
| Uruguay | 10 | 20 | 565 | 76 | 122 | 204 | 186 |
| Panama | 9 | 167 | 229 | 22 | 50 | 106 | 50 |
| Jamaica | 6 | 132 | 307 | 9 | 15 | 77 | 70 |

| | | | | | | | |
|---|---|---|---|---|---|---|---|
| USA | 254 | 368 | 950 | 265 | 546 | 535 | 794 |
| Canada | 215 | 612 | 682 | 136 | 417 | 551 | 541 |

Welt in Zahlen (Fernsehgeräte), Welt in Zahlen (PKW), Welt in Zahlen (Computer) and calculations based on Mitchell (1998), 626,631,588-598 and Maddison (Population).

Table 20: Employment in Manufacturing in Latin America Around 1990
(Percent of Economically Active Population)

| Argentina (1980) | 20.9 | Bolivia (1991) | 17.0 |
|---|---|---|---|
| Brazil (1990) | 16.2 | Chile (1994) | 16.6 |
| Ecuador(1990) | 11.2 | Colombia (1992) | 23.7 |
| Mexico (1990) | 18.6 | Paraguay (1994) | 17.5 |
| Peru (1991) | 10.0 | Uruguay (1992) | 21.6 |
| Venezuela (1991) | 16.6 | | |

My calculations are based on Mitchell (1998), 105-110.

Table 21: Population of Africa, 1950-2009 (Larger Countries, Millions)

| | 1950 | 1980 | 2009 |
|---|---|---|---|
| **Nigeria** | 31.8 | 74.8 | 149.2 |
| **Ethiopia** | 20.2 | 36.0 | 85.2 |
| **Egypt** | 21.2 | 42.6 | 78.9 |
| **Congo (Dem. Rep.)** | 13.6 | 29.0 | 68.7 |
| **South Africa** | 13.6 | 29.3 | 49.1 |
| **Sudan** | 8.1 | 19.1 | 41.1 |
| **Tanzania** | 7.9 | 18.7 | 41.0 |
| **Kenya** | 6.1 | 16.3 | 39.0 |
| **Algeria** | 8.9 | 18.8 | 34.2 |
| **Uganda** | 5.5 | 12.4 | 32.4 |
| **Morocco** | 9.3 | 19.5 | 31.3 |
| **Ghana** | 5.3 | 11.0 | 23.9 |
| **Mozambique** | 6.3 | 12.1 | 21.7 |
| **Madagascar** | 4.6 | 8.7 | 20.7 |
| **Ivory Coast** | 2.9 | 8.6 | 20.6 |
| **Cameroon** | 4.9 | 8.8 | 18.9 |
| **Burkina Faso** | 4.4 | 6.3 | 15.7 |
| **Niger** | 3.3 | 6.1 | 15.3 |
| **Malawi** | 2.8 | 6.3 | 15.0 |
| **Senegal** | 2.7 | 5.8 | 13.7 |
| **Mali** | 3.7 | 6.8 | 13.4 |
| **Angola** | 4.1 | 6.7 | 12.8 |
| **Zambia** | 2.6 | 5.7 | 11.9 |
| **Zimbabwe** | 2.9 | 7.2 | 11.4 |
| **Rwanda** | 2.4 | 5.1 | 10.7 |
| **Tunisia** | 3.5 | 6.4 | 10.5 |
| **Chad** | 2.6 | 4.5 | 10.3 |
| **Guinea** | 2.6 | 4.4 | 10.1 |
| **Africa** | **227.9** | **478.1** | **990.4** |

Maddison (Population)

Table 22: Cities with Over a Million Inhabitants in Africa, 1950 and 1980 (Thousands)

|              | 1950  | 1980  |              | 1950 | 1980  |
|--------------|-------|-------|--------------|------|-------|
| Cairo        | 2 091 | 5 875 | Alexandria   | 919  | 2 705 |
| Casablanca   | 682   | 2 409 | Kinshasa     | 209  | 2 174 |
| Algiers      | 498   | 1 740 | Giza         | 66   | 1 640 |
| Johannesburg | 884   | 1 536 | Cape Town    | 578  | 1 440 |
| Abidjan      | 56    | 1 423 | Addis Ababa  | 400  | 1 277 |
| Lagos        | 267   | 1 061 |              |      |       |

Mitchell (2007), 41.

Table 23: Consumer Durables per 1,000 Inhabitants in Africa, 1970-2006
(Larger Countries)

| | Television Sets | | | Passenger Cars | | | Computers |
|---|---|---|---|---|---|---|---|
| | 1985 | 1995 | 2006 | 1970 | 1990 | 2006 | 2006 |
| **Nigeria** | 6 | 56 | 81 | 1 | 4 | 7 | 8 |
| **Egypt** | 77 | 108 | 254 | 4 | 19 | 22 | 29 |
| **Ethiopia and Eritrea** | 2 | 4 | 7 | 1 | 1 | 1 | 6 |
| **Congo (Dem. Rep.)** | 0.4 | 2 | 146 | 3 | 2 | 17 | 2 |
| **South Africa** | 87 | 106 | 237 | 68 | 88 | 99 | 99 |
| **Sudan** | 47 | 74 | 400(?) | 2 | 8 | 9 | 16 |
| **Tanzania** | 0.4 | 2 | 31 | 2 | 2 | 2 | 13 |
| **Kenya** | 5 | 18 | 36 | 5 | 7 | 10 | 10 |
| **Algeria** | 68 | 89 | 126 | 10 | 29 | 73 | 19 |
| **Uganda** | 6 | 12 | 31 | 3 | 1 | 3 | 6 |
| **Morocco** | 53 | 91 | 226 | 14 | 27 | 47 | 39 |
| **Ghana** | 11 | 90 | 113 | 5 | 5 | 7 | 6 |
| **Mozambique** | 1 | 4 | 25 | 8 | 7 | 4 | 7 |
| **Madagascar** | 5 | 22 | 29 | 7 | 4 | 4 | 13 |
| **Ivory Coast** | 48 | 57 | 59 | 10 | 12 | 12 | 21 |
| **Cameroon** | 12(88) | 23 | 34 | 5 | 5 | 10 | 16 |
| **Burkina Faso** | 5 | 6 | 17 | 1 | 2(87) | 3 | 3 |
| **Niger** | 2 | 11 | 77 | 1 | 5 | 4 | 16 |
| **Malawi** | 0.5 | 2 | 6 | 2 | 2 | 3 | 2 |
| **Senegal** | 29 | 34 | 38 | 9 | 8 | 26 | 28 |
| **Mali** | | | 70 | 1 | 2 | 4 | 3 |
| **Angola** | 5 | 10 | 22 | 15 | 15 | 26 | 7 |
| **Zambia** | 13 | 28 | 180 | 14 | 9 | 18 | 12 |
| **Zimbabwe** | 21 | 29 | 219(?) | 24 | 19 | 58 | 138 |
| **Rwanda** | | | 13 | 1 | 1 | 4 | 5 |
| **Tunisia** | 54 | 89 | 244 | 13 | 23 | 63 | 64 |
| **Chad** | | | 3 | 1 | 1(91) | 3 | 2 |
| **Guinea** | 2 | 9 | 47 | 3 | 3(95) | | 7 |
| **Libya** | 64 | 118 | 183 | 50 | 108 | 173 | 66 |

Welt in Zahlen (Fernsehgeräte), Welt in Zahlen (PKW), Welt in Zahlen (Computer) and calculations based on Mitchell (2007), 788, 795, 854-857 and Maddison (Population)

Table 24: Sectoral Distribution of GDP in Africa, 1965-2008
(Larger Countries, Percent of Total)

|  | Secondary Sector | | | Tertiary Sector | | |
|---|---|---|---|---|---|---|
|  | 1965 | 1987 | 2008 | 1965 | 1987 | 2008 |
| **Nigeria** | 13 | 43 | 24 | 33 | 27 | 34 |
| **Ethiopia** | 14 | 18 | 13 | 28 | 40 | 42 |
| **Egypt** |  |  | 38 |  |  | 49 |
| **Congo (De. Rep.)** | 26 | 33 | 28 | 53 | 35 | 32 |
| **South Africa** |  |  | 34 |  |  | 63 |
| **Sudan** | 9 | 15 | 34 | 37 | 48 | 40 |
| **Tanzania** | 14 | 8 | 17 | 40 | 31 | 38 |
| **Kenya** | 18 | 19 | 19 | 47 | 50 | 54 |
| **Algeria** |  |  | 62 |  |  | 31 |
| **Uganda** | 13 | 5 | 26 | 35 | 19 | 51 |
| **Morocco** |  |  | 24 |  |  | 63 |
| **Ghana** | 19 | 16 | 25 | 38 | 33 | 41 |
| **Mozambique** |  | 12 | 24 |  | 38 | 47 |
| **Madagascar** | 16 | 16 | 17 | 53 | 42 | 58 |
| **Ivory Coast** | 19 | 25 | 26 | 33 | 39 | 49 |
| **Cameroon** | 20 | 32 | 31 | 47 | 45 | 49 |
| **Burkina Faso** | 20 | 25 | 22 | 27 | 38 | 45 |
| **Malawi** | 13 | 18 | 21 | 37 | 45 | 45 |
| **Senegal** | 18 | 27 | 22 | 56 | 52 | 62 |
| **Mali** | 9 | 12 | 24 | 25 | 35 | 39 |
| **Angola** | 7 | 23 | 67 | 42 | 31 | 26 |
| **Zambia** | 54 | 36 | 46 | 32 | 52 | 33 |
| **Tunisia** |  |  | 35 |  |  | 54 |
| **Chad** | 15 | 18 | 49 | 43 | 39 | 37 |
| **Libya** |  |  | 70 |  |  | 27 |

Sub-Saharan Africa (1989), 224 f. and Fischer Weltalmanach (2011).

Table 25: Population of North and Central Asia, 1950-2009 (Millions)

|  | 1950 | 1980 | 2009 |
|---|---|---|---|
| **Russian Federation (Asian part and the Urals)** | ca. 27.6 | ca. 37.7 | 38.0 |
| **Uzbekistan** | 6.3 | 16.0 | 27.6 |
| **Kazakhstan** | 6.7 | 15.0 | 15.4 |
| **Tajikistan** | 1.5 | 4.0 | 7.3 |
| **Kyrgyzstan** | 1.7 | 3.6 | 5.4 |
| **Turkmenistan** | 1.2 | 2.9 | 4.9 |
| **Mongolia** | 0.8 | 1.7 | 3.0 |
| **North and Central Asia** | **ca. 45.8** | **ca. 80.9** | **101.7** |

Maddison (Population) and Wikipedia (Asia and Russia).

Table 26: Sectoral Distribution of Employment in North and Central Asia, 1990-2004
(Percent of Economically Active Population, Annual Averages)

| | Primary Sector | | Secondary Sector | | Tertiary Sector | |
|---|---|---|---|---|---|---|
| | 1990-99 | 2000-04 | 1990-99 | 2000-04 | 1990-99 | 2000-04 |
| **Mongolia** | 47.1 | 45.9 | 21.8 | 14.4 | 31.1 | 39.7 |
| **Kazakhstan** | 23.2 | 35.4 | 26.8 | 16.5 | 50.0 | 48.0 |
| **Kyrgyzstan** | 43.1 | 49.6 | 18.7 | 12.0 | 38.2 | 38.5 |
| **Uzbekistan** | 42.5 | 34.4 | 20.9 | 20.3 | 36.6 | 45.3 |
| **Turkmenistan (1991 and 1998)** | 43.0 | 48.5 | 20.0 | 18.2 | 37.0 | 33.2 |
| **Tajikistan (1991 and 2001)** | 43.0 | 66.0 | 22.0 | 9.2 | 35.0 | 24.8 |

Growth Amid Change (2007), 50, Fischer Weltalmanach (1995) and Fischer Weltalmanach (2008).

Table 27: Population of West Asia, 1950-2009 (Millions)

| | 1950 | 1980 | 2009 |
|---|---|---|---|
| Turkey | 21.1 | 45.0 | 76.8 |
| Iran | 16.4 | 39.4 | 66.4 |
| Iraq | 5.2 | 13.2 | 28.9 |
| Saudi Arabia | 3.9 | 10.0 | 28.7 |
| Yemen | 4.8 | 9.1 | 22.9 |
| Syria | 3.5 | 8.8 | 21.8 |
| Azerbaijan | 2.9 | 6.2 | 8.2 |
| Israel | 1.3 | 3.7 | 7.2 |
| Jordan | 0.6 | 2.2 | 6.3 |
| United Arab Emirates | 0.1 | 1.0 | 4.8 |
| Georgia | 3.5 | 5.0 | 4.6 |
| Lebanon | 1.4 | 3.1 | 4.1 |
| West Bank and Gaza | 1.0 | 1.5 | 4.0 |
| Armenia | 1.4 | 3.1 | 3.0 |
| Oman | 0.5 | 1.2 | 2.9 |
| Kuwait | 0.1 | 1.4 | 2.7 |
| Qatar | 0.03 | 0.2 | 0.8 |
| Bahrain | 0.1 | 0.3 | 0.7 |
| West Asia | 67.6 | 154.5 | 294.9 |

Maddison (Population).

Table 28: Cities with Over a Million Inhabitants in West Asia, 1950 and 1980 (Thousands)

|          | 1950     | 1980      |         | 1950       | 1980     |
|----------|----------|-----------|---------|------------|----------|
| Teheran  | 619      | 4 530     | Baghdad | 352        | 3 206    |
| Istanbul | 983      | 2 773     | Ankara  | 289        | 1 878    |
| Damascus | 335      | 1 112     | Riyadh  | 120        | 1 300    |
| Baku     | ca. 600  | 1 022     | Yerevan | 509 (1959) | 1 019    |
| Beirut   | 201      | ca. 1 000 | Jeddah  | 60         | ca.1 000 |
| Tbilisi  |          | ca. 1 000 |         |            |          |

Mitchell (2007), 42-46 and List of cities (individual countries).

Table 29: Manufacturing Production in West Asia, 1960-1999
(Select Countries, 1980 = 100)

|        | 1960 | 1970 | 1980 | 1990 | 1999       |
|--------|------|------|------|------|------------|
| Iran   | 14   | 46   | 100  | 130  | 234 (1998) |
| Israel | 20   | 60   | 100  | 132  | 212        |
| Syria  | 21   | 45   | 100  | 186  | 262 (1998) |
| Turkey | 22   | 50   | 100  | 211  | 296        |

Calculations based on Mitchell (2007), 367-370.

Table 30: Consumer Durables per 1,000 Inhabitants in West Asia, 1970-2006

| | Television Sets | | | Passenger Ccars | | | Computers |
|---|---|---|---|---|---|---|---|
| | 1980 | 1995 | 2006 | 1970 | 1990 | 2006 | 2006 |
| Turkey | 75 | 313 | 516 | 4 | 29 | 72 | 61 |
| Iran | 51 | 71 | 191 | 10 | 27 | 46 | 94 |
| Iraq | 31 | 82 | 78 | 7 | 37 | 40 | 15 |
| Saudi Arabia | 210 | 235 | 234 | 11 | 91 | 95 | 195 |
| Yemen | 1 | 28 | 267 | | 8 | 21 | 39 |
| Syria | 44 | 66 | 246 | 5 | 10 | 9 | 32 |
| Azerbaijan | | | 308 | | | 53 | 52 |
| Israel | 241 | 299 | 416 | 52 | 181 | 290 | 286 |
| Jordan | 79 | 102 | 154 | 10 | 53 | 49 | 54 |
| UAE | 93 | 93 | 511 | | | 95 | 292 |
| Georgia | | | 496 | | | 97 | 54 |
| Lebanon | 243 | 330 | 369 | 74 | 347 | 418 | 106 |
| Armenia | | | 343 | | | 62 | 114 |
| Oman | 29 | 680 | 529 | | | 167 | 81 |
| Kuwait | 258 | 438 | 554 | 151 | 257 | 340 | 161 |
| Qatar | 338 | 422 | 830 | | | 346 | 234 |
| Bahrain | 216 | 468 | 454 | 45 | 198 | 279 | 199 |

Welt in Zahlen (Fernsehgeräte), Welt in Zahlen (PKW), Welt in Zahlen (Computer) and calculations based on Mitchell (2007), 796-803, 858-861 and Maddison (Population).

Table 31: Population of South Asia, 1950-2009 (Millions)

|  | 1950 | 1980 | 2009 |
|---|---|---|---|
| **India** | 359.0 | 679.0 | 1 156.9 |
| **Pakistan** | 39.4 | 85.2 | 174.6 |
| **Bangladesh** | 45.6 | 87.9 | 156.1 |
| **Afghanistan** | 8.2 | 15.1 | 38.4 |
| **Nepal** | 9.0 | 14.7 | 28.6 |
| **Sri Lanka** | 7.5 | 15.1 | 21.3 |
| **Bhutan** | 0.2 | 0.4 | 0.4 |
| **Maldives** | 0,1 | 0.2 | 0.4 |
| **South Asia** | **469.0** | **897.6** | **1 576.9** |

Maddison (Population)

Table 32: Cities with Over a Million Inhabitants in South Asia, 1950 and 1980 (Thousands)

|  | 1950 | 1980 |  | 1950 | 1980 |
|---|---|---|---|---|---|
| Calcutta | 4 578 | 9.194 | Bombay | 2 839 | 8 227 |
| Karachi | 1 068 | 5 208 | Delhi | 914 | 4 884 |
| Dhaka | 336 | 3 459 | Madras | 1 416 | 3 277 |
| Lahore | 1 068 | 2 953 | Faisalabad | 179 | 2 953 |
| Bangalore | 779 | 2 629 | Hyderabad (I) | 803 | 2 093 |
| Ahmedabad | 788 | 2 060 | Kanpur | 636 | 1 428 |
| Chittagong | 290 | 1 388 | Nagpur | 449 | 1 219 |
| Pune | 481 | 1 203 |  |  |  |

Mitchell (2007), 42-46.

Table 33: Consumer Durables per 1,000 Inhabitants in South Asia, 1970-2006

| | Television Sets | | | Passenger Cars | | | Computers |
|---|---|---|---|---|---|---|---|
| | 1985 | 1995 | 2006 | 1970 | 1990 | 2006 | 2006 |
| India | 5 | 51 | 98 | 1 | 3 | 10 | 14 |
| Pakistan | 13 | 21 | 170 | 2 | 6 | 10 | 20 |
| Bangladesh | 3 | 6 | 1 | 0.4 | 0.4 | 7 | 7 |
| Afghanistan | 7 | 9 | 22 | 3 | 2 | 2 | 1 |
| Nepal | 1 | 5 | 8 | | | 3 | 4 |
| Sri Lanka | 28 | 80 | 149 | 7 | 10 | 32 | 39 |

Welt in Zahlen (Fernsehgeräte), Welt in Zahlen (PKW), Welt in Zahlen (Computer) and calculations based on Mitchell (2007), 798 f., 801 f., 858, 860 and Maddison (Population).

Table 34: Population of South East Asia, 1950-2009 (Millions)

|                 | 1950  | 1980  | 2009  |
|-----------------|-------|-------|-------|
| Indonesia       | 82.6  | 147.5 | 230.6 |
| Philippines     | 21.1  | 50.9  | 98.0  |
| Vietnam         | 25.3  | 53.7  | 88.6  |
| Thailand        | 20.0  | 47.0  | 66.0  |
| Myanmar         | 19.5  | 33.1  | 52.2  |
| Malaysia        | 6.4   | 13.8  | 25.7  |
| Cambodia        | 4.5   | 6.9   | 14.5  |
| Laos            | 1.9   | 3.3   | 6.8   |
| Singapore       | 1.0   | 2.4   | 4.7   |
| South East Asia | 182.4 | 358.6 | 587.7 |

Maddison (Population)

Table 35: Cities with Over a Million Inhabitants in South East Asia, 1950 and 1980 (Thousands)

| | 1950 | 1980 | | 1950 | 1980 |
|---|---|---|---|---|---|
| Jakarta | 1 861 | 6 503 | Bangkok | 621 | 4 697 |
| Saigon | 1 179 | 3 420 | Hanoi | 238 | 2 571 |
| Rangoon | 712 | 2 513 | Singapore | 680 | 2 414 |
| Surabaya | 1 008 (1960) | 2 028 | Manila | 984 | 1 630 |
| Bandung | 686 | 1 463 | Medan | 250 | 1 379 |
| Quezon City | 108 | 1 166 | Semarang | 503 (1960) | 1 027 |
| (Kuala Lumpur) | 176 | 920 | | | |

Mitchell (2007), 42-46.

Table 36: Sectoral Distribution of Employment in South East Asia Around 2000
(Percent of Economically Active Population)

|             | Primary Sector | Secondary Sector |
|-------------|----------------|------------------|
| Philippines | 39             | 16               |
| Indonesia   | 44             | 19               |
| Vietnam     | 63             | 13               |
| Thailand    | 42             | 25               |
| Myanmar     | 70             | 12 (1996)        |
| Malaysia    | 15             | 37               |
| Cambodia    | 74             | 8                |
| Laos        | 76             |                  |
| Singapore   | 0.3            | 25               |

Fischer Weltalmanach (2000) and Fischer Weltalmanach (2005).

Table 37: Consumer Durables per 1,000 Inhabitants in South East Asia, 1970-2006

| | Television Sets | | | Passenger Cars | | | Computers |
|---|---|---|---|---|---|---|---|
| | 1985 | 1995 | 2006 | 1970 | 1990 | 2006 | 2006 |
| Indonesia | 39 | 67 | 163 | 0.4 | 7 | 16 | 15 |
| Philippines | 26 | 45 | 188 | 2 | 7 | 10 | 45 |
| Vietnam | 34 (88) | 43 | 216 | 0.2 | | 9 | 15 |
| Thailand | 97 | 127 | 322 | 0.5 | 22 | 48 | 84 |
| Myanmar | 2 (88) | 96 | 11 | 0.4 | 26 (94) | 8 | 6 |
| Malaysia | 101 | 168 | 275 | 4 | 105 | 257 | 197 |
| Cambodia | 7 | | 8 | 0.3 | | 24 | 4 |
| Laos | | | 12 | 0.2 | | 8 | 6 |
| Singapore | 182 | 339 | 314 | 18 | 94 | 98 | 666 |
| Brunei | 160 | 243 | 682 | 2 | 423 | 643 | 105 |

Welt in Zahlen (Fernsehgeräte), Welt in Zahlen (PKW), 423Welt in Zahlen (Computer) and calculations based on Mitchell (2007), 796-803, 858-861 and Maddison (Population).

Table 38: Population of East Asia, 1950-2009 (Millions)

|             | 1950  | 1980    | 2009    |
|-------------|-------|---------|---------|
| **China**       | 546.8 | 981.2   | 1 331.4 |
| **Japan**       | 83.8  | 116.8   | 127.1   |
| **South Korea** | 20.8  | 38.1    | 48.5    |
| **North Korea** | 9.5   | 17.1    | 22.7    |
| **Taiwan**      | 7.5   | 17.8    | 23.0    |
| **East Asia**   | **668.4** | **1 171.1** | **1 552.7** |

Maddison (Population)

Table 39: Consumer Durables per 1,000 Inhabitants in East Asia, 1970-2006

| | Television sets | | | Passenger cars | | | Computers |
|---|---|---|---|---|---|---|---|
| | 1985 | 1995 | 2006 | 1970 | 1990 | 2006 | 2006 |
| **China** | 10 | 310 | 515 | 0.3 (78) | 1 | 12 | 58 |
| **Japan** | 580 | 682 | 835 | 60 | 284 | 528 | 456 |
| **South Korea** | 189 | 332 | 374 | 2 | 48 | 285 | 616 |
| **Taiwan** | | | 577 | 3 | 112 | 245 | 546 |

Welt in Zahlen (Fernsehgeräte), Welt in Zahlen (PKW), 423Welt in Zahlen (Computer) and calculations based on Mitchell (2007), 798, 800, 803, 858 f. and Maddison (Population).

Table 40: Cities with Over a Million Inhabitants in East Asia, 1950 and 1980 (Thousands)

| | 1950 | 1980 | | 1950 | 1980 |
|---|---|---|---|---|---|
| Shanghai | 5 407 | 11 185 | Beijing | 1 940 | 9 180 |
| Seoul | 1 446 | 8 364 | Tokyo | 6.778 | 8 352 |
| Tianjin | 1 786 | 5 152 | Hong Kong | 2.265 | 5 110 |
| Shenyang | 1 551 | 5 055 | Dalian | 1 054 | 4 619 |
| Wuhan | 1 008 | 3 288 | Guangzhou | 1 496 | 3 182 |
| Busan | 474 | 3 160 | Yokohama | 951 | 2 774 |
| Chongqing | 1 039 | 2 673 | Osaka | 1 956 | 2 648 |
| Harbin | 1 163 | 2 519 | Chengdu | 750 | 2 499 |
| Xi'an | 559 | 2 252 | Taipei | 503 | 2 220 |
| Zibo | 184 | 2 198 | Nanjing | 1 020 | 2 519 |
| Nagoya | 1 031 | 2 088 | Changchun | 855 | 1 747 |
| Taiyuan | 721 | 1 746 | Daegu | 314 | 1 605 |
| Kyoto | 1 102 | 1 473 | Kunming | 309 | 1 419 |
| Tangshan | 693 | 1 408 | Zhengzhou | 595 | 1 404 |
| Sapporo | 314 | 1 402 | Kobe | 765 | 1 367 |
| Lanzhou | 224 | 1 364 | Jinan | 680 | 1 359 |
| Guiyang | 242 | 1 350 | Pyongyang | 388 | 1 280 |
| Qiqihar | 345 | 1 209 | Anshan | 185 | 1 196 |
| Fushun | 679 | 1 185 | Qingdao | 884 | 1 172 |
| Hangzhou | 697 | 1 171 | Fuzhou | 553 | 1 112 |
| Fukuoka | 393 | 1 089 | Jilin | 435 | 1 088 |
| Incheon | 266 | 1 084 | Nanchang | 508 | 1 076 |
| Baotou | 149 | 1 076 | Shijiazhuang | 373 | 1 069 |
| Changsha | 651 | 1 066 | Kitakyushu | 711 | 1 065 |
| Kawasaki | 319 | 1 041 | Huainan | 287 | 1 025 |

Mitchell (2007), 42-46.

Table 41: Cities with Over a Million Inhabitants in Australia and New Zealand, 1950-2012 (Thousands)

|  | 1950 | 1980 | 2012 |
|---|---|---|---|
| **Sydney** | 1 484 | 2 877 | 4 667 |
| **Melbourne** | 1 226 | 2 578 | 4 246 |
| **Brisbane** | 402 | 942 | 2 190 |
| **Perth** | 273 | 809 | 1 898 |
| **Adelaide** | 382 | 883 | 1 277 |
| **Auckland** | 329 | 770 | 1 208 (2006) |

Mitchell (2007), 47 and List of cities (Australia and New Zealand).

# BIBLIOGRAPHY

Acemoglu/Robinson (2014) = Daron Acemoglu and James A. Robinson. *Warum Nationen scheitern. Die Ursprünge von Macht, Wohlstand und Armut.* Frankfurt am Main: Fischer Taschenbuch, 2014

Agrawal (1995) = Pradeep Agrawal. „Singapore: Export-Oriented Industrialization,“ in *Economic Restructuring in East Asia and India. Perspectives and Policy Reform.* ed. Pradeep Agraval. Basingstoke: Macmillan, 1995. 54-102

Agrawal (1995a) = Pradeep Agrawal. „Crisis and Response,“ in *Economic Restructuring in East Asia and India. Perspectives and Policy Reform,* ed. Pradeep Agraval et al. Basingstoke: Macmillan 1995, 159-216

Albertini (1985) = Rudolf Albertini. *Europäische Kolonialherrschaft: 1880-1940 (Beiträge zur Kolonial- und Überseegeschichte 14).* Stuttgart: Steiner, 1985

Allen (2009) = Robert C. Allen. *The British Industrial Revolution in Global Perspective.* Cambridge: Cambridge University, Press 2009

Amin (1997) = A. T. M. Nural Amin. „An enduring lesson from Thailand's economic performance,“ in *The ASEAN Region in Transition, ed.* Abu Wahid. Aldershot: Ashgate, 1997, 109-130

Amin (1997a) = Samir Amin. *Die Zukunft des Weltsystems. Herauforderungen der Globalisierung.* Hamburg: VSA-Verlag. 1997

Andrejew (1993) = Wladislaw Andrejew, Michail Sarafanov, and Valerij Oreskin. *Stand und Perspektiven der Wirtschaftsreform in der Russischen Föderation.* Cologne: Deutscher Instituts-Verlag, 1993

Austen (1987) = Ralpf A. Austen. *African Economic History. Internal Development and External Dependency.* London: Heinemann Education Books, 1987
Bairoch (1975) = Paul Bairoch. *The Economic Development of the Third World since 1900.* London: Methuen, 1975

Bairoch (1982) = Paul Bairoch. „International Industrialization Levels from 1750 to 1980," in: *Journal of European Economic History 11 (1982),* 269-310

Bairoch(1991) = Paul Bairoch. *Cities and Economic Development. From the Dawn of History to the Present.* Chicago: University of Chicago Press, 1991

Bairoch/Batou/Chèvre (1988) = Paul Bairoch, Jean Batou, and Pierre Chèvre. *La Population des villes européennes. Banque de donnés et analyse sommaire des résultats.* Geneva: Librairie Droz, 1988

Barbero/Rocchi (2003) = Maria Ines Barbero and Fernando Rocchi. „Industry," in *A New Economic History of Argentina, ed.* Gerardo della Paolera and Alan M. Taylor. Cambridge: Cambridge University Press, 2003, 261-294

Bauer (1988) = Michael Bauer. *Die Entwicklung der Industrie in ihrer räumlichen Differenzierung auf den Philippinen (Europäische Hochschulschriften, Reihe V, 883).* Frankfurt am Main: Lang, 1988

Bayly (2006) = Christopher A. Bayly. *Die Geburt der modernen Welt. Eine Globalgeschichte 1780-1914.* Frankfurt am Main: Campus, 2006

Berend (2006) = Ivan T. Berend. *An Economic History of Twentieth Century Europe. Economic Regimes from Laissez-Faire to Globalization.* Cambridge: Cambridge University Press, 2006
Berend/Ránki (1985) = Ivan T. Berend and György Ránki. „Ungarn, Rumänien, Bulgarien, Serbien und Montenegro 1850-1914,“ in *Handbuch der europäischen Wirtschafts- und Sozialgeschichte, Bd. 5 (Europäische Wirtschafts- und Sozialgeschichte von der Mitte des 19. Jahrhunderts bis zum Ersten Weltkrieg),* ed. Wolfram Fischer. Stuttgart: Klett-Cotta, 1985, 601-648

Bernecker/Segura (1985) = Walther L. Bernecker and Francisco Simón Segura. „Spanien 1850-1914,“ in *Handbuch der europäischen Wirtschafts- und Sozialgeschichte, Bd. 5 (Europäische Wirtschafts- und Sozialgeschichte von der Mitte des 19. Jahrhunderts bis zum Ersten Weltkrieg),* ed. Wolfram Fischer. Stuttgart: Klett-Cotta, 1985, 665-686

Bértola/Ocampo (2012) = Luis Bértola and José Antonio Ocampo. *The Economic Development of Latin America since Independence.* Oxford: Oxford University Press, 2012
Bértola/Williamson (2006) = Luis Bértola and Jeffrey G. Williamson. „Globalization in Latein America before 1940,“ in *The Cambridge Economic History of Latin America, vol. 2 (The Long Twentieth Century),* ed. Victor Bulmer-Thomas et al. Cambridge: Cambridge University Press, 2006, 11-56

Beschäftigungsstruktur 2013 = wko.at/statistik/eu/europa-beschaeftigungsstruktur.pdf
BIP pro Kopf 2015 = BIP pro Kopf im Jahr 2015 in 276 Regionen der EU – Europa EU. http://ec.europa.eu/eurostat/documents/2995521/7962769/1-30032017-AP-DE.pdf

Blanchard (1995) = Oliver Blanchard et al. „Unemployment and Restructuring in Eastern Europe and Russia,“ in *Unemployment, Restructuring, and the Labor Market in Eastern Europe and Russia,* ed. Simon  Commander and Fabrizio Coricelli. Washington, D.C.: World Bank, 1995, 289-329

Boehm (1971) = E. A. Boehm. *Twentieth Century Economic Development in Australia.* Camberwell: Longman, 1971

Braun/Grotz (2002) = Boris Braun and Reinhold Grotz. „Die Wirtschaft," in *Australien. Eine interdisziplinäre Einführung*, ed. Rudolf Bader. Trier: WVT, 2002, 163-203

Brink (2013) = Tobias ten Brink. *Chinas Kapitalismus. Entwicklung, Verlauf, Paradoxien (Schriften aus dem Max-Planck-Institut für Gesellschaftsforschung 78)*. Frankfurt am Main: Campus, 2013

Broadberry/O'Rourke (2010a) = Stephen Broadberry and Kevin O'Rourke (eds.). *The Cambridge Economic History of Modern Europe, vol. 1 (1700-1870)*. Cambridge: Cambridge University Press, 2010

Broadberry/O'Rourke (2010b) = Stephen Broadberry and Kevin O'Rourke (eds.). *The Cambridge Economic History of Modern Europe, vol. 2 (1870 to the Present)*. Cambridge: Cambridge University Press, 2010

Bronger (2004) = Dirk Bronger. *Metropolen. Megastädte, Global Cities. Die Metropolisierung der Erde*. Darmstadt: Wissenschaftliche Buchgesellschaft, 2004

Bronger/Trettin (2011) = Dirk Bronger and Trettin Lutz. *Megastädte – Global Cities heute: Das Zeitalter Asiens? (Asien, Wirtschaft und Entwicklung 5)*. Berlin: LIT Verlag, 2011

Buchheim (1994) = Christoph Buchheim. *Industrielle Revolutionen. Langfristige Wirtschaftsentwicklung in Großbritannien, Europa und Übersee*. Munich: Deutscher Taschenbuch-Verlag, 1994

Buchmann (1980) = M. Buchmann. „Die wirtschaftliche Entwicklung," in *Thailand. Geographie – Geschichte – Kultur – Religion –Staat – Gesellschaft –Wirtschaft (Buchreihe Ländermonographien 13)*, ed. Jürgen H. Hohnholz. Tübingen: Erdmann, 1980, 416-435

Buchmann (1980a) = M. Buchmann. „Die wirtschaftliche Entwicklung,“ in *Thailand. Geographie – Geschichte – Kultur – Religion –Staat – Gesellschaft –Wirtschaft (Buchreihe Ländermonographien 13),* ed. Jürgen H. Hohnholz. Tübingen: Erdmann, 1980, 436-452

Bulmer-Thomas (1994) = Victor Bulmer-Thomas. *The Economic History of Latin America since Independence.* Cambridge: Cambridge University Press, 1994

Cameron/Neal (2003) = Rondo Cameron and Larry Neal. *A Concise Economic History of the World. From Paleolithic Times to the Present.* New York: Oxford University Press, 2003
Canada Year Book (1997) = Statistics Canada (eds.). *Canada Year Book 1997.* Ottava: 1997
Cardin/Couture (1997) = Jean-François Cardin and Claude Couture. *Histoire du Canada. Espace et différence.* Québec: Presses de l'Université Laval, 1997

Cerman (2011) = Markus Cerman. „Vorindustrielles Gewerbe und Proto-Industrialisierung,“ in *Wirtschaft und Gesellschaft Europa 1000-2000 (VGS Studientexte 2),* ed. Markus Cerman et al. Vienna: StudienVerlag, 2011, 211-227

Chandler/Fox (1974) = Tertius Chandler and Gerald Fox. *3000 Years of Urban Growth.* New York: Academic Press, 1974

Chapman (1990) = S. D. Chapman. „The Cotton Industry and the Industrial Revolution,“ in *The Industrial Revolution. A Compendium,* ed. L. A. Clarkson. London: Macmillan, 1990, 1-64

Cheng (2002) = Hung-Chang Cheng. *International Trade, Productivity and Economic Growth: An Empirical Study on Economic Development of Taiwan.* Diss. Innsbruck, 2002
Cheng/Fung (2001) = Leonard K. Cheng and William K. Fung. „The Globalization of Trade and Production: A Case Study of Hong Kong's Textile and Clothing Industries“, in *Global Production and Trade in East Asia,* ed. Leonard K. Cheng and Henryk Kierzkowski. Boston: Kluwer Academic Publ., 2001, 227-248

China (2012a) = China –Bevölkerung nach Provinzen 2012 (de.statista.com > Branchen > Länder > China)

China (2012 b) = China – Bruttoinlandsprodukt (BIP) nach Provinzen 2012 (de.statista. com > Länder > China)

Chowdhury (1997) = Anis Chowdhury. „Malaysia in transition," in *The ASEAN Region in Transition,* ed. Abu N. Wahid. Aldershot: Ashgate, 1997, 43-64

Clark (2007) = Gregor Clark. *A Farewell to Alms. A Brief Economic History of the World.* Princeton: Princeton University Press, 2007

Clayton/Conniff (1999) = Lawrence Clayton and Michael Conniff. *A history of modern Latin America.* Fort Worth: Harcourt Brace College Publ., 1999

Collier/Sater (2004) = Simon Collier and William F. Sater. *A History of Chile, 1808-2000 (Cambridge Latin American Studies).* Cambridge: Cambridge University Press, 2004

Commander (1995) = Simon Commander et al. „Russia," in *Unemployment, Restructuring, and the Labor Market in Eastern Europe and Russia,* ed. Simon Commander and Fabrizio Coricelli, Fabrizio. Washington, D.C.: World Bank, 1995, 147-191

Cooper (2002) = Frederick Cooper. *Africa since 1940. The Past of the Present.* Cambridge: Cambridge University Press, 2002

Couturier (1994) = Jacques Paul Couturier. *L' expérience canadienne, des origines à nos jours.* Moncton: Éd. d'Acadie, 1994

Couturier (1996) = Jacques Paul Couturier. *Un passé composé. Le Canada de 1850 à nos jours.* Moncton: Éd. d'Acadie, 1996

Delivanis/Sundhausen (1985) = Dimitrios Delivanis and Holm Sundhausen. „Griechenland 1830-1914," in *Handbuch der europäischen Wirtschafts- und Sozialgeschichte, Bd. 5 (Europäische Wirtschafts- und Sozialgeschichte von der Mitte des 19. Jahrhunderts bis zum Ersten Weltkrieg)*, ed. Wolfram Fischer. Stuttgart: Klett-Cotta, 1985, 649-663

Diamond (1998) = Jared Diamond. *Arm und Reich. Die Schicksale menschlicher Gesellschaften*. Frankfurt am Main: S. Fischer, 1998

Donghi (1985) = Tulio Halperin Donghi. „Economy and Society in post-Independence Spanish America," in *The Cambridge History of Latin America, vol. 3*, ed. Leslie Bethell. Cambridge: Cambridge University Press, 1985, 299-345

Eaton/Newman (1994)   = Diane F. Eaton and Garfield Newman. *Canada, a nation unfolding*. Toronto: McGraw-Hill Ryerson, 1994

Ehmer (2011) = Josef Ehmer. "Bevölkerung und historische Demographie, in *Wirtschaft und Gesellschaft Europa 1000-2000 (VGS Studientexte 2)*, ed. Markus Cerman. Vienna: StudienVerlag, 2011, 134-160

Eigner (2011) = Peter Eigner. „Der Weg in die Industriegesellschaft," in *Wirtschaft und Gesellschaft Europa 1000-2000 (VGS Studientexte 2)*, ed. Markus Cerman. Vienna: StudienVerlag, 2011, 104-133

Elsenhans (1982) = Hartmut Elsenhans. „Grundlagen der Entwicklung der kapitalistischen Weltwirtschaft," in *Kapitalistische Weltökonomie. Kontroversen über ihren Ursprung und ihre Entwicklungsdynamik*, ed. Dieter Senghaas. Frankfurt am Main: Suhrkamp, 1982, 103-148
Eng (2002) = Pierre van der Eng. „Indonesia's Growth Performance in the Twentieth Century," in *The Asian Economies in the Twentieth Century*, ed. Angus Maddison. Cheltenham: Elgar, 2002, 143-179

Engelhard (2004) = Karl Engelhard. *Südkorea. Vom Entwicklungsland zum Industriestaat.* Münster: Waxmann, 2004

Engerman/Sokoloff (2000) = Stanley L. Engerman and Kenneth L. Sokoloff. „Technology and Industrialization, 1790-1914, in *The Cambridge Economic History of the United States, vol. 2 (The Long Nineteenth Century),* ed. Stanley L. Engerman and Robert E. Gallman. Cambridge: Cambridge University Press, 2000, 367-401

Escosura (2006) = Leandro Prados de la Escosura. „The Economic Consequences of Independence in Latin America," in *The Cambridge Economic History of Latin America, vol. 1 (The Colonial Era and the Short Nineteenth Century),* ed. Victor Bulmer-Thomas et al. Cambridge: Cambridge University Press, 2006, 463-504

Evans (1996) = Eric J. Evans. *The Forging oft he Modern State. Early Industrial Britain 1783-1870.* London: Longman, 1996

Eversley (1967) = D. E. C. Eversley. „The Home Market and Economic Growth in England, 1750-1780," in *Land, Labour and Population in the Industrial Revolution,* ed. E. L. Jones and G. E. Mingay. London: Edward Arnold, 1967, 206-259

Faria (1989) = Vilmar Faria. „Changes in the Composition of Employment and the Structure of Occupations," in *Social Change in Brazil, 1945-198,* ed. Edmar L .Bacha and Herbert S. Klein. Albuquerque: University of New Mexico Press, 1989, 99-140

Feinstein (2005) = Charles Feinstein. *An Economic History of South Africa: Conquest, Discrimination and Development.* Cambridge: Cambridge University Press, 2005

Fellmeth/Rohde (1999) = Sebastian Fellmeth and Christian Rohde. *Der Abbau eines Wohlfahrtsstaates. Neuseeland als Modell für das nächste Jahrhundert?* Marburg: Metropolis, 1999

Fessen/Kubitschek (1984) = Helmut Fessen and Hans Dieter Kubitschek. *Geschichte Malaysias und Singapurs*. Berlin: Deutscher Verlag der Wissenschaft, 1984

Fischer (1968) = Ludolph Fischer. *Afghanistan: eine geographisch-medizinische Landeskunde/A Geomedical Monograph (Medizinische Länderkunde. Beiträge zur geographischen Medizin 2)*. Berlin: Springer, 1968.

Fischer (1985) = Wolfram Fischer. „Wirtschaft und Gesellschaft 1850-1914", in Fischer, Wolfram (Hg.): *Handbuch der europäischen Wirtschafts- und Sozialgeschichte, vol. 5 (Europäische Wirtschafts- und Sozialgeschichte von der Mitte des 19. Jahrhunderts bis zum Ersten Weltkrieg)*, ed. Wolfram Fischer. Stuttgart: Klett-Cotta, 1985, 1-207.

Fischer (1987) = Fischer, Wolfram: „Wirtschaft, Gesellschaft und Staat in Europa 1914-1980", in *Handbuch der europäischen Wirtschafts- und Sozialgeschichte, vol. 6 (Europäische Wirtschafts- und Sozialgeschichte vom Ersten Weltkrieg bis zur Gegenwart)*, ed. Wolfram Fischer. Stuttgart: Klett-Cotta, 1987, 1-221.

Fischer (2011) = Karin Fischer. *Eine Klasse für sich: Besitz, Herrschaft und ungleiche Entwicklung in Chile 1830-2010*. Baden-Baden: Nomos, 2011.

Fischer Weltalmanach (1990) = *Der Fischer Weltalmanach ´90. Zahlen Daten Fakten*. Frankfurt am Main: Fischer Taschenbuch, 1989.

Fischer Weltalmanach (1992) = *Der Fischer Weltalmanach ´92. Zahlen Daten Fakten*. Frankfurt am Main: Fischer Taschenbuch, 1991.

Fischer Weltalmanach (1995) = *Der Fischer Weltalmanach ´95. Zahlen Daten Fakten*, ed. Mario von Baratta. Frankfurt am Main: Fischer Taschenbuch, 1994.

Fischer Weltalmanach (2000) = *Der Fischer Weltalmanach 2000. Zahlen Daten Fakten*, ed. Mario von Baratta. Frankfurt am Main: Fischer Taschenbuch, 1999

Fischer Weltalmanach (2005) = *Der Fischer Weltalmanach 2005. Zahlen Daten Fakten.* Frankfurt am Main: Fischer Taschenbuch, 2004.

Fischer Weltalmanach (2005a) = *Der Fischer Weltalmanach. Russland und der Kaukasus,* ed. Volker Ulrich and Eva Berié. Frankfurt am Main: Fischer Taschenbuch, 2005.

Fischer Weltalmanach (2008) = *Der Fischer Weltalmanach 2008. Zahlen Daten Fakten.* Frankfurt am Main: Fischer Taschenbuch 2007.

Fischer Weltalmanach (2011) = *Der Fischer Weltalmanach 2011. Zahlen Daten Fakten.* Frankfurt am Main: Fischer Taschenbuch 2010.

Fishlow (2000) = Albert Fishlow. „Internal Transportation in the Nineteenth and Early Twentieth Centuries", in *The Cambridge Economic History of the United States, vol. 2 (The Long Nineteenth Century),* ed. Stanley L. Engerman and Robert E. Gallman. Cambridge: Cambridge University Press 2000, 543-642.

Fitzpatrick (1969) = Brian Fitzpatrick. *The British Empire in Australia. An Economic History 1834-1939.* Melbourne: Macmillan, 1969.

Frank (1978) = Andre Gunder Frank. *Dependent Accumulation and Underdevelopment.* London: Macmillan, 1978.

Frank (1978a) = Ander Gunder Frank. *Weltwirtschaft in der Krise. Verarmung im Norden, Verelendung im Süden.* Reinbeck bei Hamburg: Rowohlt Taschenbuch, 1978.

Frank (2005) = Ander Gunder Frank. *Orientierung im Weltsystem. Von der Neuen Welt zum Reich der Mitte.* Vienna: Promedia, 2005.

Frank (2005a) = Rüdiger Frank. „Nordkoreas Wirtschaft", in *Südkorea und Nordkorea. Einführung in Geschichte, Politik, Wirtschaft und Gesellschaft*, ed. Thomas Kern and Patrick Köllner. Frankfurt am Main: Campus 2005, 235-257.

Frey (1986) = Ulrich Frey. *Entwicklungsländer im Systemvergleich. Sozialistische Verelendung und marktwirtschaftliches Wachstum. China-Taiwan, Nordkorea-Südkorea, Guinea-Elfenbeinküste, Tansania-Kenia.* Kreuzlingen: Edition Erpf bei Neptun, 1986.

Galiani/Gerchunoff (2003) = Sebastian Galiani and Pablo Gerchunoff. „The labour market", in *A New Economic History of Argentina*, ed. Gerardo della Paolera and Alan M. Taylor. Cambridge: Cambridge University Press 2003, 122-169.

Gallman (2000) = Robert E. Gallman. „Economic Growth and Structural Change in the Long Nineteenth Century", in *The Cambridge Economic History of the United States, vol. 3 (The Twentieth Century)*, ed. Stanley L. Engerman and Robert E. Gallman. Cambridge: Cambridge University Press 2000, 191-247.

Gilboy (1932) = E. W. Gilboy. „Demand as a Factor in the Industrial Revolution", in *The Causes of the Industrial Revolution in England*, ed. R. M. Hartwell. London: Methuen, 1967.

Gokarn (1995) = Subir V. Gokarn. „Industrial and Financial Restructuring", in *Economic Restructuring in East Asia and India. Perspectives and Policy Reform*, ed. Pradeep Agraval. Basingstoke: Macmillan, 1995, 22-53.

Gómez-Galvarriato (2006) = Aurora Gómez-Galvarriato. „Premodern Manufacturing", in *The Cambridge Economic History of Latin America, vol. 1 (The Colonial Era and the Short Nineteenth Century)*, ed. Victor Bulmer-Thomas et al. Cambridge: Cambridge University Press, 2006, 357-394.

Goswin (1996) = Thomas Goswin et al. „Wirtschaftsordung und Wirtschaftspolitik", in *Studien zur chinesischen Wirtschaft (Strukturen der Macht. Studien zum politischen Denken Chinas 1)*, ed. Konrad Wegmann. Münster: LIT Verlag, 1996, 8-102.

Green (2000) = Alan G. Green. „Twentieth-Century Canadian Economic History", in *The Cambridge Economic History of the United States, vol. 2 (The Long Nineteenth Century)*, Cambridge: Cambridge University Press, 2000,

Green (2003) = Duncan Green. *Silent Revolution. The Rise and Crisis of Market Economies in Latin America.* New York, 2003.

Grondana (2002) = Mariano Grondana. „Eine kulturelle Typologie der wirtschaftlichen Entwicklung", in *Streit um Werte. Wie Kulturen den Fortschritt prägen,* ed. Samuel P. Huntington and Lawrence E Harrison. Hamburg: Europa Verlag, 2002, 75-89.

Growth Amid Change (2007) = *Growth Amid Change in Developing Asia,* ed. Asian Development Bank, 2007

Haber (2006) = Stephen Haber. „The Political Economy of Industrialization", in *The Cambridge Economic History of Latin America, vol. 2 (The Long Twentieth Century),* ed Victor Bulmer-Thomas. Cambridge: Cambridge University Press, 2006, 537-586.

Hagemann (2004) = Albrecht Hagemann. *Kleine Geschichte Australiens.* München: Beck, 2004.

Haines (2000) = Michael R. Haines. „The Population of the United States, 1790-1920", in *The Cambridge Economic History of the United States, vol. 2 (The Long Nineteenth Century),* ed. Stanley L. Engerman and Robert E. Gallman. Cambridge: Cambridge University Press, 2000, 143-205.

Harberger (1988) = Arnold C. Harberger. „Growth, Industrialization and Economic Structure: Latin America and East Asia Compared", in *Achieving Industrialization in East Asia,* ed. Helen Hughes. Cambridge: Cambridge University Press, 1988, 164-194.

Hasan (1976) = Parvez Hasan. *Korea. Problems and Issues in a Rapidly Growing Economy.* Baltimore: Johns Hopkins University Press, 1976,

Hauer (1998) = Gabriele Hauer. *Direktinvestitionen im tertiären Sektor. Das Beispiel Sidney, Australien (Kölner Forschungen zur Wirtschafts- und Sozialgeographie 49).* Cologne: Wirtschafts- und Sozialgeographisches Institut der Universität Köln, 1998.

Heim (2000) = Carol R. Heim. „Structural Changes: Regional and Urban", in *The Cambridge Economic History of the United States, vol. 3 (The Twentieth Century).* ed. Stanley L. Engerman and Robert E. Gallman. Cambridge: Cambridge University Press 2000, 93-190.

Heimat und Welt (Südasien – Wirtschaft) = Heimat und Welt Weltatlas + Geschichte – Nordrhein-Westfalen – 978-3-14-100267-6, Seite 117 (www.heimatundwelt.de/kartenansicht.xtp?artId=978-3-14-100267-6)

Helmschrott (1990) = Helmut Helmschrott, Eberhard von Pilgrim, and Siegfried Schönherr. *Afrika südlich der Sahara: trotz Rohstoffreichtum in die Armut.* München: Weltforum-Verlag, 1990.

Hentschel (1986) = Volker Hentschel. *Wirtschaftsgeschichte des modernen Japans, 2 vol.. (Wissenschaftliche Paperbacks 22 and 23).* Stuttgart: Steiner, 1986.

Herrman-Pillath (1995) = Carsten Herrmann-Pillath. *Marktwirtschaft in China. Geschichte – Struktur – Transformation.* Opladen: Leske+Budrich, 1995.

Hewett (1988) = Ed A. Hewett. *Der neue Markt Sowjetunion. Effizienz und Perestroika in der sowjetischen Wirtschaft.* Landsberg am Lech: Mi-Poller, 1988.

Historical Statistics (1960) = *Historical Statistics of the United States, Colonial Times to 1957.* Washington, D.C., 1960.

Hofman (2000) = André A. Hofman. *The Economic Development of Latin America in the Twentieth Century*. Cheltenham: Edward Elgar, 2000.

Hofmeister (2002) = Burkhard Hofmeister. „Geographie: Kulturlandschaft", in *Australien. Eine interdisziplinäre Einführung,* ed. Rudolf Bader. Trier: WVT 2002, 19-35.

Hossain (1997) = Mahabub Hossain. „Economic development in the Philippines: a frustrated take-off?", in *The ASEAN Region in Transition,* ed. Abu N. Wahid. Aldershot: Ashgate 1997, 65-86.

Houtte (1980) = Jan A. van Houtte. „Europäische Wirtschaft und Gesellschaft von den großen Wanderungen bis zum Schwarzen Tod", in *Handbuch der europäischen Wirtschafts- und Sozialgeschichte, vol. 2 (Europäische Wirtschafts- und Sozialgeschichte im Mittelalter),* ed. Jan A. van Houtte. Stuttgart: Klett-Cotta 1980, 1-149.

Hübner-Schmid (2004) = Katharina Hübner-Schmid. *Studien zur länderbezogenen Konfliktanalyse. Pakistan.* Berlin: Friedrich-Ebert-Stiftung, Referat Entwicklungspolitik, 2004.

Hughes (1988) = Hughes, Helen (ed.). *Achieving Industrialization in East Asia*. Cambridge: Cambridge University Press, 1988.

Hutchings (1971) = Raymond Hutchings. *Soviet Economic Development*. Oxford: Basil Blackwell, 1971.

Ingram (1971) = James C. Ingram. *Economic Change in Thailand: 1850-1970*. Stanford: Stanford University Press, 1971.

Issawi (1982) = Charles Issawi. *An Economic History of the Middle East and North Africa*. New York: Columbia University Press, 1982.

Japan (Präfekturen) = Liste der Präfekturen Japans (de.wikipedia.org/wiki/ Liste_der_Präfekturen_Japans)

Japan-Perspektiven (1990) = *Japan-Perspektiven: Wirtschaft, Gesellschaft, Markt,* ed. Frankfurter Allgemeine Zeitung GmbH Informationsdienste, Frankfurt am Main, 1990.

Johnson/Kaufmann (2001) = Simon Johnson and Daniel Kaufmann. „Institution and the Underground Economy", in *A Decade of Transition: Achievements and Challenges,* ed. Oleh Havrylyshyn and M. Saleh. Washington, D.C.: International Monetary Fund 2001, 212-228.

Jones (1981) = Eric Jones. *The European Miracle. Environments, Economies and Geopolitics in the History of Europe and Asia.* Cambridge: Cambridge University Press, 1981.

Jones (2002) = Eric Jones. *The Record of Global Economic Development.* Cheltenham: Edward Elgar, 2002.

Kafle (2007) = Agni Prasad Kafle. *Workforce Development in Nepal. Policies and Practices.* Tokio: Asian Development Bank Institute, 2007.

Kahan (1985) = Arcadius Kahan. „Rußland und Kongreßpolen 1860-1914", in *Handbuch der europäischen Wirtschafts- und Sozialgeschichte, vol. 5 (Europäische Wirtschafts- und Sozialgeschichte von der Mitte des 19. Jahrhunderts bis zum Ersten Weltkrieg),* ed. Wolfram Fischer. Stuttgart: Klett-Cotta, 1985, 512-600.

Katzmann (1989) = Martin T. Katzman. „Urbanization since 1845", in *Social Change in Brazil, 1945-1985,* ed. Edmar L. Bacha and Herbert S. Klein. Albuquerque: University of New Mexico Press 1989, 99-140.

Kerr (1990) = Donald Kerr et al. (eds.). *Historical Atlas of Canada, vol. 3. Addressing the Twentieth Century: 1891-1961.* Toronto u.a.: University of Toronto Press, 1990

Kim (1990) = Young-Yoon Kim. *Die asiatische Pazifikregion. Entstehung eines neuen Weltwirtschaftsraumes (Studien zur Bremer Gesellschaft für Wirtschaftsforschung 1).* Frankfurt am Main: Lang, 1990.

Kim (2001) = Hyecheong Kim. *The ,Chaebol-Economy'. Its Role and Impact for the Economic Development of South Korea.* Dipl. Innsbruck, 2001.

Kingston (1988) = Beverley Kingston. *The Oxford History of Australia, vol. 3. (1860-1900: glad, confident, morning).* Melbourne: Oxford University Press, 1988.

Knapman/Quiggin (1997) = Bruce Knapman and John Quiggin. *The Australian Economy in the Twentieth Century.* Bremen: LIT Verlag, 1997.

Köllmann (1965) = Wolfgang Köllmann. *Bevölkerung und Raum in Neuerer und Neuester Zeit (Raum und Bevölkerung in der Weltgeschichte. Bevölkerungs-Ploetz 4).* Würzburg: A. G. Ploetz, 1965.

Kötter (1979) = Herbert Kötter et al. (eds.). *Indonesien. Geographie, Geschichte, Kultur, Religion, Staat, Gesellschaft, Bildungswesen, Politik, Wirtschaft.* Tübingen: Erdmann, 1979.
Kolb (1984) = Frank Kolb. *Die Stadt im Altertum.* München: Beck, 1984.

Kolb (2006) = Frank Kolb. „Die ,Hauptstadt der Welt' – Flaniermeilen, Tempel und Wohnquartiere", in *Antike Metropolen,* ed. Walter Ameling. Darmstadt: Wissenschaftliche Buchgesellschaft 2006, 92-108.

Kratoska (1998) = Paul H. Kratoska. *The Japanese Occupation of Malaya. A Social and Economic History.* London: Hurst, 1998.

Kraus (1979) = Willy Kraus. *Wirtschaftliche Entwicklung und sozialer Wandel in der Volksrepublik China.* Berlin: Springer, 1979.

Kreisel (2009) = Werner Kreisel. „Die wirtschaftliche Entwicklung der pazifischen Inselländer 1750-2000", in *Ozeanien 18. Bis 20. Jahrhundert. Geschichte und Gesellschaft,* ed. Hermann Mückler et al. Vienna: Promedia 2009, 246-266.

Kuchis (Afghanistan) = Kuo (1982) = Kuo, Xing-Hu: *Freies China. Asiatisches Wirtschaftswunder.* Stuttgart: Seewald 1982.

Kwack (1986) = Sung Yeung Kwack. „The Economic Development of the Republic of Korea", in *Models of Development. A Comparative Study of Economic Growth in South Korea and Taiwan,* ed. Lawrence Lau (ed.). San Francisco: ICS Press 1986, 65-135.

Lal (1988) = Deepak Lal. „Ideology and Industrialization in India and East Asia", in *Achieving Industrialization in East Asia,* ed. Helen Hughes. Cambridge: Cambridge University Press, 1988, 195-240.

Lamoureux (2003) = Florence Lamoureux. *Indonesia. A Global Studies Handbook.* Santa Barbara: ABC Clio, 2003.

Landes (1969) = David Saul Landes. *The Unbound Prometheus. Technological change and industrial development in Western Europe from 1750 to the present.* Cambridge: Cambridge University Press, 1969.

Landes (1973) = David Saul Landes. *Der entfesselte Prometheus. Technologischer Wandel und industrielle Entwicklung in Westeuropa von 1750 bis zur Gegenwart.* Cologne: Kiepenheuer & Witsch, 1973.

Landes (1998) = David Saul Landes. *The Wealth and Poverty of Nations: Why Some Are So Rich and Some So Poor.* New York: W. W. Norton, 1998.

Landes (2002) = David Saul Landes. *Armut und Wohlstan der Nationen. Warum die einen reich und die anderen arm sind.* Berlin: Berliner Taschenbuch-Verlag, 2002.

Larsen (1996) = Sven Larsen. „Die demographische Entwicklung der Volksrepublik China", in *Studien zur chinesischen Wirtschaft (Strukturen der Macht. Studien zum politischen Denken Chinas 1)*, ed. Konrad Wegmann. Münster: LIT Verlag 1996, 142-187.

Lechleitner (1972) = Herwig Lechleitner. *Die Rolle des Staates in der wirtschaftlichen und sozialen Entwicklung Libanons (Wiener geographische Schriften 36/37)*. Vienna: Hirt, 1972.
Linteau/Brown (1988) = Paul-André Linteau and Robert Craig Brown. *Histoire générale du Canada*. Montreal: Boréal, 1988.

Lions (2010) = *Lions on the move: The progress and potential of African economies*. Ed. McKinsey Global Institute, 2010.

Lipsey (1972) = Robert Lipsey. „Foreign Trade", in *American Economic Growth. An Economist's History oft he United States*, ed. E. Davis Lance. New York: Harper & Row, 1972, 548-581.

List of cities = List of cities in Albania to List of cities and towns in Zimbabwe. https://en.wikipedia.org/wiki/List_of_cities_in_Albania   to   https://en.wikipedia.org/wiki/List_of_cities_and_towns_in_Zimbabwe

List of countries (GDP) = List of countries by GDP (PPP) per capita – Wikipedia. https://en.wikipedia.org/wiki/List_of_countries_by_GDP_(PPP)_per_capita

List of countries (Steel) = List of countries by steel production  Wikipedia. https://en.wikipedia.org/wiki/List_of_countries_by_steel_production

List of metropolitan areas in Africa  =  https://en.wikipedia.org/wiki/List_of_metropolitan_areas_in_Africa

Looney (1977) = Robert L. Looney. *A Development Strategy for Iran through the 1980's*. New York: Praeger, 1977

Lopez (1971) = Robert S. Lopez. *The Commercial Revolution of the Middle Ages 950-1350.* Englewood Cliffs, N.J.: Prentice Hall, 1971.

Mabro/Radwan (1978) = Robert Mabro and Samir Radwan. *The Industrialization of Egypt 1939-1973. Policy and Performance.* Oxford: Clarendon Press, 1978.

Mackie (1988) = J. A. C. Mackie. „Economic Growth in the ASEAN region: the political underpinnings", in *Achieving Industrialization in East Asia,* ed. Helen Hughes. Cambridge: Cambridge University Press, 1988, 283-326.

Maddison (Per Capita GDP) = Historical Statistics of the World Economy. www.ggdc.net/maddison/historical_statistics/horizontal-file_02-2010.xls

Maddison (Population) = Historical Statistics of the World Economy. www.ggdc.net/maddison/historical_statistics/horizontal-file_02-2010.xls

Maddison (2001) = Angus Maddison. *The World Economy: A Millenial Perspective.* Paris: OECD, 2001.

Maddison (2007) = Angus Maddison. *Contours of the World Economy, 1-2030 AD.* Oxford: Oxford University Press, 2007.

Malanima (2010) = Paolo Malanima. „Urbanization", in *The Cambridge Economic History of Modern Europe, vol. 1 (1700-1870),* ed. Stephen Broadberry and Kevin H. O'Rourke. Cambridge: Cambridge University Press 2010, 235-264.

Mansfield (1980) = Peter Mansfield (ed.): *The Middle East. A Political and Economic Survey.* Oxford: Oxford University Press, 1980.

Margo (2000) = Robert A. Margo. „The Labor Force in the Nineteenth Century", in *The Cambridge Economic History of the United States, vol. 2 (The Long Nineteenth Century)*, ed. Stanley L. Engerman and Robert E. Gallman. Cambridge: Cambridge University Press, 2000, 207-243.

Mathieu (2011) = Jon Mathieu. *Die dritte Dimension. Eine vergleichende Geschichte der Berge in der Neuzeit (Wirtschafts-, Sozial- und Umweltgeschichte 3)*. Basel: Schwabe, 2011.
Mathis (2006) = Franz Mathis. „Insel und Industrialisierung. Japan und Großbritannien im Vergleich", in *Bericht über den 24. Österreichischen Historikertag in Innsbruck,* ed. Verband Österreichischer Historiker und Geschichtsvereine. Innsbruck: 2006, 222-235.

Mathis (2007) = Franz Mathis. „Erste Welt und Dritte Welt in einem Land. Zum Nord-Süd-Gefälle in der Wirtschaft Italiens", in *Politik-Konflikt-Gewalt (Innsbrucker Historische Studien 25),* ed.: Robert Rebitsch and Elena Taddei. Innsbruck: StudienVerlag 2007, 333-341.
Mathis (2011) = Franz Mathis. „Industrialisierung in der Antike – zum Scheitern verurteilt?", in *Gegenwart und Altertum. 125 Jahre Alte Geschichte in Innsbruck*, ed. Robert Rollinger and Gundula Schwinghammer. Innsbruck, 2011, 97-114.

Mathis (2012) = Franz Mathis. „Wirtschaftliche Entwicklung - ein regionaler statt nationaler Prozess", in *Internationale Studien zur Geschichte von Wirtschaft und Gesellschaft, part 1,* ed. Karl W. Hardach. Frankfurt am Main: Peter Lang 2012, S. 589-601.

Mathis (2013) = Franz Mathis. „No Industrialization without Urbanization: The Role of Cities in Modern Economic Development", in *Globalization and the City. Two Connected Phenomena in Past and Present*, ed. Andreas Exenberger et al. Innsbruck: innsbruck university press 2013, 23-38.

Matis (1988) = Herbert Matis. *Das Industriesystem: Wirtschaftswachstum und sozialer Wandel im 19. Jahrhundert*. Vienna: Ueberreuter, 1988.

Matis/Bachinger (1973) = Herbert Matis and Karl Bachinger, Karl. „Österreichs industrielle Entwicklung", in *Die wirtschaftliche Entwicklung (Die Habsburgermonarchie 1848-1918)*, ed. Herbert Brusatti. Vienna: Österreichische Akademie der Wissenschaften, 1973, 105-232.
McAuley (1992) = Alastair McAuley. „The Central Asian economy in comparative perspective", in *The Disintegration of the Soviet Economic Syste*, ed.: Michael Ellman and Vladimir Kontorovich. London: Routledge, 1992, 138-156.

McInnis/Horn (1982) = Edgar McInnis and Michiel Horn. *Canada: A Political & Social History*. Toronto: Holt, Rinehart & Winston of Canada, 1982.

McInnis (2000) = Marvin McInnis. „The Ecomomy of Canada in the Nineteenth Century", in *The Cambridge Economic History of the United States, vol. 2 (The Long Nineteenth Century)*, ed. Stanley L. Engerman and Robert E. Gallman. Cambridge: Cambridge University Press, 2000, 57-107.

Mauro (1984) = Frédéric Mauro. *Die europäische Expansion (Wissenschaftliche Paperbacks 17)*. Wiesbaden: Steiner, 1984.

Menzel (1985) = Ulrich Menzel. *In der Nachfolge Europas. Autozentrierte Entwicklung in den ostasiatischen Schwellenländern Südkorea und Taiwan*. München: Simon & Magiera, 1985.

Menzel (1993) = Ulrich Menzel. *Geschichte der Entwicklungstheorie. Einführung und systematische Bibliographie (Schriften des Deutschen Übersee-Instituts Hamburg 18)*. Hamburg :Deutsches Übersee-Institut, 1993.

Menzel/Senghaas (1986) = Ulrich Menzel and Dieter Senghaas. Dieter: *Europas Entwicklung und die Dritte Welt: Eine Bestandsaufnahme*. Frankfurt am Main: Suhrkamp, 1986.
Merl (1987) = Stephan Merl. „Rußland und die Sowjetunion 1914-1980", in *Handbuch der europäischen Wirtschafts- und Sozialgeschichte, vol.. 6 (Europäische Wirtschafts- und Sozialgeschichte vom Ersten Weltkrieg bis zur Gegenwart)*. ed. Wolfram Fischer. Stuttgart: Klett-Cotta 1987, 640-728.

Merrick/Graham (1979) = Thomas W. Merrick and Douglas H. Graham. *Population and Economic Development in Brazil. 1800 to the Present*. Baltimore, 1979.

Mishra (1995) = Veena Mishra. „Adjustement in the 1980s", in *Economic Restructuring in East Asia and India. Perspectives and Policy Reform,* ed. Pradeep Agraval et al. Basingstoke: Macmillan 1995, 103-133.

Mitchell (1975) = Brian R. Mitchell. *International Historical Statistics: Europe, 1750-1970.* London and Basingstoke: Macmillan, 1975.

Mitchell (1992) = Brian R. Mitchell. *International Historical Statistics: Europe, 1750-1988.* Basingstoke: Macmillan, 1992.

Mitchell (1998) = Brian R. Mitchel. *International Historical Statistics: The Americas, 1750-1993.* London: Macmillan. 1998.

Mitchell (2003) = Brian R. Mitchell.: *International Historical Statistics: Europe, 1750-2000.* Basingstoke: Palgrave Macmillan, 2003.

Mitchell (2007) = Brian R. Mitchell. *International Historical Statistics: Africa, Asia & Oceania, 1750-2005.* New York: Palgrave Macmillan, 2007.

Mitterauer (2003) = Michael Mitterauer. *Warum Europa? Mittelalterliche Grundlagen eines Sonderweges.* München: Beck, 2003

Moreno-Brid/Ros (2009) = Juan Carlos Moreno-Brid and Jamie Ros. *Development and Growth in the Mexican Economy: A Historical Perspective.* Oxford: Oxford University Press, 2009.

Moyo (2011) = Dambisa Moyo. *Dead Aid. Warum Entwicklungshilfe nicht funktioniert und was Afrika besser machen kann.* Berlin: Haffmans & Tolkemitt, 2011.

Myers (1986) = Raymon H. Myers. „The Economic Development oft he Republic of China on Taiwan, 1965-1981", in *Models of Development. A Comparative Study of Economic Growth in South Korea and Taiwan,* ed. Lawrence Lau. San Francisco: ICS Press, 1986, 13-64.

Nadal (1977) = Jordi Nadal. „Der Fehlschlag der Industriellen Revolution in Spanien 1830-1914", in *Die Entwicklung der industriellen Gesellschaften (Europ*äische Wirtschaftsgeschichte 4), ed. Carlo M. Cipolla and Knut Borchardt. Stuttgart: Gustav Fischer, 1977, 341-401.

Naya (1988) = Seiji Naya. „The Role of Trade Policies in the Industrialization of rapidly growing Asian developing countries", in *Achieving Industrialization in East Asia,* ed. Helen Hughes. Cambridge: Cambridge University Press, 1988, 64-94.

Newson (2006) = Linda A. Newson. „The Demographic Impact of Colonization", in *The Cambridge Economic History of Latin America, vol. 1 (The Colonial Era and the Short Nineteenth Century),* ed. Victor Bulmer-Thomas et al. Cambridge: Cambridge University Press, 2006, 143-184.

Niemi (1997) = Albert W. Niemi. *Economic History: A Survey of the Major Issues.* Chicago: Rand McNally College Publishing Company, 1997.

Noor (1974) = Abdul Sami Noor. *Die Rolle des Außenhandels in der wirtschaftlichen Entwicklung Afghanistans.* Diss. Bonn, 1974.

North (1961) = Douglas C. North. *The Economic Growth of the United States, 1790–1860.* Upper Saddle River, N.J.:, Prentice Hall, 1961

North (1988) = Douglas C. North. *Theorie des institutionellen Wandels. Eine neue Sicht der Wirtschaftsgeschichte.* Tübingen: Mohr, 1988.

North (2005) = Douglas C. North. *Understanding the Process of Economic Change.* Princeton: Princeton University Press, 2005..

Nove (1982) = Alec Nove. *An Economic History of the U.S.S.R.* Harmondsworth: Penguin Books, 1982.

O'Brien (1982) = Patrick O'Brien. „European Economic Development: The Contribution of the Periphery", in *The Economic History Review 35 (1982)*, 1-18.

Ochel (1978) = Wolfgang Ochel. *Die Industrialisierung der arabischen OPEC-Länder und des Iran. Erdöl und Erdgas im Industrialisierungsprozess (Ifo-Studien zur Entwicklungsforschung 5)*. Munich: Weltforum, 1978.

OECD Australia = *OECD Economic Surveys. Australia.* Paris, 1976-2001.

OECD (2002) = *OECD Economic Surveys 2001-2002. Russian Federation.* Paris, 2002.

OECD Turkey = *OECD Economic Surveys. Turkey.* Paris, 1990/91-2002.

Osterhammel (2010) = Jürgen Osterhammel. *Die Verwandlung der Welt. Eine Geschichte des 19. Jahrhunderts.* Munich: Beck, 2010.

Outlook (2013) = International Monetary Fund (ed.): *Regional Economic Outlook: Sub-Saharan Africa – Keeping the Pace. 2013* (Regional Economic Outlook, October 2013: Sub-Saharan…https://www.imf.org/external/pubs/.../longres.aspx?s...)

Paolera/Taylor (2003) = Gerardo della Paolera and Alan M. Taylor (eds.). *A New Economic History of Argentina.* Cambridge: Cambridge University Press, 2003.

Pascha (1990) = Werner Pascha. „Dritte Welt im Aufbruch: Ostasiatische Schwellenländer als neue weltwirtschaftliche Entwicklungspole?", in *Wirtschaftssysteme im Umbruch. Sowjetunion, China und industrialisierte Marktwirtschaften zwischen internationalem Anpassungszwang und nationalem Reformbedarf,* ed. Dieter Cassel. Munich: Vahlen, 1990, 92-120.

Pascha (2005) = Werner Pascha. „Südkoreas Wirtschaft", in *Südkorea und Nordkorea. Einführung in Geschichte, Politik, Wirtschaft und Gesellschaft,* ed. Thomas Kern and Patrick Köllner. Frankfurt am Main: Campus, 2005, 87-120.

Phyllis (1998) = Deane Phyllis. „Die Industrielle Revolution in Großbritannien", in *Die Industrielle Revolution in England, Deutschland und Italien.* ed. Roy Porter and Mikulas Teich. Berlin: Wagenbach, 1998, 33-57

Pierenkemper (1996) = Toni Pierenkemper. *Umstrittene Revolutionen. Die Industrialisierung im 19. Jahrhundert.* Frankfurt am Main: Fischer Taschenbuch, 1996.

Pilat (2002) = Dirk Pilat. „The Long-Term Performance of the Japanese Economy", in *The Asian Economies in the Twentieth Century,* ed. Angus Maddison, Cheltenham: Edward Elgar, 2002, 180-225.

Pockney (1991) = Bertram Patrick Pockney. *Soviet Statistics since 1950.* Dartmouth: Aldershot, 1991.

Pollard (1981) = Sidney Pollard. *Peaceful Conquest. The Industrialization 1760-1970.* Oxford: Oxford University Press, 1981.

Pomeranz (2000) = Kenneth Pomeranz. *The Great Divergence: China, Europe and the Making of the Modern World Economy.* Princeton: Princeton University Press, 2000.
Pomfret (1996) = Richard Pomfret. *Asian Economies in Transition. Reforming Centrally Planned Economies.* Cheltenham: Edward Elgar, 1996.

Quest Trend Magazin = http://www.quest-trendmagazin.de/wirtschaftstrends/china/industrieproduktion.html

Raffer (1996) = Kunibert Raffer. „Exportorientierte Entwicklung und Weltmarkt – Das Beispiel der asiatischen ‚Tiger',“ in *Das pazifische Jahrhundert? Wirtschaftliche, ökologische und politische Entwicklung in Ost- und Südostasien (Beiträge zur Historischen Sozialkunde 10)*, ed. Edith Binderhofer et al. Vienna: Südwind, 1996, 41-58.

Randall (1977a) = Laura Randall. *A Comparative Economic History of Latin America: 1500-1914, vol. 1 (Mexico)*. Ann Arbor: University Microfilms International, 1977.

Randall (1977b) = Laura Randall. *A Comparative Economic History of Latin America: 1500-1914, vol. 2 (Argentina)*. Ann Arbor: University Microfilms International, 1977.

Randall (1977c) = Laura Randall. *A Comparative Economic History of Latin America: 1500-1914, vol. 3 (Brazil)*. Ann Arbor: University Microfilms International, 1977.

Randall (1977d) = Laura Randall. *A Comparative Economic History of Latin America: 1500-1914, vol. 4 (Peru)*. Ann Arbor: University Microfilms International, 1977.

Ranis (1979) = Gustave Ranis. „Industrial Development“, in *Economic Growth and Structural Change in Taiwan. The Postwar Experience of the Republic of China*, ed. Walter Galenson. Ithaca: Cornell University Press, 1979, 206-262.

Raupach (1964) = Hans Raupach. *Geschichte der Sowjetwirtschaft*. Reinbeck bei Hamburg: Rowohlt Taschenbuch, 1964.

Reichart (1993) = Thomas Reichart. *Städte ohne Wettbewerb. Eine Untersuchung über die Ursachen der Ballung von Wirtschaft und Bevölkerung in Südkorea und in Kolumbien (Beiträge zur Wirtschaftspolitik 58)*. Bern: Haupt, 1993.

Resch (2011) = Andreas Resch. „Neue Institutionenökonomik und Wirtschaftsgeschichte“, in *Wirtschaft und Gesellschaft Europa 1000-2000 (VGS Studientexte 2)*, ed. Markus Cerman. Vienna: StudienVerlag, 48-56.

Riedel (2009) = James Riedel. „Economic Development in East Asia: doing what comes naturally", in *Achieving Industrialization in East Asia,* ed. Helen  Hughes. Cambridge: Cambridge University Press, 1988, 1-38.

Roberts (1986) = A. D. Roberts. *The Cambridge History of Africa, vol. 7 (c. 1905-c.1940).* Cambridge: Cambridge University Press, 1986.

Rocchi (2005) = Fernando Rocchi. *Chimneys in the Desert: Industrialization in Argentina During the Export Boom Years, 1870-1930.* Stanford: Stanford University Press, 2005.

Röpke (1982) = Jochen Röpke. *Die unterentwickelte Freiheit. Wirtschaftliche Entwicklung und unternehmerisches Handeln in Indonesien (Organisation und Kooperation in Entwicklungsländern 20).* Göttingen: Vandenhoeck & Ruprecht, 1982.

Roesler (2009) = Jörg Roesler. *Kompakte Wirtschaftsgeschichte Lateinamerikas vom 18. Jahrhundert bis zum 21. Jahrhundert.* Leipzig: Leipziger Uni-Verlag, 2009.

Ros/Bouillon (2002) = Jaime Ros and César Bouillon. „Mexico: trade liberalization, growth, inequality and poverty", in *Economic Liberalization, Distribution and Poverty. Latin America in the 1990s,* ed. Rob Vos et al. Cheltenham: Edward Elgar, 2002, 347-389.

Rothermund (1985) = Dieter Rothermund. *Indiens wirtschaftliche Entwicklung: von der Kolonialherrschaft bis zur Gegenwart.* Paderborn: Schöningh, 1985.

Rule (1992) = John Rule. *The Vital Century. England's Developing Economy, 1714-1815.* London: Routledge, 1992.

Sachs (2002) = Jeffrey Sachs. „Bemerkungen zu einer neuen Soziologie der wirtschaftlichen Entwicklung", in *Streit um Werte. Wie Kulturen den Fortschritt p*rägen, ed. Samuel Huntington and Lawrence Harrison. Hamburg: Europa Verlag, 2002, 57-74.

Sachs (2005) = Jeffrey D. Sachs. *The End of Poverty. How We Can Make It Happen in Our Lifetime*. London: Penguin Books, 2005.

Salisbury (1996) = Neal Salisbury. „The History of Native Americans from Before the Arrival of the Europeans and Africans Until the American Civil War", in *The Cambridge Economic History of the United States, vol. 1 (The Colonial Era)*. ed. Stanley L. Engerman and Robert E. Gallman. Cambridge: Cambridge University Press, 1996, 1-52.

Salvatore/Nowland (2003) = Ricardo D. Salvatore and Carlos Nowland. „Between Independence and the golden age: The early Argentine economy", in *A New Economic History of Argentina*, ed. Gerardo Paolera and Alan M. Taylor. Cambridge: Cambridge University Press, 2003, 19-45.

Salvucci (2006) = Richard Salvucci. „Export-Led Industrialization", in *The Cambridge Economic History of Latin America, vol. 2 (The Long Twentieth Century)*, ed. Victor Bulmer-Thomas et al. Cambridge: Cambridge University Press, 2006, 249-292.

Sautter (2000) = Zdo Sautter. *Geschichte Kanadas*. München: Beck, 2000.

Schmid (2013) = Dominik Schmid. *Der ländliche außerlandwirtschaftliche Sektor in Thailand und Vietnam – Struktur, Krisenanfälligkeit und institutionelles Umfeld (Giessener Geographische Schriften 83)*. Bonn: Scientia Bonnensis, 2013

Schmidt (1974) = Waltraud Schmidt. „Zu den Beziehungen zwischen dem Urbanisierungsprozess und der Herausbildung des inneren Marktes in Indien", in: *Jahrbuch für Wirtschaftsgeschichte 1974*, II, 83-97.

Schuman (2009) = Michael Schuman. *The Miracle. The Epic Story of Asia's Quest for Wealth*. New York: Harper Business, 2009.

Schuster (1979) = Wolfgang Schuster. *Wirtschaftsgeographie Saudi Arabiens mit besonderer Berücksichtigung der staatlichen Wirtschaftslenkung (Dissertationen der Wirtschaftsuniversität Wien 27)*. Vienna: VWGÖ, 1979.

Scitovsky (1986) = Tibor Scitovsky. „Economic Development in Taiwan and South Korea, 1965-1981", in *Models of Development. A Comparative Study of Economic Growth in South Korea and Taiwan*, ed. Lawrence Lau. San Francisco: ICS Press 1986, 135-195.

Sen (1995) = Kunal Sen. „Stabilization with Growth", in *Economic Restructuring in East Asia and India. Perspectives and Policy Reform*, ed. Pradeep Agraval. Basingstoke: Macmillan, 1995, 134-158.

Senghaas (1981) = Dieter Senghaas (ed.). *Peripherer Kapitalismus. Analysen über Abhängigkeit und Unterentwicklung*. Frankfurt am Main: Suhrkamp, 1981.

Senghaas (1982) = Dieter Senghaas. „Dissoziation und autozentrierte Entwicklung. Eine entwicklungspolitische Alternative für die Dritte Welt", in *Kapitalistische Weltökonomie. Kontroversen über ihren Ursprung und ihre Entwicklungsdynamik*, ed. Dieter Senghaas. Frankfurt am Main: Suhrkamp, 376-412.

Serrao/Thomas (1985) = Joel Serrao and Georg Thomas. „Portugal 1830-1910", in *Handbuch der europäischen Wirtschafts- und Sozialgeschichte*, vol. 5 (*Europäische Wirtschafts- und Sozialgeschichte von der Mitte des 19. Jahrhunderts bis zum Ersten Weltkrieg*), ed.. Wolfram Fischer. Stuttgart: Klett-Cotta, 687-704.

Siddiqui (1997) = Shamim Siddiqui et al. „Economic and social policies of Brunei", in *The ASEAN Region in Transition*, ed. Abu Wahid. Aldershot: Ashgate, 1997, 1-23.

Siew-Yean/Zainal-Abidin (1999) = Tham Siew-Yean and Mahani Zainal-Abidin. „Industrial Institution: The Case of Malaysia", in *Institutions and Economic Change in Southeast Asia. The Context of Development from the 1960s to the 1990s*, ed. Colin Barlow. Cheltenham: Edward Elgar, 1999, 55-71.

Shoup (1981) = Paul S. Shoup. *The East European and Soviet Data Handbook. Political, Social, and Developmental Indicators, 1945-1975*. New York: Columbia University Press, 1981.

Sivasubramonian (2002) = Siva Sivasubramonian. „Twentieth Century Economic Performance in India", in *The Asian Economies in the Twentieth Century*, ed. Angus Maddison, Cheltenham: Edward Elgar, 2002.

Skidmore/Smith (2001) = Thomas E. Skidmore and Peter H. Smith. *Modern Latin America*. Oxford: Oxford University Press, 2001.

Sowjetunion (1992) = Statistisches Bundesamt (ed.*). Sowjetunion 1980-1991. Bilanz der letzten Jahre*. Wiesbaden, 1992.

Sri Lanka Industry Country Studies = http://countrystudies.us/sri-lanka/52.htm

Stahl (Tabellen und Grafiken) = http://de.wikipedia.org/wiki/Stahl/Tabellen_und_Grafiken
State of World Population (2010) = United Nations Population Fund (ed.): *State of World Population 2010*.

Statistisches Jahrbuch = Statistik Austria (ed.): *Statistisches Jahrbuch Österreichs 1993-2013*. Vienna: Verlag Österreich GmbH, 1993-2013.

Sub-Saharan Africa (1989) = The World Bank (ed.): *Sub-Saharan Africa. From Crisis to Sustainable Growth*. Washington, D.C., 1989.

Suh (1978) = Sang-Chul Suh. *Growth and Structural Changes in the Korean Economy 1910-1940 (Harvard East Asian Monographs 83)*. Cambridge, Mass.: Harvard University Press, 1978.

Summerhill (2006) = William R. Summerhill. „The Development of Infrastructrure", in *The Cambridge Economic History of Latin America, vol. 2 (The Long Twentieth Century)*, ed. Victor Bulmer-Thomas et al. Cambridge: Cambridge University Press, 2006, 293-326.

Sutter/Menck (1973) = Rolf Sutter and Karl Wolfgang Menck. *Investieren in Südostasien. Investitionsbedingungen in Indien, Indonesien, Korea, Malaysia, Philippinen, Singapur, Sri Lanka, Taiwan, Thailand.* Hamburg: Verlag Weltarchiv, 1973.

Taiwan Data Book (2013) = Council for Economic Planning and Development (ed.): *Taiwan Statistical Data Book.* Taipei, 2013

Taylor (2003) = Jean Gelman Taylor. *Indonesia. Peoples and Histories.* New Haven: Yale University Press. 2003.

Textilindustrie in Bangladesch = de.wikipedia.org/wiki/Textilindustrie_in_Bangladesch
Thorp (1998) = Rosemary Thorp. *Progress, Poverty and Exclusion: An Economic History of Latin America in the 20th Century.* Washington, D.C., 1998.

Tischner (1981) = Helmut Tischner. *Die wirtschaftliche Entwicklung Indiens in den Jahren 1951-1978 unter besonderer Berücksichtigung der Auslandshilfe (Volkswirtschaftliche Schriften 303).* Berlin: Duncker & Humblot, 1981.

Transition report (2003) = European Bank for Reconstruction and Development (ed.): *Transition report 2003. Integration and regional cooperation.* London, 2003.

Tucher (1999) = Mathias von Tucher. *Die Rolle der Auslandsmontage in den internationalen Wertschöpfungsnetzwerken der Automobilhersteller (Wirtschaft und Raum 5).* Munich: VVF-Verlag Florentz, 1999.

Uhlig/Lange (1983) = Christian Uhlig and Michael Lange. *Internationale Produktionskooperation im Vorderen Orient. Joint Ventures und andere Formen unternehmerischer Zusammenarbeit.* Tübingen: Erdmann, 1983.

Urbanisierung (2011) = Urbanisierung in Afrika Informationen des BMZ (PDF 276 KB) Valmonte (2007) = Ligaya Valmonte. *Workforce Development in the Philippines. Policies ans Practices.* Tokio: Asian Development Bank, 2007.

Vittinghoff (1990) = Friedrich Vittinghoff. „Wirtschaft und Gesellschaft des Imperium Romanum. Gesellschaft", in *Handbuch der europäischen Wirtschafts- und Sozialgeschichte, vol.. 1 (Europäische Wirtschafts- und Sozialgeschichte in der römischen Kaiserzeit),* ed. Friedrich Vittinghoff. Stuttgart: Klett-Cotta, 1990, 161-373.

Vorlaufer (2009) = Karl Vorlaufer. *Südostasien. Brunei, Indonesien, Kambodscha, Laos, Malaysia, Myanmar, Osttimor, Philippinen, Singapur, Thailand, Vietnam.* Darmstadt: Wissenschaftliche. Buchgesellschaft, 2009.

Vos (2002) = Rob Vos et al. (eds.). *Economic Liberalization, Distribution and Poverty. Latin America in the 1990s.* Cheltenham: Edward Elgar, 2002.

Vries (1984) = Jan de Vries. *European Urbanization 1500-1800.* London: Methuen, 1984.
Vries (2011) = Peter Vries. „Europa und die Welt", in *Wirtschaft und Gesellschaft Europa 1000-2000 (VGS Studientexte 2),* ed. Markus Cerman. Vienna: StudienVerlag, 2011, 411-438.
Wagener (1972) = Hans-Jürgen Wagener. *Wirtschaftswachstum in unterentwickelten Gebieten. Ansätze zu einer Regionalanalyse der Sowjetunion (Veröffentlichungen des Osteuropa-Institutes München: Wirtschaft und Gesellschaft 12).* Berlin: Duncker & Humblot, 1972.

Wallerstein (1989) = Immanuel Wallerstein. *The Modern World-System, Bd. 3 (The Second Great Expansion of the Capitalist World-Economy, 1730–1840's).* San Diego: Academic Press, 1989.

Weber (2006) = Max Weber. *Die protestantische Ethik und der „Geist" des Kapitalismus. Textausgabe auf der Grundlage der ersten Fassung von 1904/05 mit einem Verzeichnis der wichtigsten Zusätze und Veränderungen aus der zweiten Fassung von 1920.* Munich: FinanzBuch-Verlag, 2006.

Weigl (2011) = Andreas Weigl. „Wirtschafts- und Sozialpolitik", in *Wirtschaft und Gesellschaft Europa 1000-2000 (VGS Studientexte 2)*, ed. Markus Cerman. Vienna: StudienVerlag, 2011, 305-322.

Weitensfelder (2011) = Hubert Weitensfelder. „Technologische Entwicklungen", in *Wirtschaft und Gesellschaft Europa 1000-2000 (VGS Studientexte 2)*, ed. Markus Cerman. Vienna: StudienVerlag, 2011, 161-177.

Weitz (1987) = Bernd O. Weitz. *Die Türkei. Soziale, ökonomische und politische Strukturen. Eine Handreichung zum besseren Verständnis türkischer Mitbürger.* Essen: Die Blaue Eule, 1987.

Welt in Zahlen (Fernsehgeräte) = http://www.welt-in-zahlen.de/laendervergleichphtml?indicator=115.

Welt in Zahlen (Computer) = http://www.welt-in-zahlen.de/laendervergleich.phtml?indicator=117.

Welt in Zahlen (Industrieproduktion) = http://www.welt-in-zahlen.de/laendervergleich.phtml?indicator=64.

Welt in Zahlen (PKW) = = http://www.welt-in-zahlen.de/laendervergleich.phtml?indicator=126.

Wikipedia (Asia) = https://en.wikipedia.org/wiki/Asia

Wikipedia (Bangladesh) = https://en.wikipedia.org/wiki/Bangladesh

Wikipedia (Canada) = https://en.wikipedia.org/wiki/Canada

Wikipedia (Constantinople) = https://en.wikipedia.org/wiki/Constantinople

Wikipedia (Mongolia) = https://en.wikipedia.org/wiki/Mongolia

Wikipedia (Pakistan) = https://en.wikipedia.org/wiki/Pakistan

Wikipedia (Papua New Guinea) = https://en.wikipedia.org/wiki/Papua_New_Guinea

Wikipedia (Russia) = https://en.wikipedia.org/wiki/Russia

Wikipedia (Sri Lanka) = https://en.wikipedia.org/wiki/Sri_Lanka

Wirtschaftszahlen zum Automobil = http://de.wikipedia.org/wiki/Wirtschaftszahlen zum Automobil

WKO Länderprofile = wko.at/statistik/laenderprofile/lp-moldawien.pdf

wko.at/statistik/laenderprofile/lp-russland.pdf

wko.at/statistik/laenderprofile/lp-ukraine.pdf

wko.at/statistik/laenderprofile/lp-weissrussland.pdf

Wolffsohn (1991) = Michael Wolffsohn. *Israel. Grundwissen – Länderkunde. Geschichte – Politik – Gesellschaft – Wirtschaft*. Opladen: Leske + Budrich, 1991.

Wontroba/Menzel (1978) = Gerd Wontroba and Ulrich Menzel. *Stagnation und Unterentwicklung in Korea. Von der Yi-Dynastie zur Peripherisierung unter japanischer Kolonialherrschaft (Transfines 9)*. Meisenheim am Glan: Hain, 1978.

World Pig Iron Producing Countries = https://www.mapsofworld.com/minerals/world-pig-iron-producers.html

Woronoff (1992) = Jon Woronoff. *Asia's ,Miracle' Economies*. New York: Armonk, 1992.
Wu (2002) = Harry X. Wu. „Industrial Output and Labour Productivity in China 1949-94: A Reassessment", in *The Asian Economies in the Twentieth Century*, ed. Angus Maddison). Cheltenham: Edward Elgar, 2002, 82-101.

Zeleza (1993) = Paul Tiyambe Zeleza. *A Modern Economic History of Africa, vol 1 (The Nineteenth Century)*. Oxford: CODESRIA, 1993.

Zimmermann (2003) = Gerd R. Zimmermann. *Indonesien. Eine geographische Landeskunde*. Nackenheim am Rhein: Edition Matahari, 2003.

Zingel (1979) = Wolfgang-Peter Zingel. *Die Problematik regionaler Entwicklungsunterschiede in Entwicklungsländern: eine theoretische und empirische Analyse, dargestellt am Beispiel Pakistans unter Verwendung der Hauptkomponentenmethode*. Stuttgart: Steiner, 1979.

# PLACE INDEX

## A

## B

# C

## D

# E

## F

## L

# M

# N

# R

# S

# T

# W

## Z